CHICAGO PUBLIC L

R00939 38886

HC
681
.B87
1992

Burnett, Alan
  Alexander.

The Western Pacific.

$69.95

DATE			

D1445504

BAKER & TAYLOR BOOKS

The Western Pacific

The Western Pacific

Challenge of Sustainable Growth

Alan Burnett

The Australian National University
Canberra, Australia

Edward Elgar

©Alan Burnett 1992

All rights reserved. No part of this publication may be reproduced, stored in a retrieval system, or transmitted in any form or by any means, electronic, mechanical, photocopying, recording, or otherwise without the prior permission of the publisher.

Published by
Edward Elgar Publishing Limited
Gower House
Croft Road
Aldershot
Hants GU11 3HR
England

Edward Elgar Publishing Company
Old Post Road
Brookfield
Vermont 05036
USA

A CIP catalogue record for this book
is available from the British Library

Library of Congress Cataloging-in-Publication Data

Burnett, Alan Alexander.
    The Western Pacific: challenge of sustainable growth / Alan
Burnett.
        p.   cm.
    Includes bibliographical references and index.
    1. Pacific Area - Economic conditions. 2. Pacific Area - Economic
policy. 3. Environmental policy - Pacific Area. 4. Economic
development - Environmental aspects. I. Title.
HC681.B87 1992   92-10389
338.99 - dc20   CIP

ISBN 1 85278 367 2

Printed and bound in Great Britain by
Billing and Sons Ltd, Worcester

Dedication

This book is dedicated to friends and colleagues who served with the former New Zealand Department of External Affairs, the former Australian Department of Trade and Resources, and at the Australian National University.

Contents

List of Tables and Figures

Tables

Figures

Acknowledgements

My colleague Coral Bell, whose capacity to anticipate significant trends in international relations is almost unrivalled, triggered a process which led to the completion of this book. Responding several years ago to a seemingly casual suggestion, I found myself writing a chapter entitled 'Defence of the Environment—The New Issue in International Relations' for a book *Agenda for the 90s* which Coral edited for publication in 1991. Not only is Coral a distinguished author, she has an extraordinary gift for inspiring work in others.

I am also grateful for the assistance I have received from other colleagues at the Australian National University: Mitchell Bernard, Stuart Harris, Geoffrey Jukes, Lynne Payne (who produced the camera -ready version), John Ravenhill of the Department of International Relations, and Christine Wilson (who prepared the index). I also received a great deal of invaluable help from colleagues in other parts of the University notably the Departments of Political and Social Change, Human Geography, Demography, Forestry and the Centre for Resource and Environmental Studies. The late Dr Gurdip Singh of the Department of Biogeography and Geo-morphology was especially helpful in enabling me to crystalize the argument in the concluding chapters.

I should also like to thank those who helped me during my visits to Asia, especially members of the staff of the Australian Embassies in Seoul and Tokyo. Others include people who spared me their valuable time in the Ministry of International Trade and Industry, the Institute of Energy Economics and the Environment Agency, Tokyo; the Ministry of Energy and Resources and the Korea Energy Economics Institute, Seoul; the Centre of Asian Studies, University of Hong Kong; the Institute of Southeast Asian Studies, Singapore; the International Tropical Timber Organisation, Yokohama; the United Nations Economic Commission for Asia and the Far East, Bangkok.

Foreword

The twentieth century will doubtless be regarded as unique in the span of history because it is the century of nuclear science. Weapon systems have been developed which have the capacity to destroy most if not all forms of life. Beyond that we can now see that during the final quarter of this tumultuous century more and more of us are coming to understand that humanity is faced with both immediate and more distant threats. We are increasingly realizing the nature of the longer-term peril. The biosphere, especially its land, vegetation, water systems, as well as the atmosphere, is being adversely affected by our collective economic activities, and especially our insatiable demand for energy. In other words we have to face up to the probability that the planet might not be capable of indefinitely supporting a population of the present size, let alone the ten billion that demographers predict will be demanding the material benefits of industrial society not many decades hence.

In this book I have endeavoured to challenge the assumption that the present pattern of economic growth in the countries of the Western Pacific is ushering in an era of unparalleled prosperity. High rates of growth are bound to continue for many years, but evidence is accumulating that the process itself is causing such extensive degradation of the fundamentals of existence, fertile soils, fresh water and clean air, that it is inherently unsound. In other words the processes of economic development on the scale to which we now have become accustomed everywhere are in conflict with the actual preservation of the fundamentals of existence.

I suggest that it is unfortunate at this stage that the international debate about the consequences of large-scale economic development is primarily focusing on whether the utilization of fossil fuels in the enormous quantities needed to keep the international economy going, has triggered global warming. That is a distinct possibility, and its consequences could be very grave for humanity. Nevertheless data are still being accumulated and analysed. It is easy to rush to premature judgements on this issue.

But I suggest that it is not premature to attempt to form judgements at this stage about the consequences of increasing numbers of people and their demand for energy on the soils, vegetation and water systems. A process of degradation is under way which will have enormous significance for people everywhere. If this process is not taken properly into account, there is a risk that governments will be overwhelmed by circumstances which could prove largely to be beyond their capacity to control.

It seems appropriate to test this proposition by considering the present and likely future circumstances of the countries of the Western Pacific and, as part of the exercise, to compare the situations of the rich —Japan, South Korea, Taiwan, Singapore, Australia and New Zealand —with the relatively poor and poor countries of this increasingly important part of the world—China, Vietnam, Indonesia, the Philippines, Malaysia, Thailand and Papua New Guinea.

We now know that the combined populations of these countries will exceed two billion early in the next century. Not only will numbers increase, so will economic activity. An enormous process of transition is under way as country after country seeks to emulate Japan and transform itself from being predominantly agricultural to creating the industrial and commercial structures necessary to provide employment for their expanding labour forces.

This book poses some fundamental questions. Is that part of the biosphere which the countries of the Western Pacific share, capable of withstanding, say, a quadrupling of economic activity? Will the major countries prove capable of evolving both a coherent philosophy of sustainable economic growth (or change and adaptation)? More importantly, will they be able to adapt their agricultural and industrial practice to ways which are much less stressful for their environments? Is it possible to redirect a process of industrial development which has already generated such colossal momentum? Will China and Japan, with their fundamentally different philosophies, and entrenched enmity towards one another, be able to forge a basis for cooperation with each other and with their neighbours in Northeast and Southeast Asia?

Alan Burnett
Canberra, March 1992

Percentages of Population, Gross Domestic Product and Utilization of Energy

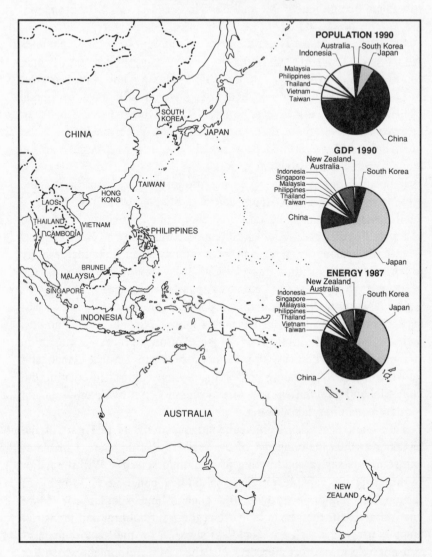

The percentages of total population and gross domestic product expressed in $US have been derived from data in Regional Performance Figures in *ASIA 1991 YEARBOOK* published by the Far Eastern Economic Review, Hong Kong. The percentages of utilization of energy were derived from data calculated as tonnes of oil equivalent by the Institute of Energy Economics, Tokyo.

1. Introduction

The countries of the 'Western Pacific', especially Japan and China, have come to have profound significance in world affairs. They include the continental and island countries on the Western rim of the Pacific Ocean—Japan, the Koreas, China and Hong Kong (Northeast Asia), Vietnam, Cambodia, Laos (Indochina), Indonesia, Malaysia, the Philippines, Thailand and Singapore (Southeast Asia) and below the equator, Australia and New Zealand with the Melanesian and Polynesian islands to their north and east.

Despite great differences in culture and religion, differing stages of development, wars, revolutions, the continuing impoverishment of a large proportion of big and growing populations, the Asian countries of the Western Pacific have successfully asserted themselves to the point where commentators speak, often loosely, of the twenty-first century being a 'Pacific Century'. That would seem to imply an era where Japan and other Asian countries of the Western Pacific, which have emulated to a greater or lesser extent Japan's pattern of economic development, could eventually constitute an area of greater collective economic significance than North America or Western Europe.

During the second half of this century a major advanced industrial area has emerged in Northeast Asia. It is based of course on Japan but now comprises Taiwan and Hong Kong, so closely linked in trade with China, and South Korea. It seems now inevitable that other countries will extend progressively and strengthen this industrial area. China may adapt and change. Its growing export industries may continue to expand providing it with the resources needed to renew its obsolescent and inadequate energy, transport and heavy industrial sectors. North Korea may escape the ideological cage in which it has been imprisoned by the Kim Il Sung regime. Thailand and Malaysia-Singapore, which are industrializing rapidly, along with Indonesia seem likely to extend significantly the East Asian industrial area. The size and scale of a modern, high technology industrial area spanning both Northeast and

1

Southeast Asia could further transform the economic geography of the world by strengthening the already considerable power and influence of Northeast Asia.

The future of other Asian countries bordering the Pacific Ocean is less certain. The political and economic outlook for the Indochinese trio, Vietnam, Cambodia and Laos, and for the Philippines is uncertain. Because of the resilience of the peoples of Indochina—especially the Vietnamese—there should be a gradual transformation which will enable those countries to break clear of the terrible legacy of war and to free themselves from the dogmatism of Marxist-Leninist ideology. The process could be slow. In the case of the Philippines the future is obscure. We have learned, since the fall of the Marcos regime, that the predominant position of the élite families of that country almost precludes any possibility of a government in Manila addressing effectively the serious problems that affect that island country.

It is evident that the pace of economic development accelerated in many Western Pacific countries while it faltered in the United States and Western Europe and seems to have ceased in Central Europe and the Soviet Union. The relative positions of the major economies and those clustered about them have shifted. It is significant historically that for the first time a major industrial area without a European base or heritage has emerged with consequent powerful effects on the world economy. As one commentator has put it there has been an historic shift in the centre of gravity of economic production and power towards Northeast Asia. The countries of this grouping have caught up or are in the process of catching up technologically and have based their economic policies on high investment, increasing international orientation and willingness to foster rapid structural change (Garnaut, 1989, p. 36).

In other words the distribution of world economic activity has changed as a result of the progress made during the past four decades by Japan and its neighbours. The emergence of a region of great industrial capacity in Asia is only partly attributable to the surge of industrial growth from the time Japan began its postwar recovery. It also owes much to the development of an interdependent world trading environment following the gradual elimination mainly by Western European and North American countries of systems of foreign exchange control, reductions of tariff rates and other methods of restricting trade in industrial and semi-industrial goods. This enabled first Japan and then newly industrializing countries, notably South Korea and Taiwan, to take advantage of market opportunities around the world, especially in the United States.

It is easy to exaggerate the prospects of the Western Pacific. It is vast, heavily populated and diverse. It lacks historical linkages. It has been racked by war and revolutions and is divided by race and religions (Segal, 1990). It has come to be regarded, following the retreat of the colonial powers after 1945, as an area with the capacity to develop its considerable material and vast human resources in ways which might progressively solve problems of poverty, reduce gross inequalities between rich and poor in some countries and make good lack of educational opportunities and comparative lack of technology.

That may be so, but assessments such as this neglect to take into account the damage growth of population and the pursuit of economic growth has done to the land and water systems which sustain vast and still increasing numbers of people. There is an important environmental dimension which needs to be fully considered. The ramifications of these problems are beginning to be widely understood, notably in China and Japan. Nevertheless the urgency of initiating remedial policies is still largely unacknowledged as the drive for economic growth, almost regardless of consequences, has possessed the minds of policy-makers everywhere.

It is probably best to be more than ordinarily cautious about the political and economic prospects of the Asian countries of the Western Pacific. They are too heavily populated, too divided politically, socially and by religion and ideology. Economic progress has been achieved at a relatively high price using a predominant model, that of Japan, which, despite many stunning achievements, holds equal numbers of dangers.

In his conclusion to the book he entitled *Pacific Destiny*, Robert Elegant suggests a more sombre assessment of Japan's future which puts assertions about its capacity for exercising leadership in the Western Pacific in a realistic if harsh light:

> ... Japan's search for cheap labour, new markets, and homes for its surplus capital will not stop until it has exhausted most of the world's human and natural resources. Japan is not deterred by the ecological disasters that result from its despoiling the world's forests and oceans. Nor is Japan deterred by the extremely high toll its compulsive expansion imposes on its own people, as well as

outsiders. Neither principles nor premonitions of a dolorous future deter Japan.
Charging head-down towards their goal, the ruthlessly pragmatic Japanese see
only what lies directly ahead (Elegant, 1990, p. 507).

There may be some deliberate exaggeration involved in this as he
refrains from mentioning the equally rapacious practices of much
American and European economic activity in the Third World. He
nevertheless brings out an underlying reality which is becoming more
and more apparent to people in other countries of the Western Pacific.
Japanese (and South Korean and Taiwanese) economic activity can be
very destructive and heedless of the interests of the supplying or
customer countries. They are understood to be ruthlessly self-seeking
but that is the way of all powerful economies. These three countries are
in the game of consolidating their economic influence with the
Japanese clearly in a position where they are now acknowledged to
have attained predominance. They are coming increasingly to be feared
because aspects of their economic activity (and that of other foreign
and domestic entrepreneurs) are contributing to processes of
exploitation and unsustainable development, which are increasingly
regarded as damaging the long-term capacity of other countries to
sustain the well-being of their growing populations.

The view that the twenty-first century will in some way be 'the
century of the Pacific' is simplistic. The industrial progress of several
countries along its north-western shores has been phenomenal but there
is little justification at this stage for assuming that their further
industrialization will bring about a fundamental change in the scheme
of things. The relative importance of North America, Western Europe
and Northeast Asia may continue to change but not to the extent that
the latter may become predominant as distinct from more important.

If the twenty-first century can at this stage be characterized in a few
words it is far more likely that it will be the century of the great global
environmental crisis. Far from being the century of any particular part
of the planet, it is likely to be the era when the consequences for the
biosphere of the growth of the human population and its still rapidly
increasing economic activity will have to be addressed. Perhaps it will
come to be seen that the Asian countries of the Western Pacific have
special significance as we move into the next century because they will
have to solve problems caused by continuing growth of already large

populations and by the consequences of their headlong rush to achieve improvements in the material conditions of their peoples.

Are the processes of development which have generated such a powerful momentum sustainable? In other words is it possible for the material circumstances of growing populations continually to improve without the processes of economic growth actually undermining the capacities of economies, individually and collectively, to sustain people not just for a few decades but for many centuries?

That is something about which there should be great doubt given the way in which economic development involves increasing use of fossil fuels for the generation of energy and as feedstock for an increasing range of products and the generation of huge quantities of wastes.

It is evident that the concept of sustainable growth (or development), in the sense of pragmatic adaptation and change with the objective of ensuring over time that the requirements of economies do not over-extend available resources, has not adequately been thought through. That seems to be especially true in relation to the long-term survival of industrial/agricultural societies such as Japan and Korea and agricultural/industrial societies such as China, Vietnam and the countries of Southeast Asia. What chance will there be of change to policies based on sustainable growth when some of the consequences of present policies are exhaustion of some mineral resources, rapid loss of vegetation, loss of soil fertility, degradation of fresh water resources, pollution of coastal waters, depletion and extinction of species and deterioration of air quality?

The theme of this book is that it is unwise to assume that sustainable growth is a viable concept, given that modern societies need increasing amounts of energy to increase their present rates of economic activity. Utilization of more energy when population and economic activity are increasing is inescapable. That is the paradox of modern economic development. The sources of energy are for the meantime readily available, but the adverse consequences for the biosphere of their even more extensive use are becoming better understood. This is posing a dilemma for all countries, but especially for those like China and Indonesia where millions of people are understandably trying to escape from poverty and deprivation.

It is important at least to try to grasp the practical problems involved for any grouping of countries as they respond to the problems posed by the pressures which their growing populations are putting on the environments which sustain them. It is also necessary to avoid drawing artificial distinctions between groupings of countries which are often carelessly described as regions. The countries which form the basis of this study do not form a coherent region, although some of them, notably the ASEAN countries—Brunei, Indonesia, Malaysia, the Philippines, Thailand, Singapore—increasingly think of themselves as a regional grouping. Links between the countries of the Western Pacific are developing, but for the meantime they are all participants to a greater or lesser extent in the international economy. It could become fractured into regional groupings but it is more likely to further develop as a partially integrated whole. The collapse of the centrally planned command economy system of the Soviet Union, following its abandonment by the countries of Central Europe, may mean that all economies will before long participate to a greater or lesser extent in an immense linked system. A greater European economy, including Russia, could extend from the Atlantic to the Pacific, and develop closer links with the countries of its western rim. China is becoming more and more involved in world trade and finance. Vietnam is likely to follow, leaving the economic future of North Korea, alone among the Western Pacific countries, obscure.

Nothing in history provides anything like a model for the change which has taken place in the second half of this century. An international economic juggernaut has developed which has astonishing momentum. Northeast Asia has become an increasingly important part of it. It is difficult to comprehend how that momentum could be slowed down through a process of change and adaptation, so as to avoid the possibility of the totality of global economic activity gradually reducing the capacity of the biosphere to sustain the growing human population. As The World Commission on Environment and Development (WCED), which reported to the United Nations in 1987, has expressed it:

> We have in the more recent past been forced to face up to a sharp increase in economic interdependence among nations. We are now forced to accustom ourselves to an accelerating ecological interdependence among nations. Ecology and economy are becoming even more interwoven—locally, regionally, nationally, and globally—into a seamless net of causes and effects (WCED, 1987, p. 5).

It would be impossible fully to describe that web of causes and effects in the Western Pacific. At this stage a beginning has been made, largely by United Nations agencies, to elucidate them but governments still, it seems, have only a rough understanding of what might be involved. I have attempted, in the next chapter, to explore the contradiction inherent in the words 'sustainable growth' to help the reader grasp what might be involved for the countries of the Western Pacific should a consensus eventually be reached among them that their economic activity should adapt and change to keep it within the capacity of land, water and vegetation to support growing populations.

In Chapter 3, I describe the main features of the Western Pacific countries to demonstrate their great variety in both geographical and human and political terms. A multifaceted picture emerges covering the features of continental and archipelagic countries, racial and religious differences and economic prospects. The characteristics of the various systems of government are also summarized. That is intended to provide a basis for subsequent assessments of the extent to which they may be able to effectively address the problems which are piling up as they pursue economic growth.

Chapter 4 provides an overview of the demographic state of the Western Pacific using forecasts of population growth and the way in which people are changing from largely agricultural to much more urban modes of existence. Special attention is paid to the growth of rural and forest dwelling populations and to the development of the great cities of the Western Pacific as the proportion of urban dwellers continues to increase.

In Chapter 5, I turn to the demand for and the provision of energy in Western Pacific countries. The purpose is to describe how the lifeblood of economic growth is provided, to consider likely future requirements and what might be the consequences of big increases in the use of fossil fuels. In this chapter I also describe the energy resources available in the Western Pacific and the extent to which they may be sufficient to meet future needs.

Chapters 6 and 7 summarize the environmental consequences of economic development in the area and examine the capabilities of governments to respond. Chapter 6 describes the way in which forests are being lost or threatened, the state of and prospects for agricultural land, the condition of rivers, lakes, estuaries and coastal seas and the state of urban environments.

Chapter 7 examines whether governments have the capability to effectively respond to the problems of environmental degradation. Special attention is paid to the present situation in and prospects for China. It is the dominating presence among the countries of the Western Pacific. Its circumstances indicate, because of its huge population and its substantial dependence on coal as a source of energy, the enormous practical difficulties of shifting from the pursuit of material growth to sustainable development policies. I also examine the scope for and the significance of intergovernmental cooperation on environmental problems among the countries of the Western Pacific.

Chapter 8 is entitled 'The Future of the Western Pacific'. I revert to the forecasts for the growth of population and demand for energy and examine the overall prospects for the countries of the Western Pacific should the projections for the opening decades of the next century prove to be reasonably close to the mark.

In the concluding chapter I attempt an assessment of whether sustainable growth is within the bounds of possibility for the countries of the Western Pacific. In other words will it be feasible for governments to reorder policies over time to greatly reduce pressures on the environment and to bring about a situation where the countries of the Western Pacific will be able to avoid serious problems of instability during the period of time in the twenty-first century when their populations pass through a peak?

2. Sustainable Economic Growth

Conventional economic assumptions about the wisdom of countries seeking the highest possible rates of economic growth came under increasing challenge during the 1980s. They had earlier been subject to scrutiny and criticism on the ground that they almost completely neglected consequences of productive processes in the technological age for local and regional environments, and for the biosphere as a whole (Daly, 1977; Rivkin, 1980). The reverberations from the academic circles in which the debates largely occurred were for long neither taken very seriously, nor considered relevant, by governments of the major powers and the powerful international economic institutions they dominate, like the Organisation for Economic Cooperation and Development (OECD) or the World Bank.

Nevertheless the growing accumulation of evidence about the likely adverse consequences for mankind of the increasing economic activity of a growing world population for land, fresh water systems, seas, oceans and, of course, the atmosphere has brought about a change. In 1968 some countries successfully pressed the point during discussions in the United Nations that environmental problems could pose a long-term threat. At the initiative of the Swedish Government, the United Nations decided to call a conference on the human environment. The Stockholm Conference, as it became known, met in 1972 to review the work of a preparatory committee which had spent the intervening years formulating recommendations under the following headings:

- Planning and management of human settlements, together with non-economic factors such as educational, social and cultural aspects.

- Natural resources and aspects of development.

- Identification and control of pollutants and organizational implications of the measures proposed.

The conference adopted no less than 106 resolutions which were labelled the international 'Action Plan' for the environment. The practical outcome was: (1) a global assessment known as 'Earthwatch' whose purpose is to identify and measure environmental problems of international importance and to warn against impending crises; (2) the establishment (following the passing of a resolution by the United Nations (No. 2997) in 1973), of the United Nations Environmental Programme; and (3) support activities such as educational, financial and organizational measures (Keesings, 1972, pp. 25476-8; 1973, pp. 25728, 26165).

Governments are now aware that continuing economic growth, which demands increasing use of very large quantities of fossil fuels and other materials, may have disastrous long-term consequences for the biosphere. In 1989 it was acknowledged by the Group of Seven (United States, West Germany, Japan, France, Britain, Italy and Canada), which forms the core of the OECD, that the international community was facing a set of problems of profound significance. The leaders of those countries agreed that decisive action is urgently needed to understand and protect the earth's ecological balance and, in particular, the depletion of the ozone layer. They also acknowledged the need to define policies based on the concept of sustainable economic activity, and to ensure the compatibility of economic growth with the protection of the environment (Keesings, 1989, p. 36802).

It is now more widely appreciated that the biosphere is being adversely affected by the more routine, peaceful economic activities of mankind. In other words, most governments recognize that it might not be able to support the present population indefinitely at anything like present average standards of living let alone a still rapidly increasing population. As an American writer has expressed it:

> The planet today is inhabited by somewhat more than five billion people who each year appropriate 40 per cent of the organic material fixed by photosynthesis on land, consume the equivalent of two tons of coal per person and produce an average of 150 kilograms of steel for each man, woman and child on the earth (Clark, 1989, p. 20).

If the population should increase to eight or ten billion, pressures on resources are bound to increase greatly. We are now beginning to understand the consequences of the European industrial revolution for the world at large. The extension and adaptation of systems developed in Western Europe and North America using vast amounts of energy, especially by big economies like the Soviet Union, China, Japan, Brazil, Mexico, India and South Korea, poses a gradually increasing threat to all societies. The overarching danger is that burgeoning industrial production and the loss of vegetation, especially virgin forests, through excessive exploitation may have triggered a process of adverse climate change which has been labelled 'the greenhouse effect'. Growing discharges of gases, notably carbon dioxide, methane, nitrous oxide and the notorious chlorofluorocarbons, are now widely believed to have precipitated warming of the atmosphere by gradually altering its composition. There could be profound and adverse changes in precipitation, weather patterns, decline of the ice caps and general rises in sea levels (Pearman, 1988; Daly, 1989; Arrhenius and Waltz, 1990).

There is also the related threat that the damage to the ozone layer through the use of chlorofluorocarbon and halon gases could endanger human health by making exposure to direct sunlight distinctly more dangerous than it is at present. The possibility of damage through increasing levels of ultra-violet radiation to microscopic organisms like oceanic plankton, which are known to have a vital role in the food chain, cannot be ruled out (Graedel and Crutzen, 1989, p. 31).

Although the International Panel on Climate Change reported to governments in late 1990 that the great weight of scientific evidence supports predictions of an increasing rate of global warming during the next century, there will be debate about the scientific validity of such predictions and still more about what, if anything, should be done to reduce the danger of adverse changes in climate.

The issue of the 'greenhouse effect' has tended to mask a whole range of immediate environmental problems which are the direct and incontestable consequence of the vast extension of economic activity which has now to a greater or lesser degree influenced the lives and will affect the futures of people everywhere.

These problems are manifest in the loss of forests, the increasing desertification of drier areas, degradation of agricultural land through erosion and misuse, the loss of plant and animal species, pollution of freshwater systems, the proliferation of human and industrial wastes for which adequate systems of disposal do not exist, deterioration of air quality especially in urban and industrial areas, pollution of estuaries and coastal seas and even the deterioration of oceanic waters through spillage of oil and the incineration and dumping of wastes.

The Western Pacific has its share of these problems. Indeed they are becoming so serious that they should be addressed in a systematic and effective way through combinations of national and international action if the region is going to avoid the risk of undermining the economic gains it has made during the past forty years of impressive economic growth.

It is here that we run into a fundamental problem of terminology. The word 'growth' used in the term 'economic growth' is a metaphor. The underlying image is the biological growth of plants and animals which increase in size at stages or throughout their life cycles. One imagines that 'economic growth' is most likely akin to the metaphor of the growth of a giant tree which will mature over hundreds of years. But economists, whatever their persuasion, seem seldom to have given serious consideration to what economic maturity might involve— presumably an era which might be regarded as stable, capable of continuing more or less indefinitely without over-expending the non-renewable, non-substitutable resources which have to be exploited so as to enable growth to continue and on which economies are by definition dependent. Similarly a sustainable economy would not have done anything to diminish the capacity of its land and water resources to provide a continuing and adequate supply of renewable resources, especially agricultural, fisheries and forest products.

On the contrary, economic advice, whether based on private property and market or socialist concepts, has been to pursue material growth measured in output of goods and services largely regardless of consequences. The primary objective of all our societies has, quite understandably, been to create the circumstances where more people escape poverty and better enjoy the material benefits of industrial civilization.

During the past decade it has become increasingly understood that some of the fundamental assumptions on which economic thinking has been based since the eighteenth century are no longer adequate either for the analysis of current developments or as a basis of future policy. It is now necessary to accept as a basic principle that the balance of the biosphere should not be disturbed as it is fundamental to the survival of human societies.

We seem to be moving towards a new synthesis, or philosophic framework about economic activity, at all levels. That framework is being slowly developed. It must focus on the way in which societies should change and adapt so as to enable them to shift from being exceptionally careless about the way they use energy and materials to produce goods and services, to being exceptionally careful (Daly and Cobb, 1989; Pearce et al., 1989).

The way the word 'growth' has been used by economists and political leaders has itself created problems. There is now an assumption that the pursuit of economic growth is an ultimate good, something that brings benefits to everybody in a reasonably equitable society. The problem is that economic growth, measured by the statistical techniques by which gross domestic product (GDP) numbers are calculated, involves only estimates of increases and decreases in outputs of goods and services. Admittedly, the pursuit of material growth has brought innumerable benefits to large numbers of people. So important has it become that a decline in percentage increases in GDP, or worse a decrease, spells political problems for governments, manifest in industrial stagnation and rising unemployment.

Only recently has it come to be appreciated that calculations such as GDP do not take adequately into account the adverse consequences of economic activity, such as pollution of water and the degradation of land. Furthermore if these and objective considerations, such as the excessive loss of forests, loss of soil fertility, pollution of water and the growth of vast slums around the mega-cities of Asia and elsewhere, are largely ignored, then the pursuit of economic growth is likely to prove illusory over time. In other words, the increasing provision of material goods and improved services based on increasing production of energy to make more goods and to provide more and better services could ultimately fail to benefit societies. Instead their economies could slowly be undermined because of the degradation of their fundamental resources—land, water and vegetation.

What the international economy, which has developed during this century, may in fact be doing is slowly undermining the basis of those societies whose improvement has been its primary objective. This may be a devastating concept for the mature industrial societies of Europe and North America and for Japan. It must be even more so for newly-industrializing countries and developing countries in the Western

Pacific and elsewhere. It forces reexamination of the philosophic bases of policies which have been embraced and pursued with varying degrees of success for decades. The difficulty is that while the dangers inherent in present policies are coming to be understood, no coherent alternative approach has yet been articulated. Moreover, there is still no proper understanding of how to slow down the momentum which has been generated by policies of economic growth, or of the adaptation and change which will be needed to move to policies based on the avoidance of unsustainable outcomes.

The 1987 report by WCED, *Our Common Future*, has turned out to have an unexpected influence on attitudes of governments to the pursuit of economic growth. The task set the Commission by the United Nations was:

- to propose long-term environmental strategies for achieving sustainable development by the year 2000 and beyond;

- to recommend ways concern for the environment may be translated into greater co-operation among developing countries and between countries at different stages of economic and social development and lead to the achievement of common and mutually supportive objectives that take account of the interrelationships between people, resources, environment and development;

- to consider ways and means by which the international community can deal more effectively with environmental concerns;

- to help define shared perceptions of long-term environmental issues and the appropriate efforts needed to deal successfully with the problems of protecting and enhancing the environment, a long-term agenda for action during coming decades, and aspirational goals for the world community (WCED, 1987, p. ix).

The authors of *Our Common Future* exposed the dilemma implicit in policies which are based on the pursuit of economic growth, expressed largely as the provision of increasing quantities of goods and a wider range of services, largely regardless of consequences for the environment. They might take the form of land degradation in all its manifestations, problems of the disposal of solid wastes, atmospheric pollution by petrol and diesel engines, gaseous discharges from the burning of coal and hydrocarbons for power generation and other purposes and the accumulation of nuclear wastes. WCED chose to use these blunt words:

Growth has set no limit in terms of population and resource use beyond which lies ecological disaster (WCED, 1987, p. 45).

The second chapter of the report is entitled 'Towards Sustainable Development'. That is very broadly defined as development which meets the needs of the planet without compromising the ability of future generations to meet their own needs. The Commission goes on to express the following general propositions:

... Sustainable development clearly requires economic growth where ... needs (such as those of the world's poor) are not being met.

... High levels of productive activity and widespread poverty can coexist and can endanger the environment. Hence sustainable development requires that societies meet human needs both by increasing productive potential and by ensuring equitable opportunities for all.

... Sustainable development can only be pursued if demographic developments are in harmony with the changing productive potential of the ecosystem.

... Land should not be degraded beyond reasonable recovery.

... With mineral and fossil fuels, the rate of depletion and the emphasis on recycling and economy of use should be calibrated to ensure that the resource does not run out before acceptable substitutes are available.

... the rate of depletion of non-renewable resources should foreclose as few future options as possible.

... Adverse impacts on the quality of air, water, and other natural elements are minimized so as to sustain the ecosystem's overall integrity (WCED, 1987, pp. 44-6).

The Commission seems therefore to define sustainable development (or growth) as a process of change in which the exploitation of resources, the direction of investments, the orientation of technological development and institutional change are basically in harmony so as to meet current and future human needs and aspirations, while at the same time gradually arresting and eliminating activity which is progressively leading to the unacceptable degradation of the environment.

Another important point is stressed in *Our Common Future*. That is the linkage between the natural world and human activity. As some people appreciate, agricultural practices, although often based on politically acceptable policies, ultimately, sometimes all too quickly, contribute to the degradation of land, water and forests. Beyond that, estuaries and coastal seas can be adversely affected. Even more dramatically, energy policies and practices, which are based on the utilization of vast quantities of fossil fuels, pollute the air, acidify soils and lakes, degrade seas and even oceans given the huge quantities of oil which have to be moved to fuel modern economies (WCED, 1987, pp. 37-8).

This brings out the enormous philosophic and practical difficulties involved in the concept of sustainable growth, especially for a world where the population is likely to reach eight billion and could exceed ten billion.

If the current policies of the Western Pacific grouping of countries, or any other grouping for that matter, are based on unsustainable increases in the production of the goods and services because of serious irreversible damage over time to their environments, what changes should be made to avoid that threat?

Some general principles have been suggested. For example there is a need for governments to have regard to the basic premises behind the concept of ecological sustainability. That involves the way people react with the biosphere to ensure that its capacity to support us in our teeming millions will not progressively deteriorate to the point where it is incapable of providing that support. Again, some general principles have been enunciated and are gaining general acceptance.

- Biological diversity should be preserved.

- The stock of ecological resources, soil, ground and surface water, land and water biomass, should not be degraded.

- Attempts at improvements in a particular area should not be made should they impact adversely on other areas.

- Because the ecosystem could be subject to profound change, there should be a general aversion to running the risk that economic activity will contribute to such changes.

- People should consciously recognize that they must minimize 'their use of mass and energy flows relative to the total mass and energy flows of the relevant ecosystem' (WCED (Australian edition), 1990, p. 29).

Such precepts should not be dismissed as unsound or irrelevant. But could they conceivably be implemented in practice?

The Asian countries of the Western Pacific comprise one of the most heavily populated areas of the world. Parts of it, such as eastern Japan, South Korea, large areas of China, Taiwan and Java are exceptionally densely populated. It is a dynamic, restless and troubled area where the pace of economic development has been forced along by governments and industrial organizations more often than not regardless of consequences for the land, water and the atmosphere. Moreover, despite some impressive work at government and intergovernmental levels, it is very unlikely that the average person, even in developed countries such as Australia and New Zealand and Japan, is much more than dimly aware of recent developments in economic thinking, notably the argument based on ecological considerations that the pursuit of conventional economic growth could in the longer run prove disastrous.

People everywhere, on the other hand, are obviously aware of the problems of pollution. They could not fail to be so in Bangkok, Shanghai, Manila, Jakarta, Tokyo and Seoul. Recent decades have, however, brought progress for many, modest wealth for others, great wealth for some, but above all a sense that Asian people are capable of great achievements through their own efforts. There has been a consensus between governments and the governed that conventional growth policies have brought tangible benefits and the pursuit of material wealth should, if anything, be intensified.

At the bottom end of the scale the age-old problem remains for a great many people, whether they are landless rural workers, slash-and-burn cultivators or slum dwellers. Life is a struggle for existence, with little scope for consideration of the consequences of individual or collective activity, let alone acquisition of many of the better things of life available to those with more or less assured incomes. That is one of the realities of the Asian countries of the Western Pacific which can scarcely be missed, but might be ignored among the bustle and impressive activity in the cities and industrial areas which is usually taken to be evidence of great progress.

Our Common Future is an impressive call for national and international action. At WCED's final meeting in Japan on 27 February 1987, it issued the Tokyo Declaration (annexed to this chapter). The choice of Tokyo seems to have been deliberate. While Japan has made vast progress in material terms since 1945, it has experienced, and in some cases successfully addressed, many difficult economic problems. It has succeeded in becoming the leading economy in many areas of technology and, largely as a result, has come to play an important role in international trade and finance. It has shown capacity for adaptation and change which has shocked and challenged other big industrial countries, not least the United States. It has contributed massively to the development of the Western Pacific countries.

Although some of its international activity can fairly be characterized as rapacious, Japan will be, for the foreseeable future, the predominant economy in the Western Pacific, and will have a major influence on world economic development policy. Its policies have been emulated, its technological successes much admired, and its capacity to play a leading role in international economic and financial policy accepted by the Western European and North American powers. WCED may have reasoned, when it chose Tokyo for its concluding meeting, that it was crucial to convince the Japanese Government of the need for a gradual shift to sustainable economic policies. Among all the major economies, it might be the Japanese élite which has the intellectual flexibility to plan the shift to a new economic/ecological philosophy, and to see it partly as involving a great and worthwhile technological challenge rather than as an unwarranted and risky reversal of present policies.

The Tokyo Declaration is based on eight points: revive growth (in the sense of keeping the momentum of economies going albeit without demanding so much material and producing so much waste), change the quality of growth, conserve and enhance the resource base, ensure a sustainable level of population, reorient technology and the management of risk, integrate environment and management in decision-making, reform international economic relations and strengthen international cooperation (WCED, 1987, pp. 363-6).

This set of prescriptions is exemplary. It is necessary to ask whether it is realistic.

Our Common Future fails in one important respect. It does not bring out sufficiently clearly that we are probably reaching the end of an era of economic philosophy. Since the eighteenth century there have been three major streams of economic thought—mercantilist, free market (both of which allow the right to own property and the accumulation of personal wealth), and socialist. The first is based on concepts of protection and bargaining with other countries in the pursuit of national interest. It was the traditional approach of European countries like France and Germany and has been practised very successfully in recent times by Japan and South Korea. The second, deriving from the British philosopher Adam Smith, postulates that great benefit will flow to people everywhere if trade is allowed to develop nationally and internationally with the minimum of restriction. Socialism, although ostensibly international, involves in practice the adoption of policies based on the achievement of national self-sufficiency and the balancing of trade with other countries. Where it differs profoundly from the two other approaches to economic development is in rejecting private property and the formation of price structures through the operation of supply and demand in markets. They are replaced by a system of economic management, based on supposedly rational planning of every aspect of production. The end result should be an equitable society where every citizen shares appropriately in the benefits which such planning is sure to bring. We now know that this assumes the continual refinement of planning skills which is beyond the capability of bureaucratic systems.

It is however frequently overlooked that these three approaches share a common objective. That is the utilization of industrial technology to foster material economic growth. What this boils down to essentially is the development of sources of energy which will enable the production of goods and services continually to be increased, so as to achieve improvements in material benefits for the great majority of people.

Perhaps one of the lessons of recent decades is that this fundamental objective of economic systems is probably more important than the profound differences of economic doctrine and practice. They share a common assumption that greater production of goods and services will promote the welfare of the greatest number of people. Whether one system seems to be succeeding or failing is not irrelevant, but assessment of success or failure should not be allowed to obscure the fact that production, some efficient, some inefficient, has vastly increased everywhere.

There is another important assumption in *Our Common Future*. It is postulated that sustainable growth (development) is attainable and that equity between present and succeeding generations can be attained. In

other words there are ways of ensuring that present use of resources
will not deprive future generations of what they need for much more
than survival. That presupposes, among other things, that substitutes
will be found for the oil and natural gas, to use only two examples,
which are currently being consumed so rapidly.

There are, however, no grounds at this stage for assuming
substitutes will become available on a sufficient scale to make good the
foreseeable exhaustion of these precious sources of energy.

We are now having to contemplate the consequences for global,
regional and national environments of great and continuing economic
activity for the health of the biosphere. This is now influencing
economic thinking and focusing increasing attention on the essential
preliminary to the production of goods and services—the utilization of
vast amounts of energy, especially that derived from fossil fuels. This
involves simple but essential activities, such as the acquisition of
combustible materials for cooking and heating, as well as more
complex processes.

The next step is to consider the utilization of fossil fuels, notably
coal, oil and natural gas and their role in modern economies. Without
the production and distribution of these commodities in prodigious
quantities, without the products derived from them and transported
using power generated from them, the world economy could not have
developed to its present stage. Without these sources of energy it is
highly unlikely that the planet could support the present population.
Without them our present industrial societies could hardly function
(Foley, 1981, pp. 27-52).

Examination of economic processes from the perspective of
acquisition of energy materials and their utilization helps to explain the
interrelationship between the activities of people and environmental
stress no matter whether they are living in the remote valleys of Papua
New Guinea or the highly sophisticated milieu of present-day Tokyo.
At the simplest level stress can be caused if people destroy forest and
other vegetation for use as fuel or to make way for crops, and
unwittingly cause their farming land to be impaired by erosion. The
sophisticated urban dwellers collectively demand energy in such
enormous quantities that the gases and wastes coming from the use of
fossil fuels are causing a decline in the quality of air and water and are
proving harmful to soils, water systems and plant and animal life. This

demand is primarily responsible, with the burning of wood and other biomass, for the changing composition of the atmosphere.

In 1980 world energy consumption was estimated to be about ten terawatts (TW) or ten billion kilowatts. Most of this was generated from fossil fuels. If per capita use continues to increase at the rate experienced during the 1980s, WCED suggests that demand, based on assumptions that much production and use would continue to be inefficient or relatively inefficient, could reach 35 terawatts by 2030. That would mean that the world economy would use 1.6 times as much oil, 3.4 times as much gas and perhaps five times as much coal as in the mid-1980s (WCED, 1987, p. 171). Given what is already known about the harmful effects of the gases released into the atmosphere through burning fossil fuels this scarcely bears thinking about (Graedel and Crutzen, 1989, pp. 28-36). It poses a problem of a magnitude outside previous experience especially if the disturbance caused by the extension of mining and extraction to provide the quantities needed is taken into account.

This is the fundamental dilemma of the technological civilization of the twentieth century. Within a very short period of time the world population seems certain to increase to at least eight billion. Over a quarter of them will live in the countries of the Western Pacific. The question is whether or not the biosphere will be capable of sustaining so many people with a significantly enhanced level of economic activity expressed in their demand for energy, goods and services in all their forms.

An enormous and unprecedented test is coming. Perhaps the Asian countries of the Western Pacific will experience the inevitable crunch earlier than elsewhere because of extreme population pressures, especially in China, Vietnam and parts of Southeast Asia. Vast numbers of people are degrading their living space in what for many of them is a struggle to survive, and for others an understandable desire to acquire more of what they regard as the things which make for a better life.

What should be the prescriptions for a gradual shift to a new approach to economic activity based on the concepts of sustainable growth, in the light of the contemporary realities of the Western Pacific grouping of countries? It is an exceptionally diverse grouping, but one where the Japanese, through intense and sustained collective effort, have achieved a position of extraordinary influence both in trading and financial terms and also have provided a model of how to manage the transition to a high technology, high income society. Japan now has such impressive technology, capacity to deploy capital and such a highly educated and technically competent society that it could, conceivably, redefine its policies so that over time its society will be ordered in terms of an industrial philosophy which is based on or is regarded as approximating the principles of the Tokyo Declaration. That would have profound significance. It could lead first to the articulation, then to the implementation of environmentally benign technology and industrial practice.

Japan is so important to Asia and the rest of the world that such a shift in orientation would doubtless have an especially strong impact on other countries of the Western Pacific. Is such a shift conceivable? It cannot be ruled out. It would necessarily involve a profound transformation in attitudes, as it would in the United States or the European Community, which can scarcely be envisaged other than as a gradual process. Rapid transformation might only come about in the face of a series of environmental disasters which would so alarm both governments and peoples that they would accept that fundamental changes in attitudes and industrial practice were inescapable.

In order to grasp the enormous significance and difficulty of such a transformation, in Japan or any other major country or countries, it needs to be appreciated that much more than a change in the policies of governments would have to be involved. The attitudes of enterprises of every kind, regardless of their ownership, and of individuals, may turn out to be of greater importance. Idealism is a rare commodity anywhere, especially in Asian countries. A majority of Asian people are understandably preoccupied with survival in the circumstances in which they find themselves and with the task in hand. That often amounts to getting by on a day-to-day basis. For most of them government and large-scale business are outside comprehension. Life is either tolerable or a struggle. There is no scope for speculation about philosophic issues involved in macroeconomic policies and the future of the biosphere. Nevertheless they are, like people elsewhere, collectively stressing forest, land, water and air to the point where there could eventually be such a severe environmental disequilibrium that their livelihoods and societies would be endangered. Again, it may need a series of disasters to ensure that such a perception should become widely understood.

The future viability of the Western Pacific countries could depend on whether the governments and the élites which sustain them will come to be convinced of the need to develop, in response to such a threat, an entirely new basis for policy which takes fully into account the risks of undermining the gains which have been made during the past forty years. Japan is probably the only country with the necessary capacity. It has worked its way to the top of the international league. It is a member of the Group of Seven with the United States, Canada, West Germany, Britain, France and Italy. The only other Western Pacific countries, other than Singapore, which approximate its living standards and sophistication in some areas, are fellow OECD members, Australia and New Zealand. They are both slipping internationally. Their economies appear to be insufficiently strong to withstand the full force of international competitive pressures at a time when terms of trade are adverse for most of the commodities they export. They are important sources of resources for other countries of the Western Pacific, but are both geographically and economically marginal in relation to the Asian countries to their north.

Apart from the three members of the OECD and South Korea, Taiwan and Singapore, it is necessary to be realistic about the capacity of governments to give effect to basic change, even over the long term. The developing countries are confronted with great difficulties in devising and implementing policies and enforcing the law, partly because of shortages of resources and partly because they are still going through the process of building up competent and relatively honest administrations. As a consequence there are formidable difficulties in the way of achieving effective national administration and the level of international cooperation which will be an essential part of the transition to coherent economic policies let alone those based on concepts of sustainability.

Many Asian administrations are, for the meantime, capable of maintaining and improving the framework of government but that is a slow process. Enterprises and individuals often have scope to make decisions in situations where the enforcement of law is notional rather than effective. Concepts such as the rule of law and institutions such as independent judiciaries have scarcely taken hold in Asian countries.

Influence-peddling, nepotism and corruption are the rule. Government officials frequently have no alternative but to take whatever opportunities are available to supplement their meagre salaries.

Complex networks have developed nationally and internationally which are versed in exploiting loopholes in laws or the absence of effective enforcement in the pursuit of commercial objectives. The links between Japanese and overseas Chinese companies are well known, but they virtually defy analysis because most of the business-men concerned seek to avoid publicizing their activities. Whatever their faults, regardless of how nefarious aspects of their practices may seem to outsiders, the era of rapid material economic growth in the Western Pacific has produced dynamic and technically skilled enter-prises and groups of enterprises. From beginnings in Japan, China (notably Shanghai before 1949), Taiwan and Hong Kong, they have spread to South Korea, Singapore, Malaysia, Thailand and Indonesia. They are extending to other countries. There is a distinct possibility that these and other international business will be given increasing scope to operate by the governments of China and Vietnam because those countries, even should they sustain their Leninist systems for some considerable time, have no option if they wish to make rapid technological and material progress in the Asian environment.

It is probably safe to assert that the prevailing ideology of enter-prises in the Western Pacific is grounded in the belief that they need freedom to operate nationally and internationally with the objective of maximizing the production of goods and the provision of services. Indeed, demonstration of what can be achieved through the unrelenting pursuit of capacity to deliver quality goods and efficient services to national and international markets has become and remains accepted religion. Success has bred greater success. Asian enterprise has suc-ceeded in doing what most European and American industrialists for some time thought impossible. It forged to the forefront first in textiles, then in steel and shipbuilding technology, later in electronics and the production of most types of motor-powered vehicles. Inevitably lead-ing companies in Japan developed whole new ranges of products especially where the marriage of electronics and traditional engineer-ing, especially in machine tools, could improve the productivity of industry and provide new consumer goods.

By the 1980s the combination of uniformly well-educated popula-tions in Japan, South Korea and Taiwan and the availability of vast pools of labour and the progress of education in China and other Asian countries of the Western Pacific has provided the basis for the spread of the benefits of conventional economic growth. Japan, South Korea and Taiwan seized the enterprise dynamic which characterized American industry at its best and kept going when the latter faltered. Governments provided considerable protection from external competi-tion, inexpensive reliable sources of energy and low-interest finance, so as to enable businessmen to look far ahead, to plan strategies for securing shares of targeted markets without having to worry about short-term profits, to improve the quality of products and to ride out market downturns and set-backs caused by misjudgement.

It is very difficult to imagine how such a successful industrial culture could be substantially modified to enable it to more or less conform to the principles of sustainable growth. So much momentum has been generated that it would be very difficult to switch direction. Yet that is what a transition to sustainable growth necessitates. The slow process of adjustment to changing perceptions of the realities of economic processes may mean that too little is done too late to mitigate damage to the environment.

A series of calamities could accelerate reexamination of economic fundamentals, but most societies, especially those of Asia, are phleg-matic about disasters or even a series of disasters. It is more likely that a change in thinking will only come about as it gradually dawns on politicians, their advisers, the functionaries of political parties, business executives and the members of armed forces whose role extends far beyond the immediate tasks of national defence and internal stability, that the activities of the individuals which comprise the growing populations of most of the countries of the Western Pacific could be endangering their collective future.

Perhaps it is easier to grasp what the sum of these activities may actually involve by examining the human circumstances in the Western Pacific. It is home to people ranging from ancient almost untouched traditional cultures in West Irian/Papua New Guinea to among the most sophisticated urban people of modern technological civilization. On the land and in the forests there are people bridging all circumstances of the human condition from virtual stone-age cultures, slash-and-burn methods of subsistence agriculture, traditional cropping systems and plantation agriculture. Their numbers are increasing and many of them play their part in contributing to the destruction of the tropical rain-forest of Southeast Asia, Indochina, the Pacific Islands and China.

There are among these people some who make their living from producing charcoal, still the primary source of heat for vast numbers. That increases the pressures on diminishing supplies of suitable wood. Peasant farmers in their millions feed most of the people of the region in circumstances where there are fewer opportunities to bring suitable new land into production and the size of existing agricultural holdings is diminishing. They encroach on the marginal land which may erode or become desert.

Outside the agricultural/forest sectors the number of people whose incomes are adequate or substantial, given the circumstances in which they live, has created an increasingly numerous middle class. These people are rapidly acquiring the stocks of goods common in North America and Western Europe—substantial housing, vehicles and consumer goods of all kinds. It is they who provide the basis for continuing conventional economic growth as their number, incomes and savings increase. But is also they who have provided the means for the expansion of towns and cities, demanded the energy and raw materials needed for new industries, and who have contributed through their economic activity to urban congestion, pollution and proliferation of waste which characterizes so many of the cities and towns of the Western Pacific.

For the meantime, outside China and Vietnam, nearly all these people will expect to be able to continue successfully to strive for material progress within the framework which has been provided by their societies during the past three decades. After all, while development assistance programmes have been important, most economic gains have been achieved through the unremitting dedication to hard work which characterizes the Japanese, Koreans and overseas Chinese and is being emulated by people in Southeast Asia.

Proposals for a transition to policies based on concepts of sustainable growth/development need to be considered in the light of these realities. As subsequent chapters will show, it is important to consider not just populations and their growth patterns, but the economic activities of those populations and groups within them. The achievement and maintenance of material wealth by individuals can be regarded as a function of their demand for energy and raw materials. The capacity of a given population to put such stress on an environment that it will degrade, depends not just on its pattern of growth but on the way it is demanding more energy. That includes the fertility of soil itself and renewable and non-renewable materials. In the case of people living traditional lifestyles, excessive demand for the simple energy and other materials needed for the continuance of that society can cause rapid degradation.

Material progress is synonymous with the provision of more energy and the raw materials with which it is used to produce semi-finished and finished goods. It is possible to calculate the amount of materials needed to produce increasing supplies of energy and materials for industry. From that it is possible to assess the impact on the biosphere, either globally or regionally, of the processes involved in extracting materials and using them for energy production and the production of goods. In the Western Pacific demand for materials for both purposes has increased phenomenally and will continue to increase as it is the clear purpose of all governments to improve the material welfare of their peoples.

The longer-term danger is, of course, not just the depletion of regional resources, and there is ample evidence in the tropical forests of Southeast Asia. It is, as suggested earlier, that the totality of increasing economic activity, will bring about rapid and excessive degradation of the environment. In other words governments are likely to be confronted with the paradox that the pursuit of material growth as a basis for the improvement of the human condition will only provide a temporary improvement. Over the long run, increasing the economic activity of large and growing populations will prove to be unsustainable. The question whether it is realistic to expect a gradual transition to economic practice based on concepts of sustainable activity is explored in subsequent chapters

It seems especially instructive to consider the ways things could work out in the Western Pacific countries because of the sheer variety of countries in the grouping, their increasing importance in global terms, and the contrasting circumstances of the elements which make up their populations. Many locations are among the most heavily populated on earth, and in some cases support especially intense areas of economic activity. It seems likely that environmental problems attributable to the pursuit of material growth in some places and necessities of survival in others will have to be addressed sooner rather than later by Western Pacific governments. Otherwise they could face insuperable problems which will undermine their capacity even to maintain stability and order.

Annex: Tokyo Declaration

At the close of its final meeting, in Tokyo, the Commission issued the following as the Tokyo Declaration, dated 27 February 1987:

The World Commission on Environment and Development was constituted in 1984 as an independent body by the United Nations General Assembly and set out to:

(a) re-examine the critical issues of environment and development, and formulate innovative, concrete, and realistic action proposals to deal with them;

(b) strengthen international cooperation on environment and development, and assess and propose new forms of co-operation that can break out of existing patterns and influence policies and events in the direction of needed change; and

(c) raise the level of understanding and commitment to action on the part of individuals, voluntary organizations, business, institutes and governments.

As we come in Tokyo to the end of our task, we remain convinced that it is possible to build a future that is prosperous, just and secure.

But realizing this possibility depends on all countries adopting the objective of sustainable development as the overriding goal and test of national policy and international co-operation. Such development can be defined simply as an approach to progress which meets the needs of the present without compromising the ability of future generations to meet their own needs. A successful transition to a sustainable development through the year 2000 and beyond requires a massive shift in societal objectives. It also requires the concerted and vigorous pursuit of a number of strategic imperatives.

The World Commission on Environment and Development now calls upon all nations of the World, both jointly and individually, to integrate sustainable development into their goals and to adopt the following principles to guide their policy actions.

1. Revive Growth

Poverty is a major source of environmental degradation which not only affects a large number of people in developing countries but also undermines the sustainable development of the entire community of nations—both developing and industrialized. Economic growth must be stimulated, particularly in developing countries, while enhancing the environmental resource base. The industrialized countries can, and must contribute to reviving world economic growth. There must be urgent international action to resolve the debt crisis; a substantial increase in the flows of development finance; and stabilization of the foreign exchange earnings of low income commodity exporters.

2. Change the Quality of Growth

Revived growth must be of a new kind in which sustainability, equity, social justice, and security are firmly embedded as major social goals. A safe, environmentally sound energy pathway is an indispensable component of this. Education, communication, and international co-operation can all help to achieve those goals. Development planners should take account in their reckoning of national wealth not only standard economic indicators, but also of the state of the stock of natural resources. Better income distribution, reduced vulnerability to natural disasters and technological risks, improved health, preservation of cultural heritage—all contribute to raising the quality of that growth.

3. Conserve and Enhance the Resource Base

Sustainability requires the conservation of environmental resources such as clean air, water, forests and soils; maintaining genetic diversity; and using energy, water and raw materials efficiently. Improvements in the efficiency of production must be accelerated to reduce per capita consumption of natural resources and encourage a shift to non-polluting products and technologies. All countries are called upon to prevent environmental pollution by rigorously enforcing environmental regulations, promoting low-waste technologies, and anticipating the impact of new products, technologies and wastes.

4. Ensure a Sustainable Level of Population

Population policies should be formulated and integrated with other economic and social development programmes—education, health care, and the expansion of the livelihood base of the poor. Increased access to family planning services is itself a form of social development that allows couples, and women in particular, the right to self-determination.

5. Reorient Technology and Manage Risks

Technology creates risks, but it offers the means to manage them. The capacity for technological innovation needs to be greatly enhanced in developing countries. The orientation of technology development in all countries must also be changed to pay greater regard to environmental factors. National and international institutional mechanisms are needed to assess potential impacts of new technologies before they are widely used. Similar arrangements are required for major interventions in natural systems, such as river diversion or forest clearance. Liability for damages from unintended consequences must be strengthened and enforced. Greater public participation and free access to relevant information should be promoted in decision-making processes touching on environment and development issues.

6. Integrate Environment and Economics in Decision-making

Environmental and economic goals can and must be made mutually reinforcing. Sustainability requires the enforcement of wider responsibilities for the impacts of policy decisions. Those making such policy decisions must be responsible for the impacts of those decisions upon the environmental resource capital of their nations. They must focus on the sources of environmental damage rather than the symptoms. The ability to anticipate and prevent environmental damage will require that the ecological dimensions of policy be considered at the same time as the economic, trade, energy, agricultural, and other dimensions. They must be considered on the same agendas and in the same national and international institutions.

7. Reform International Economic Relations

Long term sustainable growth will require far-reaching changes to produce trade, capital and technology flows that are more equitable and better synchronized to environmental imperatives. Fundamental improvements in market access, technology transfer, and international finance are necessary to help developing countries widen their opportunities by diversifying their economic and trade bases and building their self-reliance.

8. Strengthen International Co-operation

The introduction of an environmental dimension injects an additional element of urgency and mutual self-interest, since a failure to address the interaction between resource degradation and rising poverty will spill over and become a global ecological problem. Higher priorities must be assigned to environmental monitoring, assessment, research and development, and resource management in all fields of international development. This requires a high level of commitment by all countries to the satisfactory working of multilateral institutions; to the making and observance of international rules in fields such as trade and investment; and to constructive dialogue on the many issues where national interests do not immediately coincide but require negotiation to be reconciled. It requires also a recognition of the essential importance of international peace and security. New dimensions of multilateralism are essential to sustainable human progress.

The Commission is convinced that if we can make solid progress towards meeting these principles in the balance of this century, the next century can offer a more secure, more prosperous, more equitable, and more hopeful future for the whole human family.

3. The Western Pacific Mosaic

The Western Pacific should be viewed as part of an increasingly interdependent world economy, not as an emerging region which is likely to develop into a trading bloc comparable with the European Community. Most of the countries need to trade internationally to sustain their development. Trade with the United States is especially important. The resource-rich countries, like Indonesia, Malaysia and Australia, are more likely to enhance their economic welfare by spreading their exports across international markets rather than becoming excessively dependent on Japan, South Korea and Taiwan. The same could be said of South Korea and Taiwan, *vis-à-vis* Japan, as they increase their capacity to export manufactured goods. There would be risks involved for all the countries of the Western Pacific, as well as some benefits, from the negotiation of arrangements designed to foster intra-regional trade, not least because the Northeast-Asian countries, with their instinctive protectionist orientation, are unlikely to provide market opportunities comparable with those offering in North America and Europe. Intra-regional transactions are increasing, but there is little likelihood of them becoming predominant, as distinct from increasing in relative importance, in the trade and payments of the majority of Western Pacific countries (Nakatika, 1991).

There could scarcely be a sharper contrast between the Western Pacific of the present and its political and economic geography during the imperial era which collapsed in the aftermath of the 1941-45 war. British rule in Malaysia and Singapore (and influence in Australia and New Zealand), American domination of the Philippines, Dutch and French rule in Indonesia and Indochina respectively and Japanese authority in Korea and much of China shaped the geopolitical situation. By the 1960s the imperial era was clearly over. Apart from China the now fully independent countries of the Western Pacific are, however, increasingly responsive to the economic power of Japan. Its predominance is such that it is increasingly regarded by Europeans and Americans as exercising a leadership role in the Western Pacific

(Emmott, 1989, p. 177). They point to its investment capacity, its ability to provide technical solutions for many problems, its capacity to secure strategic positions in the markets of other countries and the way in which government agencies and businesses collaborate to further Japan's power and influence.

The Japanese, seemingly working in collaboration if not in harmony, with the 'overseas' Chinese of Taiwan, Hong Kong, Singapore and other countries in Southeast Asia, have contributed significantly to the profound changes needed as the high-technology countries of the Western Pacific gradually caused a shift in the relativities of the international economic system. Japan is predominant but its style and execution of policies are tailored not just to further its own interests but also to allow for, and remedy to some extent, the deeply-rooted suspicion of its motives towards China and the other countries its forces invaded, brutalized or threatened during the past century (Whiting, 1989).

It is probably unwise to interpret the present circumstances of Asian countries or to speculate on future developments from a European or North American perspective. At this stage the importance of Japan's role in the Western Pacific is becoming better understood, especially the way it deploys its economic and financial power and the extent of its role as a model for its neighbours. But other factors need to be taken into account. Even though great economic changes have occurred since 1970, there is no certainty that the pattern of recent times will prevail during the next two, let alone, four decades.

As for China, a new regime will emerge shortly in that country as the survivors of the Long March eventually join Chairman Mao in eternal rest. Despite the suppression by the People's Liberation Army of the student protest in Beijing in 1989, and the reversion to orthodox rhetoric, no future government of China is likely to revert to policies based on self-sufficiency. China, unlike the Soviet Union, is building a significant role for itself in the international economy. A reversion to concepts of socialist self-sufficiency is probably regarded, even by the most conservative elders of the current senior leadership, as unrealistic. Although it clings to its anachronistic ideology and Communist Party-directed system, the Government of China cannot avoid responding to the challenge posed by Japan, South Korea, and other countries where ethnic Chinese financiers and industrialists are forcing the pace of economic development, of becoming an advanced industrial economy.

Progress in the southern provinces of China holds out the prospect of rates of progress which could match those of Taiwan (*Economist*, 5 October 1991, p. 21). If the authorities in Beijing were to crack down, denial of economic freedoms might trigger such widespread hostility that the system might become unworkable. Decline, collapse and a period of political instability cannot be ruled out. Neither can a transition to a less autocratic system.

While China and South Korea have reestablished cordial relations ostensibly with Japan, those relationships should be analysed with an understanding of the way in which the Asian nations interact with one another. Past excesses by Japan, although apologies have been made, will not be forgiven or forgotten. While Japan's present economic pre-eminence is accepted, it would not expect to be openly acknowledged by China and others as the leading country of the Western Pacific in a political sense. On the contrary, Japanese governments appreciate that they are expected to be sensitive and reasonably cautious in developing and executing policy, taking fully into account China's great power status, Korea's increasing importance in regional and world affairs and the need to avoid souring relations with the countries of Southeast Asia. Japan might be better described as capable of wielding great influence rather than leadership. Its neighbours, without exception, wish to avoid excessive dependence on Japan. The Japanese seem to understand China's intention to become the predominant power, no matter how long that process might take. After all it was the Japanese, through their development of the capacity to wage modern war in the Western Pacific, who ignited the powerful urge in China to transform itself into a technological society.

Furthermore, populous countries like Indonesia, grouped with other significant countries in ASEAN (the Association of Southeast Asian Nations), also serve as a counterweight in political although much less in economic terms. The former Prime Minister of Singapore, Mr Lee Kuan Yew, held the view that Vietnam's policy of seeking hegemony in Indochina was the external geostrategic consideration which provided the foundation of the collective interest of the ASEAN countries (*Asia Yearbook 1990*, p. 62). The apprehension on geostrategic grounds has receded to some extent. Now the governments of the Southeast-Asian countries are also faced in their collective interest with a need to consider together the consequences of Japanese long-term intentions and economic activities. It is probably as difficult for them as for China, South Korea and Vietnam actually to acknowledge Japan as a regional leader, as distinct from being, for the meantime, by far the most important of the economies of the Western Pacific. They have no wish again to be the creatures of any foreign power.

In Asia historical traditions and age-old concepts of behaviour exert a continuing and especially powerful influence. Diplomatic relations are conducted with a sense of and respect for protocol which dates from ancient times. It is instinctive in most circumstances to build relationships using personal contacts and networks, and frequently to avoid publicity. Understandings may be reached between countries who are deeply suspicious of each other's intentions, for example between Japan and China, Japan and South Korea, Vietnam and China, Malaysia and Indonesia which, while not diminishing suspicion or even an underlying sense of enmity, enable economic relationships to develop and subsequently to flourish.

Robert Elegant has written about what he terms 'the Asian ethos': the tenacious accretion of power and virtue. It is the core, he suggests, of the philosophy of many Asians, especially the Chinese, Japanese and Koreans. They are inclined to think instinctively in decades and generations rather than in terms of calculation of short-term advantage (Elegant, 1990, p. 511).

There is another important factor. That is the tenacity and sometimes longevity of leadership in many Asian countries. There are notable exceptions such as Japan where leadership is an elusive collective process (Van Wolferen, 1990). But in a majority of the Asian countries of the Western Pacific, the Koreas, China, Vietnam, Singapore and Indonesia, there has been firm if autocratic leadership. It has often contributed to, or enforced, stability. In some cases it has clearly assisted in fostering economic development. In others—China under Mao, Indonesia under Sukarno and the Philippines under Marcos—it has limited or misdirected economic processes. It could also mean that there could be acute problems of legitimate political succession and unrest because evolution to less authoritarian forms of government has been stifled.

I return later in this chapter to the differing characters of the governments of the Western Pacific. It seems important to understand their basically autocratic or authoritarian attributes otherwise one is likely to misinterpret political and economic developments. In this context it is particularly relevant to consider their differing capacities to effect changes to economic policy and practice which will rectify serious environmental degradation.

Geography of the Western Pacific

The countries of the Western Pacific extend over an immense continental and maritime environment. Those bordering the Pacific Ocean, China, Indochina and the Korean peninsula, are the cradles of ancient and durable civilizations. A unique geographical feature of this part of the world is the chain of archipelagoes which extends across two hemispheres. The islands of the Western Pacific are part of a great geologic rim. They abound with mountain chains, volcanoes and complex systems of reefs. They are prone to earthquakes and, like the coastal regions of their neighbouring continents, typhoons. The great chain of islands extends from the Kurile Islands north of Japan, through the Philippines and Indonesia to the Melanesian Islands and New Zealand which spans the fortieth and fiftieth parallels in the distant reaches of the temperate zone of the Southern Hemisphere. South of Indonesia and Melanesia is the sparsely populated island continent of Australia.

The continental countries of the Western Pacific, with their great mountain chains and river systems, support about a billion and a half people. It is important when considering the scale and significance of this part of Asia to disregard political boundaries and to examine the way the land itself supports its people. The importance of the river systems is virtually self-evident. There are three great rivers in China, the Huanghe (Yellow), the Changjiang (Yangtze) and the Zhujiang (Pearl); the Red River which reaches the sea in the north of Vietnam; the Mekong which, from its sources in China and Tibet, flows down between Laos and Thailand, crosses Cambodia and forms a great delta in the south of Vietnam; the Chao Phraya which drains the great basin of central Thailand.

For generations people have developed a highly productive system of agriculture based on rice and other intensively cultivated crops, supplemented by domestic livestock, notably poultry and pigs, and inland fisheries. Irrigation, which began in ancient times, enabled the fertile valleys of the river systems of both the Asian continent and the archipelagoes to support large populations in historical times and, not without great effort, the immense increases in population during this century. An overview of East Asia from a satellite would reveal the way in which the hinterland, with its great extensions of the Himalayan massif, provides the snowfields, glaciers, lakes and forested ranges which catch and conserve the water, and sustains rivers great and small. Most of the major rivers rise or flow from mountain systems which are in Chinese territory or close to it. Elsewhere, and especially on the islands, smaller river basins with headwaters in mountain spines or volcanic areas have enabled farming communities to replicate the agricultural systems of the valleys of the continent.

There is a vital connection between these mountain and river systems and the economic health of the countries of the Western Pacific. If the deserts of western China advance, if the deciduous forests of its north are depleted, and if too much of the semi-tropical and tropical forests of southern China, Indochina, Southeast Asia, Melanesia and Australia succumb to the chainsaws and heavy machinery of timber companies, peasant timber cutting and slash-and-burn agriculture, river systems will slowly cease to have the capacity to sustain the civilizations they have supported, in many cases, for thousands of years.

The rivers are not only the life-support system for agriculture, they are essential to the functioning of the industrial conurbations which have grown up around ancient and new cities. Populations are exceptionally concentrated in the lower reaches of the river systems. Beijing, Tianjin, Shanghai and Guangzhou (Canton) in China, Hanoi and Ho Chi Minh City (Saigon) in Vietnam, Bangkok in Thailand and Surabaya in Indonesia are examples. Further inland are great centres like Wuhan, Xian, Zhengzhou and Shenyang in China. They, and many other cities, are the focal points of huge concentrations of people whose long-term well-being depends on the careful management of their hinterlands.

The islands of the chain of archipelagoes provide many contrasts. The lowlands of Honshu in Japan, Taiwan and Java are among the most densely populated places on earth. The islands of Japan have been transformed during less than 150 years into what many regard as the epitome of advanced industrial development. There, nearly 130 million people crowd the coastal plains of the island of Honshu and its smaller companions Kyushu and Shikoku. The northern island of Hokkaido offers some open space and the still forested mountain chains of Honshu are largely protected from excessive human encroachment. Industrial Japan is a crowded pattern of linked cities and towns stretching from northern Kyushu to northern Honshu. It has become densely webbed with railways, highways and high-tension electricity systems. There are vast concentrations of people in greater Tokyo and greater Osaka. Japan demonstrates how extreme the pressures exerted by human populations on small land areas can be. The Japanese seem to be arriving at an understanding of the pressures they place on the limited land and water resources of their islands. Comprehending the demands that their now enormously powerful industrial civilization places on other countries from which they draw the goods that sustain that civilization, is a much slower process.

Other islands in the chain of archipelagoes provide a series of contrasts. There are the great islands of Luzon and Mindanao in the Philippines, Sumatra, Java, Borneo and Sulawesi in Indonesia, some supporting mega-cities like Manila and Jakarta and intensely cultivated river basins. Despite the advance of technological civilization, millions are living close to traditional ways. Beyond the islands running east from Java is the complex of mountains, rivers and forests of what was not so long ago the home of stone-age people now known as West Irian/Papua New Guinea. Beyond these islands the other islands of Melanesia curve away to the southeast. Similarly they were almost untouched by intruders from Asia and Europe until the nineteenth century. Their people were few and cut off from all but occasional contact with their Asian neighbours. There could hardly have been a sharper contrast between the immensely sophisticated and complex rice-growing civilization of Java, let alone modern technological Japan, and the traditional ways of the still numerous hunter-gatherer and shifting cultivation tribes of the mountain country of the archipelagoes and especially of the remote forested reaches of West Irian/Papua New Guinea.

In the southern hemisphere are Australia and New Zealand. The latter is a cool-climate example of Pacific Rim island landform with its volcanoes, mountain spines, short fast-flowing rivers and potentially fertile plains. In some ways there is a geographical twin of Japan in the remote waters of the Southwest Pacific. The difference is that it is the most remote of the large island groups and, even in this century, lightly populated.

Australia is thirty times larger. Although close to the Melanesian archipelago, it provides an almost complete contrast in its geography. It is much more ancient geologically. Its mountains are low and weathered to the point where many are mere remnants. Away from the eastern seaboard it is dry, with deserts extending through the centre to the Indian Ocean coast. There is one great river system draining the country west of the confined eastern watershed and the more amply watered southeastern corner. River flow is variable depending heavily on periodic floods. Its indigenous inhabitants lived as hunter-gatherers. Their societies are of immense antiquity. The process of European occupation began two hundred years ago, a little later in New Zealand. That inevitably triggered a transformation of unique biological environments, as forests, savannahs and grasslands provided opportunities for cereal and livestock production which adapted European methods to new and challenging conditions.

People of the Western Pacific

More than half the people of the countries of the Western Pacific regard themselves as Han Chinese. They have cultivated the coastal and central provinces of China for more than four millennia and have migrated to other countries. They are probably the largest and most homogeneous ethnic group anywhere. Even so there are pronounced differences between north and south, east and west. The spoken Chinese of the south differs markedly from the Mandarin dialect of the Beijing area which is now taught throughout the education system. As one would expect of such a vast country there are numerous dialects which add richness and variety to Han China.

Other peoples live in the perimeter of modern China. In the north there are Manchus and Mongolians, on the border of Kazakhstan, Uigars, south of them Tibetans and many other peoples along the mountainous borderlands with Vietnam, Laos and Burma.

Han Chinese have spread to Taiwan, Vietnam, Thailand, Singapore, Malaysia and, in lesser numbers, to the other countries of Southeast Asia. They are usually referred to as *Overseas Chinese*. They have always been able to maintain their links with China, despite difficulties during the time of Mao Zedong's paramountcy. Taken together with the people of Hong Kong they are a formidable element in the business and politics of the Western Pacific. In many respects Bangkok can be regarded as a Chinese city; over one-third of the population of Malaysia is Chinese; Singapore is predominantly an *Overseas Chinese* city-state. Although they comprise a small proportion of the population in the Philippines and Indonesia, where they have been subject to harassment and massacre, they play an important role in business and finance (Schwarz, 1991a, p. 40). Their connections extend not just back to China but to the growing expatriate communities in the United States, Canada and Australia. In this era of industrial and financial expansion, networks have been developed and strengthened which are pursuing international trading objectives, and serve as a partial counterweight to the economic power of Japan and the growing strength of South Korea.

Lynn Pan, herself one of the overseas Chinese, notes that such people make up a disproportionate share of the commercial class of the countries of Southeast Asia. They have built up their communities and the more prominent are big players in the economies. They have displayed will, energy and flair. The most outstanding have attained positions of power and influence despite the reluctance of the governments of their adopted countries. They have always been disliked as they are seen to have profited in environments where the local people do not share their drive to make money and build up business empires (Pan, 1990, p. 225). Lynn Pan also makes the point that:

> The Chinese businessman is no stranger to the world of bribes and back-room deal-making. He has learnt over the years, that a government policy favouring the indigenous businessman need not always be a bar to his activities; for it is certainly not beyond his ingenuity to find himself a native sleeping partner, a front man who gets the licence, takes a cut, and leaves him to run the actual

business. Very often a native suitor for a government concession is without the means or ambition to work it, and would have to pass it to a Chinese to make it operable. In much of Southeast Asia, it is well known that it takes two to get an 'Ali Baba' business off the ground—Ali the Indonesian or Malay who qualifies for the government handouts, Baba the Chinese with the capital and skill (Pan, 1990, p. 228-9).

For the present Japan and South Korea dominate Northeast Asia. Despite some cultural similarities the Japanese and the Koreans take great pains to distinguish themselves from one another and from the Chinese. Few countries would rank with the Japanese when it comes to pride in race and a (probably false) conception of their racial homo-geneity or purity. They have been protected by the sea from invasions. They chose deliberately to keep foreign influences to a minimum until the American 'black fleet' forced a change in this most basic of policies in the 1850s. Since that time the Japanese people have made the most remarkable adaptation to Euro-American technological civilization. Throughout that time they have nevertheless striven to preserve their homogeneity and to pursue with relentless persistence national objec-tives from the increasingly strong economic bastion of their home islands (Holstein, 1990).

The Koreans have not been so fortunate. Their pensinsula has been coveted by both China and Japan. They endured Japanese occupation for most of the first half of this century and their country was parti-tioned as a consequence of the Second World War. The consequence was the development of a rigid communist system in the north and a now powerful market, or more precisely mercantilist, economy in the south. The Koreans regard themselves as hemmed in by the Chinese, Russians and the Japanese. There is great frustration at the conse-quences of partition and a longing for the country to be united. Circumstances have made the people of the south ambitious for their country, and intent on matching the Japanese as an industrial and trading nation.

The Vietnamese, whose country extends from southeast China to the Gulf of Thailand, are similar to the Koreans in that their nationality has been forged in the long and continuing struggle to assert themselves as a people independent of their great neighbour. Their origins as a people go back over two millenia. They asserted their independence from China for the first time as early as the ninth century. French colonialism, which was thrown off in the 1950s, could be regarded as a relatively brief interlude in an ancient and continuing struggle. While the Vietnamese have recently dominated their neighbouring countries, Laos and Cambodia, these countries too have struggled, following the withdrawal of the French, to establish their identities as nations separate from both Vietnam and China.

The same can be said of Thailand. The Thais managed to avoid colonial rule. With the benefit of greater distance from China, they have also sought to limit external influences, but they have accepted many immigrants from China. Like the Vietnamese, they have had to acknowledge the existence of numerous smaller ethnic groups in their often unmarked remote borderlands.

In Malaysia the population comprises indigenous tribespeople, Malays, people from the Indian sub-continent and Chinese. There are strict boundaries between the major racial groups. The Malays are about as numerous as the others combined and hold firm control of political power. The Chinese dominate business and the professions and sustain close links with the Chinese city-state of Singapore.

The peoples who inhabit the Malayan peninsula and the archipelagoes of the Philippines and Indonesia are as diverse as the mountain chains, valleys and the thousands of islands which they inhabit. The use of the term Malay to describe the majority of these people is inappropriate. The peoples of these islands are a blend of indigenous peoples and waves of immigrants from India, the Middle East, China, Indochina and Europe. There is a pastiche of languages and dialects with some like Bahasa Indonesia/Malay and Tagalog used as national languages or for common parlance.

Malaysian, Filipino or Indonesian nationality is a new and probably still an artificial construction in this maritime region. It traces back after all to boundaries drawn during the centuries of Spanish, Dutch and British colonization and may not sit easily with the local cultures and aspirations of peoples who treasure their own traditions.

The population of the Philippines is concentrated on the major islands of Luzon and Mindanao. Ethnically the people are distantly related to the Malays and most Indonesians. Chinese traders first came to the Philippines about ten centuries ago and the Chinese presence, although relatively small, is important (Pan, 1990, pp. 31-4). This archipelago did not, however, come under Chinese cultural dominance, nor did it receive the waves of religious and cultural influence which had such profound effects on Japan and Indonesia. Indeed when the Spanish, as part of their great venture across the Pacific from the Americas, annexed the islands their peoples, apart from some encroachment by Islam in the south, were still practising traditional religions. Spanish rule persisted for over three hundred years. The Philippines is unique among Asian countries in being predominantly Christian.

Spanish rule collapsed at the turn of this century when that country was at war with the United States. Its cultural influence gave way to the pervasive aspects of American popular culture, with the English language eclipsing Spanish. Despite these powerful outside influences, the Philippines remains a complex Asian country, but with a traditional and still powerful landholding class. It is similar to that of some Latin American countries, and reflects their common inheritance from Spanish colonialism (McBeth, 1989, p. 36). More than seventy languages are spoken. That in itself indicates the complex character of the population and, as is especially evident in island countries, the persistence of local traditions. Islam has taken hold in the south while elswhere Communism has had a strong influence among the landless and the discontented.

The other great archipelagic country of Southeast Asia—Indonesia —provides both a comparison and a contrast to the Philippines. It has never been immune from migration flows and cultural influences from continental Asia lying as it does to the immediate south of the traditional trade route from the Indian sub-continent to China. Culturally, linguistically, and ethnically, Indonesia is especially diverse. Buddhist and Hindu culture came to the archipelago in the seventh century reaching great heights of sophistication in Java and Bali. From the fourteenth century the Islamic religion of Arab traders, who had developed a network reaching as far as China, took hold and formed a strong overlay in Sumatra, Java and some other islands. Indonesia is consequently a predominently Muslim country. But there are other religions, such as Balinese Hinduism, Christianity and persistent traditional beliefs. People in Indonesia have a capacity to synthesize their traditional beliefs with concepts and practices of newer religions. In Java the religious underlay of the culture is regarded as virtually defying classification and even understanding other than by those versed in the language and thought of Javanese civilization.

Not long after Islam began to take hold in the islands, the complex pastiche of kingdoms and sultanates was progressively subdued by the Dutch and incorporated into their colonial empire. It survived from the sixteenth century until it effectively collapsed in the face of the Japanese invasion in 1942. Indonesia is nevertheless as much a manifestation of Dutch colonialism as the Philippines is of Spanish. Its present territory comprises the territories annexed by the Dutch as they extended their colonial rule from Java and the former Portuguese colony of East Timor.

The system of rule inherited from the colonial administration has been preserved, and the concept of Indonesian nationality incorporated in the political and education systems. Dutch hegemony has been replaced by that of Java. The focal point of the entire country is now the great Javanese city of Jakarta which has emerged from the original Dutch colonial enclave of Batavia. Java is one of the most densely populated places on earth, and numerically dominates the archipelago with more than half the population concentrated on that marvellously fertile, intensely volcanic island.

Malaysia, comprising the southern half of the Malayan peninsula and two enclaves, Sarawak and Sabah, on the northern coast of the island of Borneo, which became part of the British rather than the Dutch colonial empire, can properly be regarded, with the city-state of Singapore, as part of the Southeast Asian archipelago. The Malayan people are closely related to many Sumatrans and the indigenous tribes of Sabah and Sarawak share traditions with kin who happened to live on either side of the borders eventually agreed by the British and the Dutch. In pre-colonial times the Sultanate of Malacca extended across the south of the peninsula and across the straits to large areas of central Sumatra.

The peninsula itself was the focus of conflict between the Portuguese and the Dutch in the seventeenth century. The latter eventually gave way to the British, who incorporated what are now Malaysia and Singapore into their empire. The economic development they pursued, notably the tin, rubber and palm oil industries, were labour intensive, involving work which did not appeal to Malays. The British solved this problem by recruiting Chinese and Indian workers. The consequence of that development is that contemporary Malaysia has a mixed population, comprising about 60 per cent Malays, 30 per cent Chinese and 10 per cent Indian and others. The city of Singapore, which was founded by the British, became predominently Chinese. It is now an independent, vibrant, commercial centre, of great importance to both Malaysia and Indonesia at the crossroads of Southeast Asia.

To the east and south of Indonesia lie three Western Pacific countries, Papua New Guinea, Australia and New Zealand. Their contacts with the Asian countries of the Western Pacific are relatively recent, but already their economic future seems to have become closely dependent on that of the countries to their north (Garnaut, 1989). These three countries existed ethnically and culturally apart from Asia until the consequences of Asian economic development began directly to affect them, some fifteen years after the Japanese armed forces smashed through the defences of the British, Dutch and French empires in 1941-42.

Papua New Guinea was one of the last untouched places on earth until the European powers completed the parcelling out of the few remaining islands of the Pacific a century ago. Until 1914 the northern sector was a German colony, the southern half administered by Australia. After the 1914-18 war Australia administered both sectors until independence in 1973. (The western half of the main island was part of the Dutch empire. It was ceded to Indonesia in 1963.)

The people of Papua New Guinea are Melanesian and identify with the other Melanesians of the Southwest Pacific rather than with Asia. Their kin are in Irian Jaya and others in the more distant Solomon Islands, Vanuatu and New Caledonia. The population is extremely diverse. There are hundreds of languages and dialects in Papua New Guinea and, as with all archipelagic countries, tensions arise between ethnic groups on the main island, and between them and people on other islands such as New Britain, New Ireland and Bougainville.

Most of the people of Papua New Guinea were living in traditional ways, some of them very ancient, until this century. Some knew nothing else until they were fought over during the 1941-45 war. Their country is another artificial construct based on the Australian colonial administration. Independent Papua New Guinea has endeavoured, in the face of the most formidable geographical and cultural difficulties, to develop a sense of nationhood among peoples to whom such a concept would be totally unfamiliar. At the same time a rather unstable sequence of governments has had to cope with the stresses caused by major commercial projects run by foreigners—mining, timber-getting, plantation agriculture and other forms of development. It has also had to deal with problems associated with the rapid growth of urban centres which have necessitated adaptation to lifestyles unrelated to those of traditional villages.

Papua New Guinea has resources of copper and gold, of timber, coffee and rubber which are of significance to the region. It has become part of the economy of the Western Pacific but that has brought tensions and problems for a government whose electors were unfamiliar with tertiary education and cash economy a few decades ago.

Australia and New Zealand are largely European enclaves in the Western Pacific. They are underpopulated countries to which British and other migrants spread from Europe in their search for land and industries to develop, mines to open and the chance to fashion new societies unencumbered by the ancient traditions of their homelands. Their economies flourished in the age of empire, providing food and raw materials to the industries of Great Britain. That comfortable relationship persisted until the 1950s. Since then their trading interests have shifted away from Western Europe, first towards the United States, then to Japan and other countries in Asia.

These countries are now linked by a free-trade agreement. They lie resource-rich and underpopulated—twenty million people between them—south of the heavily populated Asian countries of the Western Pacific.

While the original immigrants to Australia and New Zealand were predominantly from the British Isles, there have been important changes in the composition of their populations during the second half of this century. In New Zealand the indigenous Maori population has grown rapidly and the Polynesian element of the population has been enhanced by immigration from the Cook Islands, Samoa and Tonga. The population of Australia was significantly augmented after the Second World War by immigration from Western and Eastern Europe as well as from Britain. People came in numbers from Mediterranean countries such as Italy, Greece, Malta and Yugoslavia. Since then there have been flows from Turkey, Lebanon and other Middle Eastern countries, and from Asia, notably Vietnam, the Philippines, Hong Kong and Malaysia. The arrival of large numbers of refugees from

Vietnam—some of them the 'boat people' who made the long journey at great risk in small craft—caused Australians to realize that they could not regard themselves as safeguarded by sheer distance from Asia.

Australia's big cities have taken on a multicultural flavour. While still predominantly European, they are now further changing as a consequence of immigration from Asia. The Chinese, Filipino, Vietnamese and other Asian communities will continue to grow.

The changes in the composition of the populations of Australia and New Zealand reflect in part their growing economic involvement with the Asian countries of the Western Pacific. They also reflect their political responses to developments in Asia such as the war in Vietnam, the outflow of refugees and the uncertainty about the political future of Hong Kong.

Economic Development

While it is not easy to summarize the economic development, and the now-sophisticated trading and commercial linkages which connect the countries of the Western Pacific, it is not at all difficult to pick out the features which, taken together, bring out the area's extraordinarily dynamic character. They include the growth of agricultural, forest, mineral and industrial production; the development of capital markets; the implementation of sophisticated systems for the transport of goods and for communications; the growth of service industries and the strengthening of personal and business networks.

Each year the *Far Eastern Economic Review* presents, in its *Asia Year Book*, comprehensive data which enables one to build-up a reasonably comprehensive picture of the way in which the countries of the Western Pacific are developing. Some of these data are used in subsequent chapters to illustrate disparities between countries as well as relative economic size. They also bring out, when compared with comparable data for Western Europe or the United States-Canada, the extent to which the countries of East Asia have assumed greater relative importance in the world economy and the contrasts between the affluent, the not-so-affluent and the relatively poor. They are very sharp when the GDP estimates of Japan, Australia, Singapore, Hong Kong and New Zealand are compared with those of the poor countries, especially the Philippines, China and Vietnam. On one interpretation the future looks bright, especially if it can be safely assumed that, with some outside assistance, Vietnam and China will prove capable of solving the problems in the way of making the industrial and service sectors of their economies reasonably efficient. Sufficient progress seems to have been achieved in countries such as Thailand, Malaysia and Indonesia to enable them eventually to reduce the gap between their present levels of achievement, expressed in estimates of per capita GDP, and those of Japan and the other high income countries.

Another interpretation suggests that most analysis of the prospects for the countries of the Western Pacific is rather too narrowly based. In order to gain an adequate and balanced appreciation of the prospects for these countries during the next three or four decades it is important to consider not just data relating to industrial production, capital formation, growth of international trade in goods and services and the development of national infrastructures. What is also needed is an understanding of the state of wilderness, of agriculture and forests, of river systems, lakes, both natural and artificial, and of coastal waters. On top of that, no assessment of the economic future of the countries of the Western Pacific should ignore the consequences of further increases in populations, their demand for energy and materials, transitions from rural to urban employment, the capacity of education systems to provide the trained people needed by increasingly technological societies and the ability of individual countries to maintain and further develop essential infrastructure.

The broad assessment which would provide a fuller appreciation of prospects and problems should be a composite based on such data as are available, extrapolations from the data, and descriptive material which amplifies and may qualify what can be derived from the statistics. In other words the assessment would include both the pluses and minuses of recent development, or lack of it, and attempt judgements on serious problems such as the extent to which trained people are available to ensure the success of future projects.

In the chapters which follow I attempt to summarize the essential demographic issues and the likely consequences of the demand of growing populations in the developing countries for the commodities which provide the foundation for material economic growth, fossil fuels. I also attempt to present a realistic overview of the state of the environments of the countries of the Western Pacific which avoids the alarmist tone of some writing about the degradation of land and waters. My argument is that it is simplistic to attempt to address the prospects for the economies of the Western Pacific without taking fully into account both the positive and the negative consequences of developments which have occurred since the Asian countries began to respond to the technological challenge posed by the incursions of foreign powers from Europe and North America. They include problems associated with growth of populations and degradation of the environment which have been largely disregarded except in the work of the United Nations Economic and Social Commission for Asia and the Pacific (ESCAP) which has its headquarters in Bangkok.

It can also be argued that it is simplistic, no matter how sophisticated economic analysis may be, to attempt to assess the future of regions or of groupings as large as the countries of the Western Pacific without taking into account the nature and calibre of governments in their considerable variety. There are many difficulties in the way of sensible analysis of the capacity of governments to manage their economies and to ensure stability and transitions from one regime to another. If, however, their capacities are taken as given for the purpose of making an assessment of their capacity to effect political, legal and economic change, misjudgements may be made. If it is moreover assumed that they will continue competently to deal with problems which confront them, or will become capable of so doing in the face of present incompetence and corruption, then the future may bring unpleasant surprises for those who place an optimistic interpretation on the economic data.

Governments

The political stability of many of the countries of the Western Pacific is far from assured. Political eras are coming to an end in China, Vietnam and Indonesia. Military people are effectively in power or prop up civilian regimes in a majority of countries. There is no reason to assume that there will be a smooth transition from present governments to their successors.

The dispositions made by the United States in the immediate postwar years and expressed in a series of security arrangements with

Japan, South Korea, Taiwan, the Philippines and Australia and New Zealand, seem to have contributed to long-term stability, despite the brutality of the wars in Korea and Vietnam and the seemingly interminable period of cold war between the United States and China (Nester, 1990, pp. 13-45; Segal, 1990, p. 235). Despite the threat of political instability in many countries the American presence enabled trade and commerce to flourish. The devastation of the wars in Korea and Vietnam was catastrophic for those countries, but military outlays stimulated industrial development elsewhere. The Japanese were assured that the circumstances of the 1930s and early 1940s, when their access to raw materials was threatened, would not repeat themselves. The progressive liberalization of world industrial trade contributed to relatively rapid rates of economic growth. Although bursts of rapid growth were followed by periods of economic instability or stagnation, those periods were relatively brief. For the most part the market economies beginning with South Korea and Taiwan have been able to emulate Japan in sustaining high, or relatively high rates of growth. Thailand has performed strongly during the past decade as have Malaysia and Indonesia (Schlossstein, 1991).

While there will always be debate about the consequences of the United States' policies in the Western Pacific after 1945, there seems little doubt that the management of its relationship with Japan, its intervention to prevent the communist takeover of South Korea, its refusal to contemplate surrendering Taiwan to China and, importantly, its willingness to open up its market to foreign industrial products have made an important contribution to the rates of growth which have been achieved in Northeast Asia and to the establishment and expansion of export industries in China and the countries of Southeast Asia.

It would be unwise, however, to assume nearly two decades after the end of the vicious and, for the United States, humiliating war in Vietnam, that indefinite economic progress is assured. The post-1945 security system cannot be expected to last forever, nor can the United States or any other major market continue to absorb unlimited quantities of industrial exports.

The nature of many of the regimes of the Asian countries of the Western Pacific gives cause for concern. It would be naive to expect European-style pluralistic parliamentary democracies to take root in Asia, although some of their forms may be borrowed. They are the outcome of centuries of political development which only Australia and New Zealand, among the countries of the Western Pacific, share. Cultural and governmental traditions, especially obedience to authority, are so powerful, the societies so complex that, although liberalization of political life may gradually occur, the alternation of power following elections conducted according to law between competing national political parties capable of assuming government, as distinct from groups and factions within a dominant party, should be expected to be exceptional.

As an Asian scholar has expressed it:

> Up to now, the relevant political institutions in Asia have been largely based on Westminster or Capitol Hill or other Western models. These have not fared well. Indeed, many have been counter-productive, especially as they have been culturally alien concepts transplanted into societies which by and large have no empathetic or corresponding value systems, that is those relating to, say, individual rights or privacy. Instead, the Asian world has been based much more on values emphasizing responsibilities and duties and the 'commons'. Concepts like one man one vote, sanctity of the ballot box, and individual privacy are acquired values and desires. In any case, older, traditional world-views based on such concepts as *deva-raja*, and those relating to hierarchy and status according to one's birth, wealth and so on, have not necessarily disappeared from the scene if the readiness with which the rich buy power, and the highly-placed buy votes, are any indications to go by (Sandhu, 1992, pp. 239-40).

This brings out the need to weigh up the capacity of governments of various complexions to manage both their economies and their environments. On the one hand, autocratic or authoritarian regimes may be able to bring about changes needed and effectively reeducate and mobilize large populations. But against that, pervasive corruption and problems of legitimate succession, when ageing rulers become enfeebled or die, have to be taken into account.

Military and quasi-military governments

It is perhaps encouraging that during recent years overt military rule in countries like South Korea, Taiwan and Thailand has given place, for periods of time at least, to civilian rule and periodic elections. That should not necessarily be taken to mean that the ability of the military to exercise decisive influence, albeit from behind the scenes, has been significantly reduced.

In South Korea, for example, military action against dissenting citizens a decade ago, notably students, eventually brought discredit upon the armed forces and undermined the credibility of the governments they had imposed upon the country (Garnaut, 1989, p. 133). There was a further welling up of opposition in 1989 and the country seemed to skirt the very edge of revolution. The threat remains. Popular discontent can be traced to the way in which the military have dominated the Presidency since a military coup in 1961 and the brutal methods used to suppress militancy among students and the labour force. Three generals, Park Chung Hee, who was assassinated in 1979, Chun Doo Wan, forced out of office in 1987 and subsequently disgraced, and the present incumbent Roh Tae Woo have exercised predominent power in South Korea (*Asia Yearbook 1990*, pp. 155-7). They and their military colleagues have formed a working alliance with the families which control the major companies. It seems that fifty families in Korea control over half the country's wealth and operate through webs of obligation and patronage. That has created a problem of disparity between the haves and the have-nots which is thought to be second only to that in the Philippines (*Australian Financial Review*, 13 June 1990, p. 14). The close relations between the military and business élites means that government in South Korea is inevitably dominated by people with close family, professional and client relationships. It is a pattern which repeats itself throughout Asia, an ever-present fact of life which is at the heart of all the political systems.

There are parallels in Taiwan, Thailand and Indonesia. The Government of Taiwan persists as a manifestation of the Kuomintang Party which has always held power as an ostensibly civilian administration. It was organized over sixty years ago on Leninist lines and led by Chiang Kai Shek both in China and in exile in Taiwan. The Kuomintang was recognized as the Government of China by the United States and many countries until the 1970s. The fact that it had been discredited, beaten in civil war and expelled from the mainland by Mao Zedong's Communists who established the People's Republic of China in 1949, could not be evaded despite the formalities of diplomatic recognition. Nevertheless it has hung on and has gradually acquired respectability. That may be attributable to Taiwan's impressive industrial development.

The predominance of the Chiang family has faded since the death of Kai Shek's son Ching Kuo in 1988, but power in Taiwan is still the preserve of the Kuomintang Party and the military which have sustained it in office. As in Korea a slow process of reform is under way, but the ruling party's military wing plays an important part in electoral campaigns, providing candidates, calling on the loyalties of former soldiers and assisting with ensuring that political organization is effective. (*Asia Yearbook 1990*, p. 229; 1991, p. 219).

In Thailand, as in Japan, a respected monarchy survives and exerts a stabilizing effect on domestic politics. There is increasing public attachment to democratic processes and institutions. But the political reality is that military power predominates, and there is no evidence that the military are likely to accept subordination to civilian administrations. The senior officers have for many years established themselves at the centre of the power structure.

In one sense the political history of Thailand is a sad tale of democratic institutions not seeming to be able to take firm root. In another sense it reflects many of the understandable if, from a western democratic perspective, deplorable realities of politics in East Asia. In 1957 the authoritarian regime of Pibul Songkhram, which dated from the 1930s, fell to a coup organized by Field Marshal Sarit Thanarat. He was succeeded six years later by Thanom Kittikachorn who in 1971 annulled the constitution and exercised martial-law powers through a National Executive Council. The constitution he promulgated a year later gave Thanom dictatorial powers. Military and police representatives held 200 of the 299 seats in the national assembly. So outrageous did this arrogant assumption of power seem to people in Thailand that the regime collapsed and there was a brief period of civilian rule until 1976. That year another coup brought a return to military rule under General Prem Tinsulanond. He was Prime Minister until a second upwelling of popular pressure forced the holding of elections in 1988.

The Chart Thai Party was able to form a civilian coalition. Its leader Chatichai Choonhaven was Prime Minister until 1991 when he was forced from office by the armed forces. Ostensibly a civilian he in fact reached the rank of General in the Thai army (*Asia Yearbook 1990*, pp. 234-6). He had only brief success in persuading the military to stay in the background. He failed and Thailand once again passed into the hands of a junta which rules in the name of the 'National Peacekeeping Council' (Tasker, 1991, p. 20).

While the concepts of democratic politics seem increasingly to be understood in Thailand, it is much too early to assume that elected civilian governments will take effective control of the country in the foreseeable future. It is possible because there is a growing pool of competent professional civilians, who can provide the sinews of administration. The economy is expanding and a powerful group of families have emerged in Bangkok, many of them Thai-Chinese. Their businesses account for over half of Thailand's output. They have a strong interest in maintaining political stability and at least the appearances of democratic government (*Economist*, 26 January 1991, p. 66). A familar pattern is emerging in Thailand. Powerful business interests are linked with the Chart Thai Party and the military. Using the overlapping family, professional and client/patron networks, they seem intent on further consolidating their grip on political power. It is unlikely that a civilian government can avoid being beholden to big business and the military.

In Indonesia pervasive military influence in government dates from the collapse of President Sukarno's regime in 1965 and, especially, from the formal succession of President Suharto to the Presidency in 1968. In the intervening years Indonesia has been run by a remarkable political organization, Golkar. It is based on a political organization which reaches down to the grass roots in every village. It is partly political party and partly the political wing of the armed forces. The Indonesians use the word *dwifungsi*—twin functions—to describe the role of the military in society. It is useful in understanding the basic political facts of life in most Asian countries. There is an understandable lack of cohesion either because of the political inheritance or because of the immense practical difficulties in the way of managing archipelagic countries like Indonesia and the Philippines. The military not only help to preserve order, they also sustain and develop communications and other essential linkages.

Civilian administrators have assumed greater responsibilities in successive governments under Suharto but the system still rests on the military. In recent years a former military commander and governor of East Java, Wahono, has been elected Chairman of Golkar and the armed forces have successfully campaigned for their people to assume a number of regional chairmanships (Hill and Mackie (eds), 1989, p. 12). Judging from the results of presidential elections, President Suharto retains popular support. Although some favourites are mentioned as being groomed by Suharto the question of the succession remains obscure (*Asia Yearbook 1990*, pp. 138-40).

A process of administrative evolution is going on in Indonesia. At each step it seems that civilians are becoming better placed to counter-balance the power of the military. But, as in many other Asian countries, a familiar pattern can be observed. Great financial power is limited to a relatively few families, including that of President Suharto. A network of relationships between business, especially those managed by prominent Chinese, members of the President's family and the officer corps of the military has developed. It is likely to ensure a long-term monopoly of power by the privileged people who participate (Schwarz, 1991a, pp. 46-8). If others try to lessen the economic power of the Sukarno family when the President dies, there could be serious political repercussions throughout Indonesia.

In the Philippines the continuing power of great families may be one of the consequences of Spanish colonial rule. They have expanded from their traditional landholdings into business and dominate much of economic life. With their clients they form networks which, while often in conflict, control the mechanisms of power. Most of them have persisted in resisting land reform. In so doing they have contributed to a grave imbalance between landholders and landless which has for long been a cause of insurrection and continually threatens the stability of the country. The political reality of the Philippines is that it is ruled by shifting coalitions of the same people largely from great families which supported the Marcos regime. For the meantime the coalition goes under the name Lakas Ng Democratikong Pilipinas. The name was given by President Aquino's younger brother to the political grouping which sustains her government (*Asia Yearbook 1990*, p. 207).

Governments in the Philippines cannot in fairness be categorized as military regimes but they have a quasi-military character. There were great hopes for reform and the development of a stable democratic system after the upheavals which brought President Corazon Aquino to power in 1986. The years which have passed have disappointed hopes as the Philippines seems to be progressively descending into a state of warlordism and insurrection outside Manila. Despite the euphoria surrounding the collapse of the Marcos regime, it has become clear that the revolution of 1986 did little to break the power of the same oligarchs and big businessmen (many of them Filipinos of Chinese descent) who have always controlled the reins of power and whose commitment to the improvement of the circumstances of the majority of Filipinos is marginal at best. Apparently over 60 per cent of the politicians elected in 1986 had political experience dating back some years and a significant proportion of representatives were traditional clan leaders or their relatives (Tiglao, 1990, pp. 40-1).

The role of the military is somewhat more difficult to elucidate than in Thailand or Indonesia. Some are disaffected, as the succession of attempted coups with which President Aquino has had to deal demonstrates. Nevertheless there seems little doubt that since 1986 she has been able to survive because the majority of the senior military are supportive. On one interpretion the power behind the scenes is General Ramos, who switched support from the late President Marcos at a critical time.

One of the persistent problems in the Philippines is insurrection led by the Communist New Peoples Army. The Marcos regime was not a military one, but one which responded to the ambitions of the oligarchic families and accommodated the ambitions of senior members of the armed forces. No concept of *dwifungsi* developed as in Indonesia, nor have the military sought overt power as in Thailand. On the other hand, no government could hope to survive without their support. The question was posed some years ago by a commentator on politics in the Philippines—would military rule solve the country's problems (Crouch, 1985). It was suggested then, and it seems to be valid today, that the relatively large urban middle class and the powerful business interests would be reluctant to accept military rule. Moreover insurgency is unlikely to be reduced through increased military action unless accompanied by basic socio-economic reform (McBeth, 1991c, p. 26).

Communist regimes

Although the Communist regimes of Eastern Europe have collapsed, and the future of the Communist Party in the Soviet Union is exceptionally obscure, there is no reason to conclude at this stage that communism is the wave of the past in China, Vietnam and North

Korea. Although their Communist Parties may now be perceived by a majority of the peoples of these countries to be ideologically bankrupt, and their systems unable to guarantee them a future free from poverty and degradation, there is still a possibility that the communist regimes will adapt to changing circumstances when the present generation of ageing revolutionary and wartime leaders gives place to a new generation.

All three countries are getting very close to having to resolve problems of the political succession to the aged founding fathers of revolution in China and North Korea and the generation in Vietnam which led the country through the decades of war to reunification in the 1970s.

It has been said of China:

> The cycles in the ideological climate for economic development have been exaggerated by another characteristic of the Leninist state: instability in government deriving from heavy concentration of power in the peak organs of the party, and from the high importance of particular individuals in setting the direction of policy. The Leninist state has no smooth means of transferring power from one group to another, so that inter-generational change, and major shifts in policy in response to realisation of changed circumstances, are associated with tension, uncertainty and from time to time political instability. Hence the huge lurches in economic strategy over the past forty years marking the boundaries of the periods of high growth and stagnation in China's uneven growth path.

> Over the next few years, these three interrelated sources of economic instability in China will come together in an extreme way: the most severe economic crisis in the era of reform; the strongest pressures for political liberalisation in the history of the People's Republic; and the transition to new leadership following the debilitation or death of Deng Xiaoping, the unchallenged source of political authority during the reform era (Garnaut, 1989, p. 111).

Whatever happens in China will have powerful repercussions in North Korea and Vietnam. It may be that following the death or incapacity of Kim Il Sung, who has ruled North Korea like a monarch since 1948, and who characteristically has groomed his son Kim Jong Il to succeed him, Korea will find its way to reunification. If it takes that path North Korea could emulate the transition through which the former state of East Germany is now passing. We simply do not know enough about the feelings of the people of North Korea to make any judgements at this stage. Kim Il Sung has kept them in an ideological and economic prison. They seem to know little about conditions in the south but it would be surprising if the powerful nationalistic sentiment which animates all Koreans were not to prove decisive during the next decade or two.

There is no reason to expect, however, that either China or Vietnam will be influenced significantly by events in Central Europe and the Soviet Union. They are sufficiently distant. The Chinese Communist Party has for years kept aloof from that of the Soviet Union. The Chinese Government is underpinned by a Leninist apparatus which penetrates every aspect of society and whose *raison d'être* is to retain political control. The power of the aged leaders and the insidious processes of nepotism and corruption have damaged the credibility of party and government. There is evident dissatisfaction among younger people with the inflexibility of political doctrines which were an inspirational faith for the revolutionary generation. There is also the dichotomy between orthodox communist prescriptions and the practical steps which have been taken, or the practices which have been tolerated, in order to keep economic life from becoming moribund.

There is still much debate about whether the economic doctrines and practices of central planning and management of state enterprises should be modified or discarded if China and Vietnam are to find ways of solving the problems with which they are presently confronted. China, to give it credit, has for over fifteen years tried to find a middle way and may have escaped from the industrial disaster which overtook the Soviet Union. It has, albeit grudgingly, encouraged a private sector, while trying to improve its public sector, allowed peasants scope to earn an adequate reward for their labour and to regain a sense of ownership of land, to blend central planning with price formation by markets and developed a strong export sector with emphasis on the production of industrial products which can compete on world markets.

In Vietnam, however, the ageing leadership still clings to old hopes and the tired rhetoric of revolution. In 1989, when communist regimes were collapsing in Europe, the Vietnamese leader, Nguyen Van Linh rejected calls for 'bourgeois liberalisation, pluralism, political plurality and multi-opposition parties aimed at denying Marxism-Leninism, socialism and the party's leadership' (*Asia Yearbook 1990*, p. 241). Nevertheless the Party will have to find a way of ensuring a better life for an increasing population in a region where pragmatic if authoritarian regimes, like those of Thailand, have encouraged capitalist development. Despite exacerbation of social inequalities and the haphazard nature of much of this development, such a wide gap has opened up between the non-communist (other than the Philippines) and the communist countries that it may never be bridged.

The suppression of the student-led democracy movement by the Chinese Government in 1989 could be interpreted as exposing a reality behind the facade of the doctrine to which the Communist Parties of China, Vietnam and North Korea still cling. An important and understandable motivation at this stage seems to be self-preservation. Should the regimes continue to fail adequately to handle increasingly pressing economic problems, they will inevitably depend for their survival on the support of the armed forces and the security police. The events in Beijing in 1989 exposed that reality. Like Kim Il Sung in North Korea, the Chinese patriarch Deng Xiaoping seems unable to relinquish power. Although he has abandoned the stage to other actors, passing years seem not to have condemned him to political incapacity. However, following the intervention by the army in 1989 he may have difficulty in avoiding sharing ultimate power with General Yang Shangkun, the Head of State. His ascendancy as President, although he is in his eighties, and his capacity to provide military support to Deng when it was needed, exposed another glaring weakness of the Chinese Communist Party—it could not solve a major political problem stemming from its failure to sustain the confidence of other generations, especially today's youth. There was no alternative for the old men but repression.

Since that time the man who succeeded Deng Xiaoping as Chairman of the Central Military Commission of the Chinese Communist Party, Jiang Zemin, seems somehow to have rallied moderate support in a struggle to check the power of Yang Shangkun and his half-brother, General Yang Baibing, both of whom followed political rather than military careers in the army. The latter evidently owes much to his relative for his rise from obscurity. He was promoted from being Head of the General Political Department of the People's Liberation Army in 1987 to the General Secretaryship of the Central Military Commission. The civilian leaders seem to be trying to avoid siding with any one of the military factions. Despite the prominence of the Yangs in military affairs following the crushing of the student demonstrations in 1989, there seems to still be a chance that the military will not actually play a significant part in the processes which determine the succession to Deng Xiaoping; but the armed forces may be critical to preserving the unity of China as the Communist Party clearly has lost much of its credibility among an increasingly cynical population (Cheung, 1991, p. 16).

In both China and Vietnam the governments have inevitably been seen to become more and more reliant on military support. As that process has continued, they have increasingly run the risk of alienating the majority of people and forfeiting their claim to legitimacy. The other problem is that the communist models which they still espouse are now tainted with failure, despite adaptation in China to the realities of the 1980s and 1990s. By contrast the policies of market-economy neighbours are regarded increasingly as successful, given the aspirations of the Chinese and Vietnamese people for an adequate portion of the material comforts which many other Asians have now secured. Japan, South Korea and Taiwan are exerting an increasingly powerful attraction which is going to continue to be hard for China, Vietnam and North Korea to resist.

There is tremendous pressure on the communist regimes to change and adapt. Their problems are immense and long term. If confident and flexible governments do not emerge from the present period of transition, the stability of the Western Pacific could be at risk. On the positive side, there has been a diminution in the animosity which plagued relations between the Asian countries. Japan, South Korea and Taiwan are now better placed to play a constructive role with China and Japan in determining the future of the Western Pacific. While traditional suspicions will remain, and memories of aggression and oppression will always be a factor, a basis for economic cooperation with China is growing and developing some momentum. Before long that process may well include Vietnam. There, despite a continuing addiction to the doctrinal rhetoric of its version of communism, the government is at least capable of admitting that corruption, which affects even the armed forces, as well as incompetent managers and cumbersome bureaucracies, is threatening the limited economic progress made during the 1980s (*Asia Yearbook 1991*, p. 236).

Democratic governments

Five countries of the Western Pacific—Japan, Malaysia, Singapore, Australia and New Zealand—could be described as democratic. Of these only the last two have established parliamentary systems where governments are regularly replaced by opposition parties following general elections. The three Asian countries have, however, developed their own versions of one-party or dominant coalition governments.

In Japan the Liberal Democratic Party (LDP) has held power for nearly half a century. There is a significant Socialist Party. It provides vigorous opposition on many issues but lacks the internal cohesion and nationwide organization necessary to give it a realistic chance of displacing the LDP in government. Although it did well in elections for the upper house in 1989, it ran only 148 candidates for the 512-seat lower house in the election held in 1990 (*Asia Yearbook 1991*, pp. 132-3).

The precise character of government in Japan seems almost to defy western political analysts. That may be because most non-Japanese writers try to fit Japanese political processes into their frameworks of analysis. That clearly is inappropriate, because government in Japan reflects post-war Japanese approaches to political processes and decision-making which may not have parallels in other societies. The system seems to be based on extraordinary capacity to reach consensus in such a large society.

Government in Japan rests on an unusually close relationship between the bureaucracies of the central government, the major business firms and the factions of the LDP. This seems to provide a stable and coherent if not especially admirable political system. Corruption and political jobbery are increasingly exposed at the highest levels, but the system works. It is unique among governments in Asia in that only occasionally is there an acknowledged authority-figure like a western Prime Minister or President. Although some Prime Ministers such as Tanaka and Nakasone have been able to dominate the LDP for a few years, and to exact respect and compliance with their wishes from the bureaucracy, that has been the exception rather than the rule. More often the Prime Ministership has been held for a short period by a consensus politician, usually a faction head or his nominee, who is due for a turn in the office of Prime Minister. With the exception of

Tanaka, effective power seems to be exercised from behind the scenes, but by whom is usually never obvious (Holstein, 1990).

There is no question, however, that the Government of Japan is a civilian government. The self-defence forces have been built up to the point where they comprise one of the largest and best equipped military in the world, despite limits imposed by the Constitution. There is no evidence that they exert any significant indirect influence on government. The lessons of the years of military expansion and the eventual disasters of the 1941-45 war, seem to have convinced the Japanese people of the dangers of military influence in the political process. Japan is nevertheless, on the evidence, virtually a one-party or one-coalition state. Opposition is free to express its views, to campaign vigorously and theoretically become government following an election. But the system, with the majority party holding the reins of power and having built up a massive system of patronage, goes on, despite frequent scandals, from decade to decade. It has delivered economic growth to the point where Japan is among the richest countries in the world and preeminent in many industries. That seems to be the explanation for the political longevity of the LDP.

The Governments of Malaysia and Singapore, in some respects, fit this pattern. There is little likelihood in either country of opposition political parties actually being able to form governments. The United Malay National Organisation with its partner the Malaysian Chinese Association dominates government in Malaysia. There the constitution is designed to protect the position of the Malay people at the expense of the Chinese and Indian ethnic minorities. There is active discrimination against non-Malays in the education system and in the armed forces. Nevertheless the conservative Chinese have little alternative than to make the best of their minority role in the National Front Coalition and to consolidate their extensive grip on the business life of the country (*Asia Yearbook 1991*, pp. 158-61).

In Singapore the Peoples Action Party (PAP), whose organization is distinctly Leninist, has held government since 1957. Very few seats have been won over the years by opposition candidates. Few parties anywhere could have achieved such political dominance. The founding father of the PAP, Lee Kuan Yew, has skirted the boundaries of authoritarianism. In 1989 he handed over power as Prime Minister but he does not seem capable of standing aside completely for younger

men from the position of power and influence, leaving them to manage
the city-state which has become almost his personal fiefdom. He has
canvassed amending the constitution to provide for an executive
presidency rather than the present ceremonial position. Clearly, despite
his advancing years, it is a position which he would like to fill.

Singapore has developed strong armed forces since it ceased to be
part of Malaysia in 1965. They are based on compulsory military
training. Lee's successor as Prime Minister, Goh Chok Tong, is also
Minister of Defence with the Minister of Trade and Industry, Lee
Hsien Loong, the son of Lee Kuan Yew, and a former senior army
officer, also holding the position of Second Minister of Defence (*Asia
Yearbook 1991*, pp. 204-7). The members of the armed forces reflect
the predominantly Chinese character of the population of the city-state.

The PAP has an organization which is based on a wide membership. It has developed the closest ties with business, the branches of
government and the armed forces. It has achieved political domination.
There is still no sign of an effective political opposition developing in
the parliament. Clearly the networks of related families which dominate government and business in Singapore consider that there is no
need for change.

In the Southwestern Pacific, Australia and New Zealand have kept
the parliamentary systems of government which are part of their British
heritage. They provide examples of open, pluralistic political systems
in sharp contrast to those of most Western Pacific countries. There are
only minor ideological differences between the major political parties.
Changes of government normally reflect a view among the electorate
that a particular government has become ineffective or complacent in
office, rather than seeking a profound change in political approach to
the major questions of the day.

What is lacking in these countries, by comparison with their
neighbours in Asia, is the complex networks of family and patron-
client relationships which flow from the exercise of political and
commercial power and which may come to permeate most aspects of
society. There is also a long tradition of sustaining high-wage,
extensive welfare societies which conform to the political philosophies
of all the major political parties. During the past decade economic
growth has not been strong enough to avoid a progressive deterioration
in their balances of payments as domestic demand, propped up by

substantial public expenditure and undisciplined lending by banks, created a propensity to import which far exceeds overseas earnings. While several other Western Pacific economies forge ahead on the basis of sustained material growth, Australia and New Zealand have been drifting into indebtedness. That is doing nothing to enhance their reputations and roles in the Western Pacific. It has, however, created a situation where Japan and other countries can acquire valuable productive assets in both countries at values which are likely to turn out to be rather inexpensive.

The Asian countries of the Western Pacific are often portrayed as an especially dynamic grouping. It would however be stretching the facts and the imagination to depict their governments as other than fundamentally autocratic or authoritarian. Sometimes that is evident from the character of the leadership and the dominant political party. In other cases, such as Japan, the character of government is much more subtle involving a collective approach which nonetheless has the capacity to exercise power to stifle dissent, and especially to preserve the power of the major factions of the governing party. In the case of Japan there is unlikely to be a problem with the transference of power from one generation to another, but the same cannot be said for other countries.

Feudal systems persisted in Asia until very recent times. The concepts which underlay them are tenacious and still affect the attitudes of rulers and of those who are ruled. It would be unwise not to take fully into account the historical and philosophic legacy that informs the attitudes of people despite rapid material progress during recent decades. The other powerful factor is the sheer difficulty of governing populous, complex societies where there are frequently great disparities in power and wealth. Even in the communist countries the disparity between the privileged and many of the rest is almost as sharp as between the oligarchs of the Philippines and the landless, without being so ostentatious. In some cases outside Japan, South Korea and Taiwan large numbers are not much more than a few steps away from hunger and malnutrition. The economic dynamism which has spread throughout the Western Pacific is remedying a worrying situation but should not be allowed to disguise the complexities of the area and the processes which are causing degradation of land and water.

Up until now it seems that the prescriptions for rapid material growth have been appropriate as they have enabled country after country to break through the inertia, hopelessness and despair, of rural and urban poverty, and to achieve a large measure of self-respect especially *vis-à-vis* former colonial powers. It might be prudent, however, to allow the possibility that the application of the principles and practices of rapid economic growth, which have had such a powerful influence to date, will bring more problems than they solve in the decades ahead. The question must be asked whether the Asian countries of the Western Pacific are basically on a path to economic deterioration, not prosperity, if they pursue to the limits, as Japan, South Korea and Taiwan have done, economic policies which will cause a massive increase in demand for and consumption of energy and other materials to provide more affluent living circumstances for their growing populations. The linked problems of growth of populations and associated increases in demand for energy are examined in the following two chapters.

4. The Population Dimension

The populations of the Western Pacific countries amount in total to about a quarter of the global total of about 5.2 billion. Demographic forecasts indicate that over the next fifty years this proportion will not change greatly as the world population goes up to over 8 billion. With the official count of China's population in 1990 at 1,137 million in 1990 and growth continuing, Northeast and Southeast Asia will just about maintain their relative importance in population terms.

The World Commission on Environment and Development (WCED) in its 1987 report used two starkly worded paragraphs to make a fundamental point which is going to have to be addressed by governments everywhere:

> The planet is passing through a period of dramatic growth and fundamental change. Our human world of 5 billion people must make room in a finite environment for another human world. The population could stabilize at between eight billion and 14 billion sometime next century, according to UN projections. More than 90 per cent of the increase will occur in the poorest countries, and 90 per cent of that growth in already bursting cities.
>
> Economic activity has multiplied to create a $13 trillion world economy, and this could grow five or tenfold in the coming half century. Industrial production has grown more than fiftyfold over the past century, four-fifths of this growth since 1950. Such figures reflect and presage profound impacts on the biosphere, as the world invests in houses, transport, farms and industries (WCED, 1987, p. 4).

While Table 4.1 indicates the projection of population growth used by WCED, 'median level' population forecasts of this kind do no more than indicate possibilities, and allowance must be made for wide margins of error, there is a surprisingly close correspondence between United Nations and World Bank estimates. Both exercises were carried out using data which became available in the 1980s. Projected population for 2025 is in the range of 8.2 to 8.4 billion (Demeney, 1984, pp. 392-417). This now seems to be close to a probability rather than a possibility.

67

Table 4.1. World population—size and growth rates

Region	Population (Billion)			Annual Growth Rate (percent)	
	1985	2000	2025	1950 to 1985	2000 to 2025
World	4.8	6.1	8.2	1.9	1.2
Africa	0.56	0.87	1.62	2.6	2.5
Latin America	0.41	0.55	0.78	2.6	1.4
Asia	2.82	3.55	4.54	2.1	1.0
North America	0.26	0.30	0.35	1.3	0.6
Europe	0.49	0.51	0.52	0.7	0.1
Soviet Union	0.28	0.31	0.37	1.3	0.6
Oceania	0.02	0.03	0.04	1.9	0.9

Source: WCED, 1987, p. 101.

Longer-term projections by the World Bank indicate that, providing there is a levelling off in the second half of the next century, world population could still exceed 11 billion by 2100. There could be a substantial change in present relativities between the major regions with South Asia (largely the Indian sub-continent) reaching 3.7 billion, Africa 2.9 billion and East Asia probably exceeding 2.5 billion.

Such long-range estimates are inevitably speculative, but they serve a useful purpose in indicating the rate at which populations may increase even if fertility is declining. It is hard to imagine the population of India exceeding that of China, but that is what present trends in fertility indicate. Demographers stress, however, that the upsurge in numbers which we have been witnessing in Asia in recent decades has far from run its course. The surge of growth will continue for some time because of the proportions of fertile people in the populations at present and during the first few decades of the next century. Planners must take into account the likelihood that numbers could increase by at least 50 per cent (Demeny, 1984, p. 405).

Given what has happened this century, it can be argued that increases of this magnitude can be managed, because the world economy has already developed sufficient strength and resilience to provide much more than the basics for a considerably greater population. That might be possible in some countries of East Asia. A few of them are leaders in industrial development. But it is exceptionally hard to imagine the Indian sub-continent surviving without catastrophe a build up in numbers to the point where its inhabitants reach the equivalent of two-thirds of the present world population. If, as is possible, the growth of numbers should induce a series of disasters, their consequences would be felt in neighbouring Middle-Eastern and Asian countries. Such an enormous population could not, it seems safe to assert, be supported by the land and waters of the sub-continent. A fight for existence might develop which would have serious consequences for many countries. There could be in addition a population spill of unprecedented proportions from both China and Indochina.

Scenarios such as this can be composed for all the heavily populated countries of the Western Pacific. There seems to be no doubt that there will be rapid growth of urban populations because, in most areas, greater numbers cannot be absorbed into agriculture. Recent economic history confirms that a decline in rural populations and growth of towns and cities is inevitable as modern technological development transforms societies. Is it likely that the vast majority of these new urban dwellers will be adequately housed, clothed, fed and employed? Will there be adequate education facilities for their children? Will there be clean water, sewage facilities and adequate waste disposal? There is cause for serious doubt about that, given the present state of many cities and towns in the Third World. It is especially concerning that none of the evidence presented in recent years suggests that the disparities between rich and poor countries are actually diminishing. While some countries have made phenomenal progress, especially in Northeast Asia, progress in many developing countries is slow. Wealthy or relatively wealthy élites increase and prosper but in the face of rapid population growth the great majority struggle to survive or to maintain a modest lifestyle. It seems likely that by 2000 only 20 per cent of the world's population will be classified as living in developed countries, with the remaining 80 per cent still in those labelled developing (Schubnell, 1984, p. 7). The numbers of wealthy people who control the sources of political and economic power in those countries are likely to increase as their populations continue to grow, but they will be vastly outnumbered by the poor and dispossessed. Will they be provided with more than is necessary to survive? Will many not actually be able to survive?

Environmentalists have for some time now been stressing the importance of the concept of 'carrying capacity'. It is used by biologists to demonstrate the way living organisms exist in closed cycles. Experiments show that when their nourishment is more than sufficient living creatures will increase in number, slowly at first then rapidly, until a point is reached where the increase in numbers slows down. Decrease will follow when accumulating wastes cannot adequately be dispersed, even if the supply of nourishment remains adequate (Brown, 1991, p. 5).

Even though human beings have the capacity to modify their environments, environmentalists argue that they are not exempt from the general proposition that all creatures have the capacity, as their numbers increase, to exceed the carrying capacity of the land in a local sense, or of the biosphere in a global sense, which supports them.

At first glance it might seem unlikely that the countries of the Western Pacific could exceed the limits of carrying capacity. Although there is a big population, the land area, especially that of China, Indochina, Indonesia and Australia, is very extensive. Much of it however is mountainous, desert or semi-desert and can only support sparse populations. In the Asian countries populations are naturally concentrated in the fertile areas, especially the river valleys, which have had the capacity so far to provide somewhat more than the essential requirements for large and growing numbers.

This chapter explores the dynamics of population growth in the Western Pacific in order to open up the question whether in some places, notably China, Vietnam, Thailand, the Philippines and Java, the limits of carrying capacity are being approached or have actually been overstepped. That could be taken to mean that the land, forests and rivers on which those people depend might progressively become incapable of supporting the present populations.

The next chapter takes the analysis a step further by examining present and future demand for energy in the Western Pacific in the context of the growth of population. There is an important link between human activity and the use of energy in everyday processes both simple and complex. The use of wood in cooking is one, the burning of uranium in a nuclear reactor is at the opposite extreme. The relationship of man and environment is basically a matter of the ways in which people are using energy. The use of energy, from whatever source, wood, coal, oil, uranium, is intimately linked to environmental stress because of the consequences of the processes of extraction and because of the wastes which are inevitably generated. The processes involved may bring material wealth and be measured as economic growth. If they are carried out on an ever increasing scale, it is now more widely understood that they will impair the ability of the biosphere to support the sum of increasing human activities.

Robert McNamara, a former chief executive of the Ford Motor Company, Secretary of Defense in the United States, who was also President of the World Bank from 1968 to 1981, wrote, in 1984, of the dangers of population growth exceeding carrying capacity, although he did not use the actual term. He remarked on the fall of population growth rates in the 1970s and the tendency for some people to conclude that the world would not face serious problems of over-population. He took the view that this was totally in error, suggesting instead:

> Unless action is taken to accelerate the reduction in rates of growth, the population of the world ... will not stabilize below 11 billion, and certain regions and countries will grow far beyond the limits consistent with political stability and acceptable social and economic conditions (McNamara, 1984, p. 1107).

He went on to warn that the scale of population growth may be such as to postpone or permanently foreclose desirable patterns of development that could have been attainable with less rapid demographic expansion.

The population picture in the Western Pacific is a mixed one. At one end of the scale are countries like Japan with a seemingly stable population, although a very large one given the size of its archipelago. In the middle is China with a decreasing rate of increase as a result of active government policies. At the other end are Indonesia, Thailand and the Philippines where, although fertility is declining as the low variant forecasts in Table 4.2 suggest, there are almost certain to be very large increases between 1990 and 2025.

Table 4.2. Population—Western Pacific population outlook (millions)[1]

	1990	1995	2000	2010	2025
Northeast Asia					
China	1130.0	1201.0	1259.0	1321.0	1372.0
Japan	123.0	125.0	127.0	127.0	120.0
Korea	66.0	70.0	73.0	80.0	85.0
Hong Kong	5.5	5.8	6.1	6.4	6.5
Sub-total	**1324.5**	**1401.8**	**1465.1**	**1534.4**	**1583.5**
Indochina					
Cambodia	8.2	9.0	9.8	11.0	13.0
Laos	4.0	4.5	5.0	5.9	7.1
Vietnam	67.0	73.0	80.0	90.0	100.0
Sub-total	**79.2**	**86.5**	**94.8**	**106.9**	**120.1**
Southeast Asia					
Indonesia	178.0	190.0	201.0	216.0	228.0
Malaysia	17.0	19.0	20.0	22.0	24.0
Philippines	62.0	69.0	76.0	89.0	102.0
Singapore	2.7	2.8	2.9	3.0	3.0
Thailand	55.0	58.0	61.0	66.0	70.0
Sub-total	**314.7**	**338.8**	**360.9**	**396.0**	**427.0**
Oceania[2]	**24.0**	**27.0**	**30.0**	**30.0**	**32.0**

[1] Projections for Taiwan not available.
[2] Australia, New Zealand, Papua New Guinea.

TOTAL	**1742.4**	**1854.1**	**1950.8**	**2067.3**	**2162.6**

Source: United Nations Department of International Economic and Social Affairs: *Population Studies No.106*, 1988.

The United Nations would not claim high accuracy for its forecasts. They are based on assumptions about fertility, mortality and migration which could turn out to be wrong, and on data whose accuracy varies from country to country. However, such forecasts can help to alert governments and people to longer-term possibilities, dispel fears about circumstances which can be shown to be unlikely and identify ranges of magnitudes where choices have to be made (Demeney, 1984, pp. 292-3).

It is instructive to examine the pattern of likely population growth in the Western Pacific in terms of, first, the position of developed *vis-à-vis* developing countries, second, the changing ratios between rural and urban populations and third, the significance of the growth of cities, especially the mega-cities. It is also important to consider the situation of China separately, because of its global significance and its dominating position demographically among this grouping of countries.

Developed and Developing Countries

As mentioned in Chapter 3 there are great disparities between the developed and the developing countries of the Western Pacific. The combined populations of the six developed countries—Japan, South Korea, Taiwan, Singapore, Australia and New Zealand—were 210 million in 1989, all but 20 million in the Asian countries. The rates of increase are slow. United Nations projections suggest that their combined total in 2025, assuming that the two Koreas are unified by then, could be close to 260 million, not much more than 10 per cent of a possible total population for the Western Pacific of 2,375 million in that year. Inevitably these countries will have a disproportionately large share of the projected GDP of the Western Pacific countries with Japan's share possibly amounting to between 30 and 40 per cent of the total.

The likelihood of this disparity decreasing is limited, because of the much more rapid rate of population growth in the developing countries. China's population was officially reported to be 1,137 million in 1990. The estimates for Vietnam, Laos and Cambodia were 81 million, Indonesia 190 million, and the Philippines, Thailand and Malaysia combined a further 140 million. When the 4 million people of Papua New Guinea are included the population of the developing countries of the Western Pacific was estimated to be about 1,615 million in 1990 (*Asia Yearbook 1991*, pp. 6-7).

By 2025 the combined populations of these countries could exceed 2,000 million. Even if Malaysia and Thailand, as seems generally expected, reach income levels comparable with present-day South Korea, the disparities between the two broad categories of countries will not change appreciably.

The divide in the Western Pacific between developed and developing countries has changed but not diminished. Japan, Australia and New Zealand have been members of the rich countries' club—the OECD—for over twenty years. Others, notably South Korea and Singapore, have already acquired the credentials for membership. It is now very doubtful whether there will be a further enlargement of OECD. That will leave a number of countries like South Korea, Taiwan, which for all practical purposes is a country separate from China, Singapore and, some time in the future, Malaysia in the grey area between the OECD, the oil rich and the countries which are clearly still in the 'developing' category. With the exception, for the meantime, of Malaysia, these countries comprise the rich tier of the Western Pacific. Table 4.3 brings out the disparity between developed and developing.

The nature of the income disparities between rich and poor countries may come as a surprise to people accustomed to thinking mainly of the contrast between income levels of the countries of Europe and North America and with the developing countries of Latin America, Africa and Asia. Twelve per cent of the population of the Western Pacific grouping generates 84 per cent of the GDP; 88 per cent has to manage with 15 per cent of estimated wealth.

Data of this kind should only be taken as a guide to actual circumstances. Is the average person in Japan actually over sixty times better off than someone in China and over one hundred times better off than someone in Vietnam? It is difficult to make valid statistical comparisons between socialist and market economies. Nevertheless the table does bring out that there is a great disparity in income levels in the Western Pacific which countries with low per capita incomes are going to find difficult to bridge in the foreseeable future.

*Table 4.3. Population and gross domestic product in the Western
          Pacific countries*

	Population 1990 (millions)	% Total	GDP 1989 ($US billions)	% Total
Developed				
Japan	123.6	7.0	2830.0	65.9
South Korea	42.8	2.5	211.9	5.0
Hong Kong	5.8	0.3	55.0	1.3
Taiwan	20.2	1.1	146.9	3.0
Singapore	2.7	0.2	29.2	0.7
Australia	17.1	1.0	292.5	7.0
New Zealand	3.3	0.2	40.1	1.0
Sub-total	**215.5**	**12.3**	**3605.6**	**83.9**
Developing				
China	1119.0	64.0	413.0	10.0
Indochina				
Vietnam	70.2	4.0	14.0	0.3
Laos	4.0	0.2	0.6	0.2
Cambodia	7.0	0.4	-	-
Sub-total	**81.2**	**4.6**	**14.6**	**0.5**
Southeast Asia/Pacific				
Indonesia	189.4	11.0	100.0*	2.3
Malaysia	17.9	1.0	26.4	0.6
Papua New Guinea	4.0	0.2	3.6	0.1
Philippines	66.1	3.7	44.4	1.0
Thailand	55.7	3.2	70.0	1.6
Sub-total	**333.1**	**19.2**	**244.4**	**5.6**
Total Developing	**1533.3**	**87.8**	**672.0**	**16.1**

-   Less than 0.1 per cent.
*   Estimated.

TOTAL	**1748.8**	**100.0**	**4277.6**	**100.0**

Source: Far Eastern Economic Review, *Asia Yearbook 1991*,
          pp. 8-9.

South Korea has made the transition into the ranks of industrial countries of international significance. Taiwan too should be included. It has established an international economic identity completely independent of China and achieved a per capita income level significantly higher than that of South Korea. Likewise Singapore left the ranks of the developing countries many years ago but, as a city-state, it should, like Hong Kong, be considered in a separate category. Others, notably Thailand and Malaysia, could make the transition. But where does that leave the countries whose per capita GDP is below $US700—China, Vietnam, Indonesia, the Philippines and the smaller countries? Their combined populations are about 1,550 million. The 1990 census in China showed that the population of that country had been underestimated by about 40 million (*Beijing Review*, 12-18 November 1990, p. 5).

The overall growth of population may be slowing down as fertility rates decline. Increasing urbanization may accelerate that trend. Population data show that there is a correlation between the shift of people from rural to urban lifestyles and a decline in birth rates. Nevertheless nothing can disguise the colossal disparity between the haves and the have-nots in the Western Pacific. The billion and a half people in the developing countries are not pressed for land, but they are pressed for good land. Evidence is accumulating that they may be approaching the limits of the type of land which has traditionally supported the great rice cultures. There is, moreover, a growing conflict between the growth of cities, towns, industrial areas and transport corridors and the increasing necessity to produce more to feed increasing populations. With the highly productive land in full cultivation, there is inevitably greater pressure on forests and drier, steeper country as people try to extend the intensely cultivated areas. This can lead to less rather than more production over time as the longer-term effects may be loss of fertility, advance of deserts, and the degradation of the rich agricultural land as the flow of water to irrigation systems is disturbed and degraded by activity upstream and the loss of essential forest cover in watersheds.

Economists in China acknowledge this problem (Liu (ed.), 1987, pp. 419-36). Moreover the authorities are fully aware of the pressures of people on available land:

Although China's gross national product (GNP) has doubled over the past decade, with its vast population, its per capita GNP lags far behind the world average. Its grain production is also high at 400 billion kg a year, but divided among the population, this leaves just 370 kg per head. Similarly, the per capita share of China's huge natural resources is small, and per capita the area of cultivated land, forest, grasslands and water resources is not only below the world average but is continuing to drop.

Under these circumstances, unless population growth is curbed, China's increase in wealth will be offset by the ever-larger number of people who have to share it. Simultaneously, as the contradiction between population and resources grows, environmental deterioration will follow. If this happens, it will prove impossible to increase national strength and difficult to raise living standards (*Beijing Review*, 13-19 March 1989, p. 4).

A characteristic of development since the industrial revolution has been the tendency for the proportion of the population directly engaged in agriculture to decline. For example the percentage of the population engaged in agriculture in South Korea was estimated to be just over 78 per cent in 1950. It declined to about 45 per cent in 1980 and could be less than 30 per cent by 2000 (Schubnell, 1984, p. 27). If the percentages of the economically active engaged in agriculture are used, there might be a further decrease to perhaps 8 per cent by 2025.

Leaving the developed countries aside, the great proportion of the people of the Western Pacific countries are engaged in agriculture. For example the United Nations has estimated the following percentages of the economically active: China 67, Vietnam 61, Thailand 64, Indonesia 48 and the Philippines 47 per cent. Estimates for 2025 indicate that these proportions could fall to: China 39, Vietnam 35, Thailand 39, Indonesia 22 and the Philippines 30 per cent. That means of course that the ratio of urban and rural people among the economically active will change dramatically, and that these countries will be a long way down the road of transition which Japan and Korea have travelled. Cities and towns are expanding rapidly. The pressure of people on the land itself may decrease somewhat, enabling the size of rural holdings to rise. But this must be considered in the context of a situation where total population has risen by something like 50 per cent and nearly all of that increase is in developing countries.

Table 4.4. Economically active populations

	1990	2000	2025
Developed Countries[1]			
Agriculture	13	10	5
Other	89	108	114
Percentage in agriculture	12	9	4
China and Hong Kong			
Agriculture	459	455	317
Other	224	310	493
Percentage in agriculture	67	59	39
Indochina[2]			
Agriculture	25	28	27
Other	15	23	47
Percentage in agriculture	62	54	36
Southeast Asia[3]			
Agriculture	67	68	57
Other	65	93	195
Percentage in agriculture	51	42	23

[1] Japan, South Korea, Australia and New Zealand
[2] Cambodia, Laos, Vietnam
[3] Indonesia, Malaysia, Philippines, Singapore, Thailand

Source: United Nations, Division of Economic and Social Affairs, World Demographic Estimates and Projections, 1988.

Table 4.4, which is derived from United Nations projections, is intended to provide an appreciation of the numbers likely to be directly involved in agriculture in the more populous countries in the years through to 2025.

This table gives an indication of how a vitally important distribution within a population may change over time. In the Western Pacific a massive increase in urban populations seems almost certain during what, after all, will be a relatively short period of time.

Circumstances may improve for the majority, because productivity could further increase in the countryside and growth of exports could enable food to be imported. The question remains, however, of how the increasing numbers of people in the cities and towns will be housed, provided with basic amenities, transported and employed in the developing countries, whose gross domestic product is likely to be less than 20 per cent of the total for the Western Pacific. The capital requirements of the new and existing urban centres will be immense. Even allowing for foreign loans and inflows of investment from richer countries, it is difficult to imagine how a transition on the scale needed can be funded.

In many respects Asia is not so much farmed as gardened. Much agricultural practice, when examined closely, reveals a very close integration between humans, plants and domestic animals. There are monocultures, such as rice production, and plantations have become very important, but the populations are adequately fed because the rural people are able to provide surpluses of food, feed and livestock for urban markets. As population further increases, however, there is a risk that the marketable surplus will dwindle. The shift of vast numbers of people into expanding towns and other urban areas necessarily will absorb precious hectares of agricultural land for housing, industrial purposes, service facilities and transport. This process is accelerating in China as increasing numbers of people have no option but to turn to non-agricultural occupations (Fincher, 1991, pp. 59-84).

The United Nations Economic and Social Commission for Asia and the Pacific (ESCAP), made some telling points about the pressures of population on land in its review *State of the Environment in Asia and the Pacific* published in 1990. Average availability of land for agricultural populations declined from 0.29 hectares in 1976 to 0.27 hectares in 1986. Total croplands increased slowly while population growth continued inexorably (ESCAP, 1990, p. 132). This is understandable, because good land is close to becoming a finite resource around the world, especially in Asia. In several Southeast-Asian and Pacific countries agricultural land increased by 5 to 10 per cent between 1976 and 1986 but population growth prevented any improvement in per capita availability.

Another factor contributing to the gap between developed and developing countries is increasing numbers of landless people in the latter. Most of them have no choice but to become urban fringe-dwellers or to try to move between cities and their home villages when work is offering there (ESCAP, 1990, pp. 134-7). The only other alternative seems to be to try to exist on marginal land. This has become a major problem in the Philippines. As a Report prepared by the World Bank points out:

> Because of the availability of semi-cleared land in the uplands, on which immi-grants can build a better livelihood, the direction of migration is to the uplands, as well as the urban areas. As a result, today about 18 million people, one third of the total Philippine population live in upland areas, of which perhaps 8-10 million are farming on forest land ... if growth continues unchecked, by 2020 when the Philippine population may have doubled to nearly 120 million, the upland population could triple to as much as 50 million.

> (In these areas) ... shifting cultivation is employed because it minimizes labor and cash input requirements by substituting land for labor and fertilizer ... lack of secure tenure or titling provides no incentive for land improvement or nutrient maintenance as the viability of shifting cultivation diminishes.

> These farming techniques tend to promote very high rates of erosion.

> ... these effects (of erosion) are damaging to water conservancy systems in the lowlands, reducing productivity and increasing the cost of maintenance and restoration of irrigation and hydropower systems. Deteriorating productivity in the lowlands contributes to the migratory 'push' (completing a vicious circle) (World Bank, 1989, p. x).

ESCAP points out that in some cases, while agricultural holdings are declining in size, and landlessness is a major problem contributing to the degradation of land, there is a tendency towards the concentration of land ownership in the hands of a relatively small percentage of rural people (ESCAP, 1990, p. 134). Official data shows a disturbing trend which is likely over the longer term to threaten the stability of rural areas.

Land reform is an exceedingly difficult area of policy for politicians. Asian market economy countries have for many years been warned that the land is falling into the hands of a few, while in many countries landlessness is increasing. Forty-four per cent of the agricultural population in Indonesia is regarded as living below the absolute poverty level, 64 per cent in Thailand. Even in Malaysia the estimate is 38 per cent and in South Korea 11 per cent (ESCAP, 1990, p. 136).

Urban Populations

There is a close correlation between economic development and urbanization. That is inescapable as the process of industrial development proceeds. Table 4.5 has been designed, like others in this chapter, to bring out the differences between the situations of the developed and developing countries of the Western Pacific. The populations of the developed countries show up as exceptionally urbanized, about three-quarters, and many developing countries hover around one-quarter.

Table 4.5. Western Pacific urbanization in selected countries

	Total Population (millions)	Urban Population (millions)	% Total	Growth Rate 1985-90	Large Cities % Total Urban
Developed					
Japan	123	95	77	0.5	22
South Korea	44	31	72	3	36
Australia	17	14	86	1	26
Developing (East Asia)					
China	1136	243	21	2	5
Vietnam	67	15	22	4	22
Developing (Southeast Asia)					
Indonesia	180	52	29	4	18
Malaysia	17	7	42	4	23
Philippines	62	26	42	4	32
Thailand	56	13	23	4	57

Source: ESCAP, *State of the Environment in Asia and the Pacific*, 1990, p. 99.

A vast process of change is under way throughout the developing world. Cities have been growing at rates which are concerning, especially primary cities. They are the focus of administrative, industrial and service activities for countries, regions and provinces. Among the developing countries Malaysia and the Philippines already have large urban populations. Judging from data on urban growth rates, other developing countries are similarly experiencing rapid transitions.

There seems to be little doubt that cities and towns in the developing countries of the Western Pacific will continue to grow rapidly during the decades ahead. Urbanization is an inescapable part of the process of economic development. It is integral to industrialization which is under way everywhere. But consider the sheer numbers involved. In 1990 there were about a billion economically active people in these countries. By the year 2000 they may increase by 100 million and a further 150 million by 2025. During the intervening years the people involved in agriculture could decline by as much as 150 million. The additional people seeking employment in occupations other than agriculture could therefore number close to 400 million in the period through to 2025.

Perhaps the best way of grasping what this involves for the Western Pacific is to consider the string of major urban centres along the series of curves from north to south—greater Tokyo, Osaka-Kobe, Pusan, Seoul, Beijing, Tianjin, Shanghai, Hong Kong, Taipei, Guangzhou, Saigon, Manila, Bangkok, Kuala Lumpur, Singapore, Surabaya, Sydney and Melbourne. The western coast of Honshu, the main island of Japan, is largely urbanized and industrialized. It is a prime example of what is likely to happen in a heavily populated country as it changes from an agriculturally-based to an industrially-based society.

If the people of the Asian countries of the Western Pacific are to be usefully employed and their standards of living to rise, then urbanized/industrial areas will further extend and develop along the string which already runs from Japan across South Korea from Pusan to Seoul and then down the east coast of China to northern Vietnam. Further south the concentrations of people and industry around the major cities like Saigon, Bangkok, Kuala Lumpur, Johor Bahru and Singapore will continue to grow. The primary chain of great cities will be supplemented by others especially in central China. Similar processes are evident in the chain of islands with Taipei (Taiwan), Manila, Jakarta and Surabaya now ranked among major cities of the world.

This industrialization and urbanization can be viewed as an exciting process which is taking a much more populous group of countries than those of Europe or North America into a new era of prosperity and shared technological progress. From this one can theorize that the world's economic centre of gravity is shifting to this thickening string of industrial activity. It follows that it would not be fanciful to predict that within the next century the Asian countries of the Western Pacific will, taken together, constitute the greatest area of industrial activity in the world.

A process has been started which can hardly be arrested, but there is a largely unacknowledged downside to what is portrayed increasingly as a realistic, if optimistic, view of the future. It can be argued that it is rash to assume that these countries actually have the capacity to provide adequately for the enormous transition from the present ratios between urban and rural people which will take place as the process of industrialization proceeds.

More than half the world's largest cities are in Asia. Their number is bound to increase. Those of the developing countries of the Western Pacific will continue to experience exceptionally rapid growth. As ESCAP has pointed out:

Experience shows that although the concentration of population and economic activities in one or two large metropolitan areas may stimulate higher levels of economic growth in the short run, it has a tendency to generate spatial polarization, economic dualism, social inequity and diseconomies of scale in the long run that can slow the pace of national economic development.

In many countries with strong primate cities, few secondary and intermediate cities and towns can grow large enough to diversify their economies and attract significant numbers of rural migrants. On the other hand, concentration of people and economic activities in the primate cities continue unabated and provide an even stronger rationale for concentrating investments in these metropolitan areas rather than in other regions or cities. Social costs have often been ignored or understated and, eventually, the adversities of increasing concentration undermine the ability of countries to sustain high levels of economic growth (ESCAP, 1990, p. 101).

There is probably no better example in the Western Pacific than the Philippines. Some 20 million Filipinos presently live in cities and towns. As the process of migration from the countryside to urban areas continues, this total is likely to reach 30 million by 2000. The population of Manila now exceeds 8 million and is expected to grow to 13 million by that year. Only two regional centres, Cebu and Davao have populations of about a million. There are fewer than ten other centres of the archipelago which exceed 100,000 and only about 150 municipalities with populations in excess of 10,000 (World Bank, 1989, p. 3).

Infrastructural requirements can pose massive problems, especially if there is a backlog to make up. That is in fact the situation of most, if not all, of the great cities of the Western Pacific. Even those in the developed countries, like Tokyo and Sydney, are posing headaches for the regional authorities as they total up the funds needed to sustain infrastructures, as well as providing everything that is required as the cities continue to sprawl outwards.

There are worrying examples of every known urban problem in the great cities of the Western Pacific. The summaries which follow encapsulate the situation in five great cities. The ratio of urban to rural dwellers for the Asian countries at present, including the developed countries, is about sixty:forty. That may shift during the next half century to thirty:seventy. If the population of the Western Pacific countries is about 1.7 billion at present, the cities and towns house close to 700 million. Fifty years hence they may have to accommodate and provide amenities for well over one-and-a-half billion.

Tokyo

Tokyo is an example of a mega-city which has an enormous energy requirement and which has exerted an almost magnetic attraction to people from all over Japan. These days it is attracting immigrants from outside Japan, many of them illegal but prepared to do the menial, uncomfortable and dirty jobs which Japanese are increasingly reluctant to undertake.

Growth seems virtually to be out of control in Tokyo. It has grown in a series of concentric rings. The first was 10 to 20 kilometres from the centre of the city. The third ring, some 40 to 50 kilometres from the centre, is now being developed. If this process continues Greater Tokyo could have a radius of about 100 kilometres.

Problems of providing water and electricity are growing. Greater Tokyo requires about a quarter of the total supply of water, but its reserves are only about 27 per cent of the norm for the nation as a whole. The electricity authorities are having trouble matching supply and demand, partly because of the increasing use of appliances and the rapid increase in the installation of domestic air conditioners (Delfs, 1991).

Although the metropolitan government of Tokyo has effected many improvements, especially in the quality of air, problems such as the disposal of wastes and their impact on coastal seas from such a vast urban area are serious. There is now a shortage of sites for landfill. There is already a serious problem as drainage from existing landfills contributes many of the pollutants getting into water systems. Some of these are heavy metals, such as lead and cadmium, which are used as stabilizers in polyvinyl chloride resins and mercury from discarded batteries. Incineration of waste is necessary but adds to problems of air pollution (Murata, 1989, pp. 68-72).

A thoughtful person interviewed by Robert Elegant describes the problems of alienation which can arise even in a well regulated society like Japan:

> Human beings are alienated by such gigantism. The space of a normal home in Tokyo is one-twentieth of the space of a normal home in Los Angeles. Japanese money is coming back to Tokyo from investment abroad—and driving up land values. Land now costs so much that ordinary people suffer much deprivation. Above all, they are deprived of a normal, comfortable home life. They are making money and losing a decent life. That is an unacceptable trade-off (Elegant, 1990, p. 162).

Another Japanese expert expresses the overall problem in vivid terms:

> All of the environmental problems in Tokyo today are generally concerned with the city structure and the economic structure themselves. This is true in cases of photochemical smog, garbage, red tide, neighbour noise and other problems. From this point of view, Tokyo still faces a severe situation, and is coming to a turning point in environmental policy. The task must extend from the war on individual cases to the war on finances and the war on congestion (Shibata cited by Nakano, 1986, p. 286).

Any visitor to Tokyo would have to ask whether these wars could be won. Is not the city too big? Is it not inevitable that Tokyo will be undermined by its sheer growth? Does Japan really have the resources to sustain the infrastructure of the metropolis and other cities as well?

This concern needs to be recognized because Tokyo is, effectively, the model for Taipei and for other great cities such as Shanghai, Bangkok, Manila and Jakarta.

Taipei

The circumstances of Taiwan's great city, Taipei, bring out vividly the range of problems faced by a great urban area in a country where just about everything has been sacrificed in the pursuit of economic growth. This city occupies the delta of the Tamsui River which rises in Taiwan's central mountain range and is vital to the health of the 300 square kilometre basin which is dominated by Taipei. Some six million people live in this area, nearly a quarter of the population of the island.

Although industrial development in and around Taipei has proceeded rapidly, infrastructural development has not kept pace. Water and sewage treatment plants are inadequate. Industrial wastes are not treated. Most of them find their way into the Tamsui. Apart from that, the proliferation of vehicles in recent years and a failure to enforce the clean-up by industry of emissions into the atmosphere have caused a serious decline in air quality.

A commentator on the environmental situation in Taiwan and in Taipei in particular has stressed:

> ... the Tamsui is a microcosm of Taiwan's environmental problems. The island uses an estimated twenty thousand different industrial chemicals, six thousand of which are highly toxic. Many eventually end up in rivers and streams ... Despite the severity of the current problems there currently is no budget allocation specifically targeted to reduce industrial pollution ... laws, standards, and enforcement (of environmental regulations) all need to be improved (Mindich, 1991, p. 12).

The philosophy has been that industrial development was an essential priority and that necessarily involved the development of Taipei as a great industrial centre. Once wealth had been created there would be capital available to deal with the problems of air pollution, excessive generation of wastes, degradation of the Tamsui and the decline of the quality of life of the population of Greater Taipei.

The municipal government is beginning to address the problems which have accumulated. Theoretically it will get a large share of the $US305 billion which has been budgeted in the new Six-Year National Development Plan. Some of this enormous sum will be allocated to environmental protection. But problems of changing public attitudes are admitted. Proposals for the clean-up of the Tamsui are resisted because such a programme is still regarded as harmful to the economy. Residents are apparently reluctant to pay their share for connecting new sewage systems. They resist relatively modest garbage collection fees. Piggeries and factories dump untreated wastes into water courses at night. Even if pollution control equipment is installed it is frequently switched off to reduce costs. In other words there has to be a transformation of attitudes before a real start can be made in solving the problems which increasingly beset Taipei.

Bangkok

It has been estimated by the United Nations that 32 per cent of Thailand's gross domestic output is generated in Greater Bangkok. What was once a dense and compact city has grown so much over the past twenty-five years that it now sprawls over 1,500 square kilometres. Bangkok is probably the best example in Asia of a primate city. It is forty-five times larger than the second largest city, Chiang Mai, and has nearly six times the population of that city and eleven of the other major centres in Thailand put together. Slums have increased. About 20 per cent of households have no piped water. There is acute pollution of canals and other waterways. So much ground water has been pumped out that the water table has been driven down and whole areas are subject to subsidence. This is happening on a flood plain that is not much more than a metre above sea level.

Bangkok is dependent on the Chao Phraya River, which drains central Thailand. The great urban concentration of people is using this marvellous river as a sewer. They are also demanding too much water during the dry seasons. As depletion of ground water goes on and the process of subsidence continues, the city becomes more and more prone to flood damage during the wet seasons. The floods clean out the water courses, but over time there is a risk that large areas will become badly degraded, especially as sea water already threatens to pollute the water table.

Air pollution, largely from vast and increasing numbers of badly maintained petrol- and diesel-engined vehicles, has become a serious problem. There is only limited suburban rail transport, and little prospect of a comprehensive suburban system which would reduce congestion on roads and the narrow streets and lanes of the city. As commuters rely on buses and the city is serviced by trucks and vans, traffic congestion can be extreme. The allocation of resources by government to an expressway system seems unlikely to provide long-term relief, because of the continuing increase in the number of vehicles. As soon as new expressways and their connectors are opened they quickly reach the limit of their capacity in peak traffic periods.

Bangkok is a magnet for people from all over Thailand. Other cities are developing, especially along the southeast coast of the Gulf of Thailand, but this does not seem to have caused any perceptible slowing down in the growth of the capital. It seems to have reached a point in time where so much capital is needed to sustain and extend its infrastructure that other areas are starved of the funds they need for properly planned expansion (United Nations Population Policy Paper No.10, 1987).

Manila

This city, like Bangkok, has experienced phenomenal growth during the past three decades. It was the twenty-third largest city in the world in 1984, and may become the sixteenth by 2000. The population was increasing throughout the 1970s and 1980s at a rate of about one million people every five years. Although Manila is the centre of much of the business activity in the Philippines it was estimated in the mid-1980s that over 16 per cent of the city's population was unemployed and some 43 per cent underemployed. The situation has not improved. A World Bank study points out:

> About 35% of the MM (Metro Manila) population lives below the 1983 absolute poverty threshold of $245 per capita annually, and a high percentage of these people live in slums where population densities reach 2000 per hectare. Only 10-12% of MM households are served by waste disposal systems ... MM will generate 7,000 tons of solid waste daily in 1988 of which only 65% will be collected leaving 2,000 tons daily to be burned, thrown in waterways, or to moulder on the ground ...
>
> ... About one million vehicles, more than half the country's total, operate in the MM area of which only half are thought to meet even minimal emission standards. About 65% of the country's recognized industrial enterprises are located in the MM area, of which only 1/3 to 1/2 are thought to comply with minimal air and water pollution emission standards. Although comparable data are lacking, MM's air quality is generally believed to be among the worst in Southeast Asia.

The basic cause of MM's severe environmental problems is that eight million people are utilizing infrastructure (much of which dates from the US colonial period) estimated to be adequate for two million at most (World Bank, 1989, p. 3).

The World Bank report goes on to suggest that it can be convincingly argued that the problems of Manila cannot be solved unless (1) there are gargantuan investments in land, equipment and infrastructure; (2) there is a sweeping reform of the system of government for the metropolitan area; and (3) at the same time a massive programme of regional development is implemented which will encourage people to settle in other centres (World Bank, 1989, p. 3). The United Nations supports this view. Until there are enforceable metropolitan development strategies approved for Manila as a whole the process of deterioration is likely to continue rapidly (United Nations Population Policy Paper No. 5, 1986; ESCAP, 1990, p. 113).

Jakarta

The problems which the Indonesian capital Jakarta is facing are similar to those of Manila although they may be less severe. Indonesia has had stable government for twenty-five years and strenuous efforts have been made to plan the development of Jakarta and its neighbouring regions. It is of course the focal point of the archipelago and the great city of one of the most densely populated places on earth—the island of Java. From small beginnings as the capital of the Netherlands East Indies, the population of the city reached 7.5 million in 1985 and it could become the world's eleventh largest city by 2000 with 13 million. The annual growth rate has been 4 per cent. Population density has increased, despite the way in which the city has encroached into neighbouring provinces.

The Government of Indonesia has endeavoured to plan the development of Jakarta as part of its National Urban Development Strategy. It has had mixed results. Attempts to control migration into Jakarta have been persisted with since the 1970s without great success. Problems keep piling up no doubt because there is a limit to the funds which can be made available. Indeed the planners have now to take into account the possibility that infrastructure will have to be provided for a population of the region of Java dominated by Jakarta which could exceed 23 million in the first decade of the next century. Planning is handicapped by the absence of a regional authority with the powers necessary to implement and develop programmes for both the city and those neighbouring areas which come under the authority of provincial governments.

Industrial development has been largely left to the private sector. It has contributed significantly to the growth of Greater Jakarta. Business has taken advantage of public expenditure projects notably housing and roads, but in the process has contributed to an undesirable imbalance between Jakarta and other urban centres.

Severe environmental problems are also accumulating, such as seawater intrusion, water pollution, degradation of prime agricultural land, inadequate waste management, traffic congestion and associated air pollution. There is also a massive housing problem. It has been calculated that about 40 per cent of the housing stock is semi-permanent with a life of about fifteen years and should be replaced at about 10 per cent annually. Provision of new dwellings is lagging. There does not seem much prospect of catching up with the backlog (United Nations Population Policy Paper No. 18, 1989).

These brief summaries are designed to illustrate the extent of the urban problem which affects both developing and developed countries. ESCAP has drawn attention to the potential dangers involved in the seemingly inevitable growth of cities, especially the big ones:

> The disproportionate increase in the urban population results in urban congestion and exerts tremendous pressures on infrastructures. Consequently most of the principal cities in the Asian and Pacific region, particularly in the developing countries, face the problems of inadequate housing, resulting in the growth of slum areas and marginal settlements, a lack of water supply and sanitation, deficient solid wastes collection, treatment and disposal systems, traffic noise and congestion, air, water and noise pollution (ESCAP, 1990, p. 125).

There are few grounds for confidence that the capital will be found to make good present deficiencies, let alone progressively address worsening circumstances in most countries.

China

Nearly half China's people live in the Changjiang valley below the three gorges, its delta and in the land to its north and north east. The provinces of Zhejiang, Anhui, and Jiangsu, whose metropolitan centre is Shanghai, Henan, Shandong, Shanxi, Hebei, which surrounds the great neighbouring cities of Beijing and Tianjin, and Liaoning, are very densely populated.

The combined population of these provinces and the three great cities, which are separate administrative zones, was nearly 50 million in 1990. There is another great cluster in the south where the total population of the provinces of Guangdong, Hainan and Guangxi reached 112 million. The population of the densely peopled central province of Sichuan adds another 107 million (*Beijing Review*, 17-23 December 1990, p. 23).

The five provinces and municipalities with population densities exceeding 500 persons per square kilometre are Shanghai, Tianjin, Beijing, Shandong and Henan. They are all concentrated in the central east and northeast. Taken together with South Korea and Japan this is one of the most densely populated parts of the world. It is perhaps encouraging from the long-term point of view that recent data shows that the annual population growth rate of Shanghai was just under five per thousand and that the rates in Beijing, Zhejiang, Tianjin and Liaoning were also below ten per thousand. In the southern province of Guangdong the rate is fifteen and it goes higher in the more remote provinces especially those with significant ethnic minorities.

In 1990 the proportion of urban people was officially reckoned to be 26 per cent. That means that, of the total population of about 1,134 million, about 304 million are living in the cities and towns and 858 million are rural people (*Beijing Review*, 17-23 December 1990, p. 22). The urban proportion could be significantly understated. For example an independent assessment suggests that, depending on the definition used, between 60 and 75 per cent of the population reside in rural areas. Given the growth of non-agricultural work in villages and small towns, and the now uncontrollable movement of people into cities, perhaps as many as 40 per cent of the population are urban dwellers (Wu and Xueqiang, 1991, pp. 129-43.)

China's relatively low GDP should not be taken as an indication of its proper status in global and regional terms. The disparity in wealth between China and Japan is staggering, even allowing for the difficulty of arriving at a comparable estimate of GDP for a socialist economy. China's other attributes give it great power status. It is the only Asian country with strategic nuclear capability. It maintains very large land forces. It has developed rocketry, and is capable of launching satellites.

It ranks fourth in the world as a producer of steel. It is a permanent member of the Security Council of the United Nations. It is becoming increasingly important in world trade (Klintworth, 1989, p. 4).

China's vast and still growing population is obviously a handicap to further development. Population growth in excess of 1.1 billion was described in an official publication as grim (*Beijing Review*, 13-19 March 1989, p. 4). The Chinese Government has for many years now recognized the problem, and has tried to do something about it.

No other country has endeavoured to come to grips with its population problem especially in circumstances where it has been acknowledged that the present population is much too high. The Chinese Government appears to have accepted expert opinion that given the prospects for future economic development, the nutritional requirements of the people, resources of fresh water and environmental balance, China's optimum population would ideally be about 700 million (Song and Yu, 1984, p. 517).

That is scarcely attainable. Nevertheless a serious attempt has been sustained for more than a decade now to limit the growth of population. What follows is a summary of the key elements of the Chinese population dilemma drawn from Chinese sources:

- Originally China had planned to keep its population below 1.2 billion by the year 2000. Subsequently this was amended to around 1.2 billion.

- China is experiencing its third baby boom since 1949. The principal reason for the rise in the birth rate is that 11-13 million women are reaching child-bearing age each year. This peak will not begin to decline until 1995.

- Implementation of family planning policies across China has been uneven. In many places, particularly culturally and economically backward areas, deep-rooted traditional ideas remain stubbornly entrenched—especially the notion that 'the more sons, the more blessings'.

- Some three million babies born in 1987 were unauthorized third or fourth children and around 2.5 million people married below the legal age.

- Since China began reinvigorating its economy the floating population has risen to about fifty million. As an example, 2.5 million people have moved into the prosperous southern province of Guangdong, which is closely linked economically with Hong Kong, from neighbouring provinces. This group appears to have produced a big number of over-large families (*Beijing Review*, 1989, 1990, 1991; Wang, 1991, pp. 68-87).

The understandable flow of people from the less prosperous to the more prosperous provinces may be beyond the scope of the authorities to control. As might be expected, the problem is most serious in and about the great cities of Shanghai, Beijing and Guangzhou. A survey in the latter city indicated that about a quarter of the immigrants had no regular employment, nor permanent accommodation. Few of these people are on the register of the province in which they presently live and work. Notifications of births, deaths and marriages seem seldom to be submitted (*China News Analysis*, 15 April 1991, No. 1433, p. 2).

Since the introduction of the household responsibility system in the countryside and the leasing out of land to individuals, 180 million farm labourers have become redundant. This group may increase to 260 million by 2000 (*Beijing Review*, 13-19 March 1989, p. 4; 20-6 March 1989, p. 7). It is not difficult therefore to understand why the floating population has become so large and the magnitude of the problems it must pose for both central and provincial authorities.

The Chinese acknowledge that their policy of bringing the population under control by limiting families to one child is not entirely successful. The problem has been recognized for some time. Although the authorities know the importance of getting the rural people to accept the policy, and to understand the reasons for it, fertility, although declining, has always been higher in rural areas. In 1981 the rural fertility rate was still 2.9 per cent compared with 1.4 per cent in urban areas (Liu (ed.), 1987, p. 159). It was moreover understood that even if the one-child-per-family policy were to be successful across the country, the total population would continue to increase until about 2005. The rate of family formation would be sufficient to ensure that (Song and Yu, 1984, p. 515).

The official count in the census conducted in 1990 was 1,133.7 million (*Beijing Review*, 17-23 December 1990, p. 23). The birthrate is dropping but 'temporary' difficulties still dog the implementation of birth control and family planning in rural areas (*Beijing Review*, 19-25 November 1990, p. 20). As expected, the census also revealed that population densities have increased in coastal areas and major cities, notably Beijing, Tianjin and Shanghai. Average density in these areas exceeds 500 people per square kilometre compared with the national average of 118 (*Beijing Review*, 19-25 November 1990, p. 7).

The dangers are recognized. The authorities have pointed out:

- When China's grain production peaked at 396 kilograms per capita in 1984 it was sufficient only for minimum needs. Low per capita acreage of productive land makes it difficult to feed the population. If population further increases China could not maintain current levels of per capita acreage and grain production.

- There is still a massive problem of illiteracy—230 million in 1982. Fast population growth makes it more difficult to increase per capita expenditure on education.

- Although more people are working in industry, their poor educational attainments and out-dated ideas are likely to prove an obstacle to modernization and progress in urban areas (*Beijing Review*, 29 October-4 November 1990, p. 27).

It is in China that one finds the clear link between growth of population, their activities and deterioration of the environment. Pressures of growing numbers have forced people to cultivate marginal land, often at the expense of forest cover. Economic growth depends on the procurement and processing of increasing quantities of materials. As one commentator has described the interconnections:

> ... the growing population over the centuries has forced farmers to cultivate increasingly marginal soils, encroach on forested areas, and overgraze the grasslands. Shortage of firewood for cooking and heating has also led to encroachment on the forests, though in China the availability of coal has reduced demands on the forest, while at the same time increasing air pollution problems. Intensification of agriculture in long-settled areas has also resulted in many problems: ecological hazards from agricultural chemicals, waterlogging and salinity from irrigation.
>
> Growing urban populations have also put extreme pressures on the basic necessities of life: clean air and water. Increasing sewage and household waste pollutes the rivers and the coal burnt for heating and cooking pollutes the air. Large urban populations can only be supported in a more industrialized economy, and here again the factories contribute to the pollution of both air and water (Jones, 1991, p. 265).

It could be argued that the key to long-term stability in the Western Pacific is the achievement by China of a rate of economic growth which would enable it to attain its target of a per capita GDP equivalent to $US1,000 by early next century. That would involve something like a quadrupling of present average income.

It has been suggested that, providing the political environment in China improves, which probably depends on the Communist Party accepting political reform, relinquishing its monopoly of power and encouraging further liberalization of the economy, such an objective is attainable. Since 1977 growth in output has averaged over 9 per cent each year. This could mean that a capacity to sustain such rates is becoming entrenched in China. This achievement together with what has gone on in Korea, Taiwan and Japan has brought about the great and unique shift in the centre of gravity of global economic production and power towards Northeast Asia (Garnaut, 1989, pp. 36, 124).

While it seems quite likely that the process of industrialization will continue apace along the coast of China and in some inland centres, it is prudent to remain sceptical about the possibility that the great bulk of the work force—the peasants—will continue to achieve increases in output comparable to those which were achieved in the 1980s.

The Chinese Government is aware of the problem and it is therefore surprising that economic analysts are not more cautious in forecasting what can actually be achieved in growth of GDP. As has been emphasized, population projections from new census data pose grim realities for the authorities. The fears expressed by demographers and by those people who were charged with implementing population control programmes in China have been realized. There will be a continuing spill of people from rural to urban life. Growth targets cannot possibly be achieved unless a process of rapid and efficient industrialization continues. How is work to be provided for the vast numbers involved?

Consider the magnitude of that task in terms of the capital needed to provide the factories, businesses and infrastructure for such numbers. This is after all an age where machines continue to replace labour, and many of the jobs that are created in industry call for people with considerable educational attainment. Consider further the materials needed to sustain the activities which will provide employment for those who are able to obtain work. China is relatively resource rich, but it is already exacerbating environmental problems because of the inefficient ways in which it extracts and uses basic energy and other materials, notably wood, oil and coal. Its rate of capital formation is inadequate to modernize industries such as the energy industry and the transport system. Reform in these areas is basic to getting better performance in the economy as a whole. It also seems inadequate to provide the infrastructure needed to make good the present backlog and future requirements of the growing cities.

China might be able to avoid a dangerous deterioration of the circumstances of its urban population provided its domestic capital continues to be supplemented by foreign capital. It will however be very hard to get near to the target of the equivalent of $US1,000 per capita GDP within the foreseeable future. Even modest improvements may come at great cost, given the way the population will continue to increase and the pressures developing in urban areas. This is one of the dilemmas facing the countries of the Western Pacific. None of them can afford to be indifferent to what is happening in China. Many have comparable problems themselves, but they could be adversely affected if China begins to break down as a result of the failure of the central government to handle current problems. They trace back in large part to the phenomenal growth of population since 1950 and to the failure of the system of central planning to provide adequately for the renewal of assets and to keep pollution to a minimum.

Indochina and Southeast Asia

The problems which China is facing as a consequence of the growth of its population are paralleled by similar problems in Vietnam, on the Indonesian island of Java and in the Philippines. The population of Vietnam continued to increase during the long years of war, and has now reached the point where sheer numbers are perhaps the major problem facing a government which has become trapped by policies which led to almost total dependence on trade with and aid from the Soviet Union and former Communist countries in Eastern Europe.

A census conducted in 1989 confirmed that the population had reached 64.4 million. The annual rate of growth since 1979 had averaged 2.13 per cent (Hull, 1990). While this was lower than rates reached during the previous decade, a possibility remains that the population could increase to 100 million or even more over the next three decades. The already burdened agricultural sector of the Vietnamese economy does not seem to be capable of absorbing greater numbers. The desperate economic situation which has developed since the withdrawal of Soviet assistance makes it especially difficult for the government to create opportunities for growing numbers to find work in the cities and towns. Already tens of thousands of economic refugees have left Vietnam, many of them finding only detention compounds in Hong Kong. Unless capital begins to flow to create an efficient industrial base and service industries, what has been happening in Vietnam in recent years may be a warning of what is likely to happen to increasing populations in other countries of the Western Pacific.

Java in Indonesia and the island of Luzon in the Philippines provide other examples of how populations could build up to the point where limits of carrying capacity are approached. In Luzon a large proportion of the population of the Philippines is concentrated in the corridor which runs from the Lingayen Gulf to the north of Manila to Tabayas Bay further south. The squatter population here has grown dramatically during recent years (McBeth, 1991a, p. 35). That in itself seems to substantiate growing evidence that other parts of the island, and indeed the archipelago, are having difficulty in supporting increasing numbers of people.

In Indonesia, Java, which provides only 7 per cent of the total land area, is home to over 60 per cent of the population. Density increased from 315 per square kilometre in 1930 to 690 in 1980, and is continuing to rise (Pardoko, 1984, p. 51). The population of this island could increase by the year 2020 to about 130 million of which perhaps as many as 75 million would be classified as urban. Already Jakarta is demanding a level of investment which is adversely affecting other parts of Indonesia. Transmigration to other islands has been tried and clearly will not provide an answer. The demands of the growing population of Java evidently will cause great strain on governments in Indonesia as they attempt to deal with the problems stemming from the inevitable growth of population.

Evidence is accumulating that insufficient attention has been paid, especially by economists, to the population dimension of the countries of the Western Pacific. Although the facts and the issues have been fully documented by demographers and responsible forecasts have been made, there is an evident lack of coordination with the work of economists. The estimates of the likely growth of population are probably much more likely to prove accurate than projections of growth of GDP. We already know that, whatever happens in other aspects of their national life, China and the other developing countries of the Western Pacific are going to have to somehow accommodate very significant increases in their present populations.

There will be several major pressure points. The most serious are in China. Already, as the Government admits, the situation is almost intolerable in many places. The deltas of Vietnam are in a very serious situation. There are clear signs of stress in parts of Indonesia and the Philippines, as well as in great urban concentrations such as Bangkok, Taipei, Tokyo and Seoul. Movements of people from poorer to richer provinces are occurring in China. Filipinos and Vietnamese are seeking work elsewhere in increasing numbers. While there were outlets for Filipinos in other countries of the Western Pacific and in the Middle East, and for Vietnamese in countries of the now dismembered Soviet bloc, the problems did not seem particularly urgent. They are now increasing in intensity and could become an international problem which the Western Pacific countries will find very difficult to manage.

I will turn later in this book to examine the question of whether it is possible to base policies on concepts of sustainable growth in countries where the needs of increasing numbers of people for a better life seem incompatible with the preservation and improvement of the land and waters which have sustained their civilization for centuries. There are no grounds for optimism. Indeed, it can be argued that although the dimensions of the problem are comparatively well known, so serious are their implications that people recoil from examining the realities which are gradually being forced upon them.

5. The Energy Dimension

The economic successes of the 1980s generated an atmosphere of optimism in many of the Asian countries of the Western Pacific which has run on into the 1990s. This is reflected in the way some people expert in the economics of energy analyse developments. For example:

> The Asia-Pacific energy market is expected to grow faster than any other region of the world. Most of the so-called NICs (newly industrializing countries) of the world—namely Korea, Taiwan, Hong Kong, and Singapore—are located in this region. Emerging NICs—Thailand and Malaysia—with substantial economic growth potential and energy demand are also located in the Asia-Pacific region (Fesharaki, 1989, p. 143).

The implications of this and much other writing about the Western Pacific is that there is now an inevitability about the consolidation of industrial progress in Southeast as well as Northeast Asia. Release from poverty of increasing numbers of people in the first of those areas may not quite be guaranteed but is now defined as an immediate and realizable goal. It is difficult to argue against the now abundant evidence that the essential ingredient of material economic growth—cheap energy—can be provided. Resources are adequate. But there is no reason to assume long-term supply will be adequate to cope with likely demand. That is by no means assured.

I suggested in Chapter 2 that a revealing approach to the study of economics is to examine economic activity from the perspective of the production and the consequences of utilizing energy. Mankind has reshaped the world through its capacity to proceed from the use of simple fuels, wood and charcoal, to the exploitation and gradually the massive use of fossil fuels. It has been pointed out that there was an entropic or energy watershed in Northwestern Europe at about the middle of the millenium now ending. It occurred because of the depletion of resources of wood. There was an inevitable and serious shortage of that essential commodity for cooking, heating, glass and, especially, iron and steel making. The consequence was a change from minor exploitation of deposits of coal to the development of techniques for its large-scale extraction and transport, and the solution over time of the problems associated with the use of coal and coke, as a substitute for charcoal, in iron and steel making (Rivkin, 1980, pp. 77-93). A new applied science of metallurgy gradually became fundamental to industrial development. This and related sciences continued to develop. Eventually technology made possible the use of products refined from oil as a much more efficient and convenient substitute for coal as a source of power in transport, for the generation of power and as a basis for new materials. However supplies are bound to diminish and this contingency should be taken into account.

If this is admitted as a probability, this kind of analysis points to the approach of another and probably much more serious energy watershed as supplies of oil and natural gas come closer to exhaustion. Although reserves of coal will last for several centuries at current rates of extraction, the depletion of the hydrocarbons will pose another technological challenge if energy supplies are to be maintained at anything like the levels of abundance we have experienced during the past two centuries.

Some Asian countries of the Western Pacific are beginning to experience the consequences of a transition which is in some ways similar to the first of these watersheds as they proceed with their transformation into industrial societies. The process of profound economic change which began in Europe during the late middle ages has been explained by Jeremy Rivkin:

> While the clearing of forests for cultivation greatly reduced the available wood supply, it was the quickened pace of commercial activity that led to a timber famine. For example, the new glass works and soap industry required large amounts of wood ash. But it was the production of iron and the building of ships that made the greatest demands. By the sixteenth and early seventeenth centuries, the timber crisis was so acute in England that royal commissions were set up to regulate the cutting down of forests. The regulations proved ineffective. In the 1630s wood had become two and a half times more expensive than it had been in the late fifteenth century (Rivkin, 1989, p. 88).

In Asia, wood has been plentiful until recent times. Now resources are being depleted in ways similar to what occurred in Europe five centuries before. It remains, with other biomass, an important source of energy. Its use should be taken into account with the use of fossil fuels and the exploitation of renewable sources to get an adequate understanding of the energy situation in the Western Pacific.

The Asian countries of the Western Pacific could not have made a major impact on the world economy without having developed, or begun the process of developing, high-energy consumption economies on the model of older industrial societies. As a Chinese study stresses:

Energy is one of the basic structures of society and provides the motive force for all human economic activities ... As science and technology progress and social productive forces grow, energy will exercise a greater and greater influence on the national economy, accelerating or retarding its development or revising its structure (Liu (ed.), 1987, p. 176).

The countries of the Western Pacific are now locked into a process of development which will involve utilizing vastly increased amounts of fuel for the production of energy. Herein lies a major threat to their longer-term viability because much of that energy will be wood and charcoal derived from forests and woodlands already stressed by the exploitation of the gatherers of commercial timber as well as people who are preoccupied with day-to-day survival. The countries of the Western Pacific are just beginning to realize that vegetative, and especially forest cover, is a collective as much as a national resource. They now know that the rate of depletion has for some time been exceeding the rate of replacement. They are moreover beginning to understand that this could be disastrous because it will inevitably cause deterioration of land and of water systems which are fundamental to the sustainability of all their economies.

ESCAP summed up the situation which had been reached in 1990 in an important but largely neglected report:

Production from the land and land resources within the ESCAP region have increased substantially in recent years. This has been achieved by an extensive expansion in croplands by over 100 million hectares since 1950, as well as an increase in productivity through agricultural inputs.

However these trends are not sustainable. This fact is evident in the widespread exhaustion of resources, land degradation and desertification. A typical phenomenon of resource limitation is that the rate of expansion in croplands started levelling off in the 1980s. The average rate of deforestation of tropical forests alone was 2.0 million hectares per annum or about 5,500 hectares per day in the 1970s which has been estimated to have increased to 5.0 million hectares per annum in [sic] 1980s. The increasing pressure on forests emanates not only from agriculture, but also from fuel wood and timber demands as well as grazing (ESCAP, 1990, p. 33).

If soil is regarded along with vegetation as a source of energy, which it undoubtedly is, then this situation is becoming increasingly serious.

The pursuit of material economic growth has necessitated the fulfilment by each economy, as it proceeds with industrialization, of increasing demand for fossil fuels as well as wood. In many cases the resource needs have been much greater than domestic resources. In addition to the diminution of sources of wood and the depletion of the organic content of soils, vehicles and industries are producing so much exhaust, smoke-stack gases and waste materials that governments are now having to reckon the costs of acidification, waste management, air pollution and, in the longer-term, global warming as well as erosion and deterioration of soils and water systems.

A Japanese economist has described the complex relationships of economic growth, energy and the environment as a trilemma. He explains it thus:

> As the economy grows, energy consumption increases, producing massive impacts on the environment. SOx (sulphur dioxides) and NOx (nitrogen oxides) causing such environmental problems as acid rain are among them, while the development of technologies to remove them makes it possible to minimize such adverse impact on the environment. As for CO_2 problems, however, no technologies have been established to remove or fix CO_2 within the cost range making sense in economic terms, and it is not easy to cut off, or minimize, the vicious cycle of the linkage of economic growth-energy consumption-global warming ...

> If the situation lasts long where the trilemma cannot be eliminated by technological breakthrough, among others, the only path left would be a shock solution by soaring prices, like those triggered by an energy crisis (Fujime, 1990, p. 76).

Confronting this trilemma is going to become a major policy issue for countries everywhere. It is unlikely that it can be avoided in the Western Pacific, because it is not just global warming which poses a threat. Danger of degradation of the basics of existence, for both rural and urban people, is inextricably part of the trilemma. A convincing argument can be developed that, in the global context, the major responsibility for pollution and for the threat of global warming rests with the countries of North America and Europe who produce the greatest proportion of the gaseous and solid pollutants. In the Western Pacific, Japan and South Korea, with only small resources of domestic energy, almost entirely based on dwindling reserves of coal and some hydroelectric energy, are among the most efficient users of energy materials, and are striving to improve efficiencies. Other countries, with the exception of Taiwan, Singapore, Australia and New Zealand, are developing. They argue that for them continuing material economic growth is an imperative. (By inference that is no longer the case for developed countries.) They point out that their contribution to pollution, especially atmospheric pollution, is a relatively small proportion of the global total, and that developing countries in Asia and elsewhere should therefore be permitted to achieve a much higher stage of development before having to stabilize or reduce their consumption of fossil fuels.

This is understandable, but, if it is recognized that attention should be paid in the decades ahead to every aspect of the adverse consequences of the utilization of energy materials, then it can be argued that these consequences are becoming serious enough for the land and water of the countries of the Western Pacific to necessitate remedial action whether or not they are making a significant contribution to global warming. In order to grasp what is involved, it is important to distinguish between the immediate consequences of the utilization of sources of energy and the longer-term contribution it may make to global warming. The latter is beyond the scope of this book.

The consequences of atmospheric change could be immensely serious for mankind. But concern about this global issue should not be allowed to disguise the fact that the pursuit of material economic growth through continual increases in the production of energy from all sources and goods of all kinds, in order to make possible increases in outputs of goods and services, in the Western Pacific and elsewhere, is having direct and harmful effects on the land and marine environments as well as on the atmosphere. Pressure will have to be reduced, or it will prove impossible to resolve the trilemma mentioned above.

At the expense of being repetitive it is necessary to recognize the vital importance of forest biomass in the new complex energy equation which will have to be solved in the Western Pacific. Again, ESCAP has pointed out:

> The largest forest biomass occurs in tropical Asia where 34 per cent of land area, comprising 306 million hectares is closed tropical forest. In insular South-East Asia, closed forests cover 62 per cent of the land area, but in continental South-East Asia only 35 per cent of the land is under tropical forest, and in South Asia only 15 per cent. The average rate of deforestation in the region, according to an earlier (1980) estimate was 2.0 million hectares per annum. A more recent (1990) preliminary estimate of FAO places the figure at a high 5 million hectares per annum, which is quite alarming. In insular South-East Asia the rate is highest at over 2.0 million hectares per annum, in continental South-East Asia the rate is 1.4 million hectares annually, while in South Asia the calculation is 1.6 million hectares per annum (ESCAP, 1990, p. 2).

When the loss of forest and the deterioration of soils is considered together with the environmental consequences of the use of coal and oil in energy generation, transport and as a feedstock for other materials, a picture begins to emerge which gives cause for concern. The process of material economic growth may slowly grind to a halt because the benefits of industrial progress could be undermined by the damage being done to the land and waters which support human communities. This is more likely to become serious in densely populated countries, where there is an imperative to use every square metre of arable land as intensively as possible, and to harvest whatever resources are available from the forests. That is the situation facing intensive agriculture throughout the Asian countries of the Western Pacific. While similar problems are becoming apparent in other areas where land is also cultivated intensively, such as Europe, they are an extraordinarily important aspect of the complex of problems facing governments in Asia.

Energy Resources

Firewood, as I have stressed, is an important energy resource in Asia. The proportion of energy derived from this source reflects the economic status of individual countries. As might be expected the proportion of firewood used is below 5 per cent of total use of energy materials in the richer countries—Japan, Korea, Australia and New Zealand. It is calculated to be between 5 and 30 per cent in Malaysia and China. Shortage of supply has long necessitated the use of coal for domestic cooking and heating in China. The proportion rises to between 30 and 60 per cent in the Philippines, Vietnam, Thailand and Indonesia and to between 60 and 90 per cent in Papua New Guinea, Burma and Laos. In war-ravaged Cambodia it may be over 90 per cent.

This source of energy is becoming increasingly depleted in Indochina, as well as China, Thailand, throughout the Philippines, in parts of Indonesia, notably northern Sumatra, Java and some islands to its east and in central Burma (Seager (ed.), 1990, p. 57).

Many countries of the Western Pacific are however reasonably well endowed with resources of coal and some have abundant natural gas. Oil is much less plentiful in relation to growing demand. For the meantime the Western Pacific is heavily dependent on coal and oil. Much of the latter has to be imported.

While some countries like Japan, South Korea and Taiwan are quickly working out their coalfields, coal is abundant in China and Australia. There are also significant deposits in Southeast Asia. While much of this coal is of doubtful quality and some difficult to mine, it offers an important domestic alternative to imported fuels for the Philippines, Thailand, possibly Malaysia and especially Indonesia. Australia has been able to provide a very large proportion of the needs of the Northeast-Asian industrial countries as their capacity to supply from domestic mines has declined.

China's resources of economically recoverable coal were estimated to be 241 billion tonnes in 1985. Nearly 80 per cent of these resources are in the north and northwest, with Shanxi and Inner Mongolia dominating production. Only about 10 per cent is located in southwest China and even less in the eastern provinces where so much industry is located. Consumption of coal was about 750 million tonnes in 1985 with demand steadily increasing. Coal contributed just over three-quarters of total consumption of energy. Huge quantities have to be transported long distances to meet the needs of electricity generating plants, steel and other industries and domestic fuel. The managers of the Chinese economy are having difficulty in trying to find solutions to this problem.

Another feature of the coal industry in China is the relative importance of village or town-owned mines. These small-to-medium sized operations produce a significant proportion of total output. They pose many problems—small scale, inadequate equipment, low utilization, relatively short life-spans and variations in productive capacity (Xin, 1988, p. 50).

Australia provides an almost total contrast. Its mines operate on a large scale, many of them open cut. This enables complete extraction of large deposits lying close to the surface. Australia's resources of minable coal are thought to be about one-fifth those of China but a greater proportion of good quality coal may be economically recoverable. Australia first developed markets for metallurgical coal in Japan. One of the consequences of the first increase in the price of oil in the 1970s, and declining domestic supplies in Japan, was that demand developed for steaming coal for electricity generating plants. This trade, which is also important with South Korea and becoming so with Taiwan and Southeast-Asian countries, is now greater in volume than trade in metallurgical coal which is a function of the volume of steel production. Australia exported about 110 million tonnes of coal to Northeast Asia in 1988 and a further 5 million tonnes to Southeast Asian countries (Garnaut, 1989, p. 188).

The major Australian fields are close to the eastern seaboard. Transportation from mines to coal loaders is relatively straightforward. There has been massive investment during the past thirty years in port facilities. This has been complemented by the construction by Japanese, Korean and other companies of very large bulk carriers which move coal and other minerals with great efficiency to the centres of demand in Northeast Asia.

The coal resources of the Southeast-Asian and Indochinese countries are relatively small. Reserves are thought to be about 5 billion tonnes with economically recoverable quantities probably less than half of that. Deposits in Indonesia are much larger than those in Malaysia, the Philippines, Thailand and Vietnam. The Southeast-Asian countries are increasingly using coal for the generation of electricity. Indonesia has been able to develop exports to neighbouring countries but there is doubt about its capacity to sustain exports over the long-term. At this stage planners seem to be inclined to use coal locally so as to be better placed to increase exports of higher value oil and natural gas (Reksohadiprodjo, 1987, pp. 32-71).

The oil resources of the Western Pacific are significant, although they do not compare with those of the Middle East. There are important deposits in Indonesia, while China, Vietnam, Malaysia and

Thailand have some capacity. Some fields such as those of Burma and the south of Australia have been depleted. They have been offset to a limited extent by discoveries elsewhere in and around the Australian continent, in New Zealand and Papua New Guinea.

Exploration of off-shore resources is proceeding everywhere. There are a number of highly prospective areas especially around Sakhalin, the Russian island province north of Japan, in the coastal seas of China and Vietnam, between Australia and Indonesia, in the waters that Malaysia, Thailand and Indonesia share and in the Papua New Guinea area.

Even if all these areas were to become productive, it is unlikely that the Western Pacific could approach self-sufficiency in oil. Japan, South Korea and Taiwan are highly dependent on imports. Despite increasing emphasis on achieving greater efficiency in the use of all fuels in these countries, demand is continuing to rise. Trade-flow data show a big and seemingly permanent need for Middle-Eastern oil to be brought to Northeast Asia. Indonesia, China and Australia may be able to meet all or a major proportion of domestic needs for some time, but most of the others are expected to continue to import oil. Imports may increase in Australia and Southeast Asia as depletion of existing fields could proceed more rapidly than the discovery and development of new resources. Demand is also bound to increase in Indochina as the countries there gradually acquire more transport and farm vehicles and the industrial use of diesel engines increases.

There is a powerful incentive everywhere to reduce consumption of oil although demand pressures have been very strong. Oil has been relatively inexpensive in recent years, but memories of OPEC-induced price increases remain vivid and the cost of imports, even when prices are low, remains a burden for many countries. In addition it became evident in the 1970s that most, if not all, of the market economies of the Western Pacific were in danger of becoming excessively dependent on oil, regardless of price movements. Programmes to diversify energy supplies began more than a decade ago. Even relatively well-endowed countries like Indonesia and Malaysia are aiming to reduce their present overall dependence on oil from 78 and 91 per cent respectively to around 60 and 50 per cent in the year 2000.

There is considerable scope, however, for a significant increase in the use of natural gas from sources in the Western Pacific countries and from Soviet Pacific territories. This resource provides the key to diversification in many countries, especially those of Southeast Asia. Significant reserves, both proven and prospective, are substantially greater than those of oil. Technology has been developed in Northeast Asia for liquefying and transporting gas. Reserves have been proved in China, Thailand, Malaysia, Indonesia and Australia.

Proven resources of natural gas in Southeast Asia and Australia -New Zealand were estimated in the late 1980s to be about 1.8 times larger than reserves of oil then estimated at 15 billion barrels. Using those estimates, which may rely on information from exploration companies which is deliberately understated, oil supplies could run out in eight years in Thailand, ten in Australia, fifteen in Malaysia, eighteen in Indonesia and twenty-three in Brunei. By contrast gas supplies will hold out much longer at current rates of usage, with Australia-New Zealand having over thirty years' reserves, Indonesia more than forty, Thailand over sixty and Malaysia more than two hundred (Fesharaki, 1989, pp. 143-8).

In Malaysia's case the discovery of natural gas has greatly stimulated industrial development. The following description provides a succinct indication of why Malaysia is now firmly on the list of newly industrializing countries:

> In Malaysia, where pipeline construction to connect gas fields with industrial plants has been under way in recent years, natural gas use is becoming popular in methanol production, steel-making, thermal power generation, and fertilizer manufacturing. The share held by gas in energy mix is expected to increase from the 17 per cent level of 1987 ... to 22 per cent by the year 2000. Also, the country plans to supply 4.2 million M^3D (cubic metres per day) of gas to Singapore for the purpose of power generation, through a pipeline from Trengganu. This will become the first pipeline gas trade in the Asia-Pacific region (Toichi, 1989, p. 150).

Similar development is proceeding apace in Thailand with gas being used in the power-generation, petrochemical, cement and fertilizer industries.

Trade in natural gas is becoming increasingly important in the Western Pacific. It is clean fuel compared with oil and, especially, coal. Problems associated with its storage and transport have gradually been overcome. This is one of the major new technologies which the Japanese have mastered and on which the South Koreans and

Taiwanese are concentrating. The current position has been summarized by a Japanese energy economist:

- Gas exports in the form of liquefied natural gas have been growing
  dramatically during the 1980s. In 1986 Japan imported a total of 28.8 million
  tons of liquefied natural gas (LNG) from various countries in the Asia-Pacific
  region. Indonesia currently supplies 52 per cent of Japan's imports,
  outstripping Algeria as the largest exporter of natural gas.

- LNG exports have become the second most important earner of foreign
  currency for Southeast Asian countries after oil.

- That position could be reversed as reserves of oil are gradually depleted.

- Japan was the sole importer of LNG in the Western Pacific until 1985. Since
  1986 South Korea has entered the market. Its imports could reach 5 million
  tons by 1996. Taiwan has begun importing LNG from Indonesia. Shipments
  to that country could reach 3.5 million tons this decade.

- LNG imports by Japan, South Korea and Taiwan could exceed 45 million
  tons by 2000 (Toichi, 1989, pp. 151-2).

One of the factors providing the impetus towards greater use of
natural gas is its superiority as a relatively clean fuel. It offers in
bottled form an alternative to wood, charcoal and kerosene for cooking.
In the industrial countries it also ameliorates air pollution. It will take
on fundamental importance for the energy-endowed economies of
Southeast Asia. Their gas fields constitute a domestic source of high-
grade energy which could provide the basis for their further industrialization. Providing they husband their resources and, because of the
need to earn foreign exchange, are not compelled to sell huge quantities cheaply under long-term contracts to Japan and its neighbours in
the north, they could postpone for several decades the need to import
large quantities of coal as well as oil to meet a big percentage of their
energy needs.

The Energy Outlook in the Western Pacific

Projections of future demand for energy from conventional sources
such as coal, oil, natural gas, hydro-electricity and uranium should be
assessed with as much caution as estimates of population growth. They
may be mere extrapolations of trends during recent years or they may

involve sophisticated assumptions about movements in prices, technological parameters and substitution of the various fuels for one another.
They are unlikely to be accurate given the immense difficulty of
encompassing even the more likely probabilities over several decades.
They do, however, provide us with a valuable indication of possible
magnitudes in terms of the consumption of materials and the production of energy.

Within a few years it is likely that energy forecasts will take into
account a new set of constraints arising from the need to limit emissions of greenhouse gases. That is not yet the case. Forecasts for the
countries of the Western Pacific are based on patterns of demand
which have developed during an era when demand for energy materials
has increased rapidly literally fuelling the high rates of economic
growth which have been achieved by so many countries.

However the need to regulate emissions of greenhouse gases will
probably become a significant factor. The proportion of CO_2 discharged into the atmosphere by Asian countries in the Western Pacific
was estimated to be about 12 per cent of the global total in 1987. It
could rise to 16 per cent in 2000 and 24 per cent by 2030. This change
would reflect both economic growth in the Western Pacific as a whole
and the great dependence of China on coal as it further industrializes
(Ogawa, 1990, pp. 26-46).

The Institute of Energy Economics in Japan has published an
energy-demand forecast for the Pacific Basin which provides an
informed guess about the energy outlook as far into the future as 2030.
These forecasts are based on the following assumptions:

Western Pacific countries have great potential for economic growth as many of
them will experience an acceleration of their industrial development. That means
that there will be a substantial increase in their demand for energy.

The level of dependence on fossil fuels is likely to remain very high. There could
be a proportional decline in consumption of oil with a compensating increase in
the shares of natural gas and coal.

In quantitative terms, primary demand for energy, which reached 800 million
tonnes of oil equivalent in 1987, could reach 1250 million tonnes in 2000 and
2980 million tonnes in 2030 (Ogawa, 1990).

These assumptions provide the basis for the economic analysis which produced the forecasts from which Tables 5.1 and 5.2 are derived.

Table 5.1. Primary energy demand for selected countries in the
Western Pacific (million tons of oil equivalent)

	1987	2000	2020	2030
Developed				
Japan	410	577	709	758
South Korea	66	122	217	252
Taiwan	38	67	108	121
Australia	81	107	147	173
New Zealand	14	18	25	29
Singapore	9	15	21	23
Sub-total	**618**	**906**	**1227**	**1356**
Developing				
China	594	845	1489	1906
Indonesia	36	72	209	309
Malaysia	16	42	97	128
Philippines	13	18	34	46
Thailand	20	48	120	170
Sub-total	**679**	**1025**	**1949**	**2559**
TOTAL	**1297**	**1931**	**3176**	**3915**

Source: Institute of Energy Economics Japan, *Energy Demand Forecast for the Pacific Basin in 2000, 2030*, September 1990

The scale of the possible increases in energy demand is concerning, and not just because it might involve depletion of sources of gas and particularly oil during the next forty to fifty years. Allowance must also be made for the continuing utilization of wood and other biomass as fuel, for the consequences for the environment of such a massive increase in the conversion of coal, oil and gas to energy. To what extent will acidification increase? How are the solid wastes to be disposed of? What will this mean for air quality, especially in those areas where it is already unsatisfactory?

The conversion of Table 5.1 to the percentages in Table 5.2 provides another insight into the energy dimension of possible future development in the Western Pacific.

Table 5.2. Primary energy demand for selected countries in the Western Pacific (percentage share of demand expressed in million tonnes of oil equivalent)

	1987	2000	2020	2030
Developed				
Japan	31	30	22	19
South Korea	5	6	7	6
Taiwan	3	3	3	3
Australia	6	6	5	4
New Zealand	1	1	1	1
Singapore	1	1	1	1
Sub-total	**47**	**47**	**39**	**34**
Developing				
China	46	44	46	50
Indonesia	3	4	7	8
Malaysia	1	2	3	3
Philippines	1	1	1	1
Thailand	2	2	4	4
Sub-total	**53**	**53**	**61**	**66**
TOTAL	**100**	**100**	**100**	**100**

Source: *Energy Demand Forecast for the Pacific Basin in 2000, 2030*, Institute of Energy Economics, Japan.

This array indicates that there will be a slowing down in the rate of energy consumption in the developed countries, partly because populations will have stabilized and partly, one assumes, because greater efficiencies will be achieved.

Tables such as these should be regarded as not providing more than a broad indication of likely magnitudes if present trends continue. The assumptions on which each of the estimates are based could prove to be very wide of the mark. Nevertheless they suggest that, provided greater quantities of energy materials are available, which is possible, and provided energy consumption per capita increases, which seems to be almost certain, then incomes will grow throughout the Western Pacific. The extent of the increases is largely guesswork at this stage. It is likely that there will be a powerful incentive to increase the efficiency of energy production from fossil fuels everywhere including China. That may have a big effect on the actual demand for energy materials but it seems likely that the quantities converted into energy will increase substantially in the developing countries and probably in countries like Korea as they further industrialize.

Estimates prepared by the Institute of Energy Economics in Japan suggest that there may be a slowing down in the energy intensity of GDP in Japan. Per capita GDP may rise there by 30 per cent and energy consumption by 21 per cent between 2000 and 2020. In China, by contrast, where the population is forecast to grow well beyond the official target of 1.2 billion, the respective changes could be of the order of 250 per cent and 153 per cent respectively. That would be a very profound change indeed reflecting a big increase in purchasing power of the average person in China and availability of energy for both domestic and industrial use, although per capita income in 2020 might only be about one-twentieth that of someone in Japan.

In other cases, such as the Philippines, it seems to be assumed that more than a doubling of GDP may be achieved with only a 45 per cent increase in the use of energy per capita. That would seem to involve an assumption that the Philippines will be able to achieve greater efficiency in the use of energy than other countries. That seems unlikely. It is more likely that the forecasts for Indonesia will be closer to the mark. There income is expected to more than double between 2000 and 2020 with per capita energy consumption rising by a comparable percentage.

Income and energy disparities are almost certain to remain very significant. The per capita incomes projected for Japan and Australia will be perhaps fifteen to twenty times higher than those of countries like Indonesia and China. Incomes in South Korea could be seven to ten times higher.

The rich countries will continue to consume vast quantities of energy compared with the much more populous ASEAN grouping. For example Japan, South Korea and Australia could between them use 805 million tonnes of oil equivalent in 2000, 950 in 2010 and 1,132 in 2020. The projection for the ASEAN countries for each of these years is 180, 300 and 460 million tonnes of oil equivalent. The gap will narrow, but it will remain very significant.

The increases suggested for South Korea, from 66 million tonnes of oil equivalent in 1990 to 252 million tonnes in 2030, provide a useful indication of the extent to which the supply of energy must be increased if a nation is determined to pursue a rapid growth path. The authorities there may soon realize that consumption on this scale holds dangers for the Korean economy because of the cost of importing so much additional fuel and the certainty of a matching increase in the pollution load. Even though Korea may soon begin to work towards becoming highly energy efficient, the rate of increase could not be expected other than gradually to slow down because of the importance attached to further expansion of industry.

The virtual doubling of consumption of fossil fuel in China will be inescapable if there is to be any prospect of reaching a per capita income target close to the present objective of $US1,000. The scope for improvements in efficiency are substantial but it is very much an open question whether they can be achieved even if the Chinese version of socialism evolves into a system where prices are formed by market forces rather than by the planning system.

There will have to be massive investments in mining, transport and energy-production facilities to accommodate increasing use of fossil fuels on the scale suggested by the forecasts. That in itself could lock the countries of the Western Pacific into a pattern where demand for energy will continue to rise, although probably at a slower rate, because there is no other way to ensure the steady increase in per capita incomes which is the objective of governments everywhere. There is absolutely no reason to expect that people in China and the ASEAN countries will not want significantly to narrow the gap between their standards of living and those of Japan, South Korea, Taiwan and Singapore.

An overall increase in energy demand measured by the present level of about 1.4 billion tonnes of oil equivalent to 2 billion tonnes in 2000 and 3.2 billion tonnes thirty years later would involve a massive increase in the discharge of greenhouse and other gases into the atmosphere and more than double the present serious problem of disposing of the solid wastes of power and heat generation from coal. At one further remove in the industrial process there has to be a doubling or even tripling of industrial wastes in their myriad forms. Increased utilization of fossil fuels, especially given the scope for great improvements in efficiency in both industrialized and developing countries, should enable a more-than-proportionate increase in industrial production.

Forecasts of demand for primary energy seem to take into account constraints which may affect the demand side only to the extent that they have had perceptible influence during the historical period which provides the basis for projections which have been prepared in Japan. A major consideration is that oil prices were historically very low during the 1980s and, as a consequence, so were prices for coal and other energy materials. Despite the prospect of reserves of oil being depleted in Southeast Asia and Australia within ten to twenty years, global supplies will be adequate for some decades longer even though consumption seems certain to increase. Domestic supplies of gas will offer security of supply within the Western Pacific for considerably longer, and here the prospect of significant augmentation of reserves is much brighter than for oil. There will be plenty of coal throughout the twenty-first century. In such circumstances the price of oil would not be expected to rise sharply until demand begins to exceed the capacity of the countries of the Middle East to provide supply.

The great unknown is whether agreement will be reached during this decade on concerted international action to slow down the rate of consumption of fossil fuels, as the result of a consensus that changes in the composition of the atmosphere and more immediate forms of degradation are becoming menacing. There is no prospect of phasing out the use of oil, coal and natural gas. The industrial civilizations which have developed over the past 200 years are so highly dependent on them that their use will have to continue for as long as supplies are available, while societies develop alternative ways of accomplishing appropriate patterns of utilization. They will have to find a way of prolonging their industrial societies by moving to a situation where they are no longer consuming such quantities of energy and industrial materials that the wastes of production processes are endangering the environment. It seems likely that there will be vast investment in technology, both simple and complex, which will reduce the need to burn so much fuel. Whether this process will evolve quickly enough to enable the amount of coal and oil required greatly to be reduced during the decades immediately ahead is an unresolved question.

Disparities in Energy Supply

Most of the energy resources in the Western Pacific lie to the north and to the south in the vast coal fields of China and Australia. Between them in the equatorial region are the oil and gas fields and coal resources of Southeast Asia. The oil and gas deposits are supplemented by major fields in China and significant resources in the Southwest Pacific. There could be significant supplementation from fields in the Soviet Far East for which substantial markets can only be found to the south, especially in Japan and Korea.

These countries and Taiwan have virtually exhausted their resources of domestic coal and are almost totally dependent on imports of fossil fuels. They are now industrially rich and energy poor. They have to import to survive. This has created a dependence on the energy-rich countries of the Western Pacific, although supplies are imported from North America, Africa and, of course, the Middle East.

The other energy-poor countries are Vietnam, Laos, Cambodia and the Philippines. Their resources are limited. They are handicapped by the need to allocate a significant proportion of modest foreign earnings to imports of fuel. Circumstances such as this conspire to condemn countries to a continual struggle to survive alongside neighbours whose energy resources are adequate or plentiful.

There could be no greater contrast than that of Japan, Taiwan and South Korea with Vietnam and the Philippines. Lack of domestic energy resources is no handicap to development provided that a country has the capacity to create a technological society with great export potential, as Japan, Taiwan, Korea and Singapore have done. Dependence on imports of raw materials is a cause for concern because interruption of supply can imperil the functioning of the economy, but it does not inhibit progress. Clearly, however, poor countries which need to import fuels are handicapped compared with those that do not. Indeed it is becoming increasingly apparent that major energy-import requirements can contribute to a situation where development is stifled because the foreign exchange they consume limits the capital available for infrastructural, industrial and agricultural development.

Among the energy poor there is an instructive contrast between South Korea and Taiwan on one side of the divide and the Philippines on the other. South Korea is propelled by what comes close to a compulsion to emulate Japan. Official estimates indicate that demand for oil may double between 1988 and 2000 (33 to 66 million tonnes of oil equivalent) and imports of bituminous coal more than double, from 13 to 31 million tonnes. Korean estimates suggest that by 2010 the respective tonnages may be as high as 77 and 47 million (Choi, 1990). There will be a gradual change in the composition of fuels used with oil possibly decreasing from 52 per cent in 1995 to 44 per cent in 2010, bituminous coal increasing from 22 to 26 per cent, liquefied natural gas from 4 to 8 per cent and the contribution from nuclear and hydropower from 14 to 18 per cent. Studies by the Institute of Energy and Resources in South Korea show clearly the extent to which increases in supplies of fossil fuel are essential to the continuation of a high rate of economic growth, and the extent to which it is almost impossible for an economy like that of Korea to escape from the high-energy treadmill of the newly industrialized country.

Taiwan's 'economic miracle', too, has been achieved through establishing and exploiting to the limit an energy system capable of supporting industrialization. The basis was laid during the third, fourth and fifth four-year plans (1961-1972), when the strategy of exploiting local resources of coal and water-power, supplemented by extending the use of natural gas and permitting exports of additional coal as well as oil, was adopted. In 1972 oil met 67 per cent of primary energy supply. There was a move in subsequent plans to reduce dependence on oil. Imports of coal were increased, and a nuclear-power programme initiated. Importation of coal may grow from about 17 million tonnes in 1989 to 36 million in 2000. It is hoped to keep imports of oil down to a small increase, while imports of natural gas are planned to rise eightfold or about 10 per cent of total. As a result the share of oil in the energy mix is expected to drop from 56 per cent in 1989 to about

42 per cent in 2000, with coal increasing from 24 to 31 per cent. Nuclear power is planned to stay at about 13 per cent. Again the connection between a fast rate of economic growth and increasing consumption of fossil fuels is brought out by the way in which the annual average rate of increase in real GDP is anticipated to be 6.5 per cent during the 1990s and the growth of energy demand 4.4 per cent averaged over the decade (Yih, 1990).

The Philippines has about 300 million tonnes of recoverable reserves of coal, mostly lignitic and sub-bituminous. High-grade coal is limited to small deposits which are awkward and expensive to mine (Asian Development Bank, 1989, p. 40). In summary the energy profile of the Philippines is as follows: adequate reserves of lower quality coals, some hydro and geothermal resources, small production of oil, and considerable reliance on wood and other biomass such as bagasse (stalks of sugar cane) and agricultural waste. A nuclear-power generation programme was initiated during the last years of the Marcos regime. No power has been generated, despite outlays running into billions of dollars, and its future is uncertain. A major effort has been made to limit demand for oil and to encourage the use of imported coal as a substitute. This country has endeavoured to develop an alternative energy programme to lessen dependence on oil but the expense, especially of nuclear installations, has been high and seemingly wasted. Importing coal still imposes a burden on an economy whose export performance remains unimpressive (Reksohadiprodjo, 1987, p. 61).

Shortages of fuelwood are already posing a problem. Until recently its cost has been low relative to other sources of energy. In 1985 over 28 million cubic metres were used, more than 82 per cent by households. The annual growth of demand seems to be between two and three per cent. The consequences of excessive demand for wood fuel has been described in a World Bank Report:

> Fuel, wood or charcoal are the main cooking fuels for rural households. Historically, most of the demand could be supplied through gathering from sources outside forests proper, but increasing population pressure and deforestation in most lowland rural areas have created a lively market in fuel. This has become an important source of cash income to upland dwellers encroaching on the remaining forests or logged-over areas. As this is mainly extra-legal or illegal activity, statistics do not record the volume, but the supposition is that the degradation of second-growth forests is partly associated

with firewood gathering and charcoal making. Destruction of mangroves has also been associated with commercial demand for fuel (World Bank, 1989, p. 13).

It can be argued that the Philippines will have great difficulty in solving its energy problems as part of the process of furthering its industrialization. Substitutes will have to be found for diminishing supplies of fuelwood. They could be costly imports. The poor quality of local coals is a problem in itself. Nuclear generation seems to have been rejected as an option. Supplementation of domestic resources by imports is inescapable, but exports are insufficient to support increasing levels of imports. The problem is already sufficiently acute to put in question whether it is sensible for governments in the Philippines to pursue a high-energy future. The model of neighbouring Taiwan may be entirely inappropriate.

The countries of the Western Pacific which are well endowed with energy resources also provide interesting contrasts. In the south there is Australia, with world-scale reserves of coal and a large endowment of natural gas. The continent has a minuscule population (17 million) by Asian standards, comparable with one of the great mega-cities of Japan or China. Its increasingly threatened prosperity depends on exports of energy materials and industrial minerals, significantly supplemented by farm products. In the late 1980s the countries of Northeast Asia purchased about 40 per cent of Australia's mineral exports. Shipments of both steaming (for power generation) and coking (for steel production) coals have become more important over the decades since the great south to north trade in industrial materials began to develop in the Western Pacific (Garnaut, 1989, pp. 72-4). Australia offers virtual certainty of supply of coal for the foreseeable future, and useful supplementation of requirements for liquefied natural gas. These trades, along with those in iron ore and non-ferrous metals, are now the foundation of its relationship with Northeast Asia.

The ASEAN countries, other than Singapore and the Philippines, have substantial energy resources. Thailand, Malaysia and Indonesia are stressing their forests, but they have significant resources of coal, oil and natural gas. The quality of coal varies greatly but there are major deposits in northern Thailand, northern Malaya, Indonesian and Malaysian Borneo and in Sumatra. The oil and gas deposits appear in an arc which runs from Indonesia's Kalimantan through Brunei close to the northeastern tip of that great island along the Malayan peninsula to Southern Thailand with further resources in the northeast of that country. Exploration is proceeding throughout this region. The extent of off-shore resources is still largely unknown (Toichi, 1989, pp. 149-56).

Whereas the Philippines is likely to face great difficulties in meeting demand for energy, recent assessments for the three other big ASEAN countries are optimistic. Liquefied natural gas is beginning substantially to supplement oil as an export commodity and is providing a relatively clean source of industrial fuel. It can also be used to offset the decline in supplies of wood and charcoal which is occurring everywhere. Availability of some oil and major deposits of natural gas can be seen as providing the base enabling Thailand and Malaysia to make the transition to significantly industrializing economies. Indonesia is following along spurred by the imperative to cope with growing population pressures, especially on Java. The availability of domestic supplies of the fossil fuels should at least contribute importantly to that transition.

China is an energy-rich poor country. It has enormous resources but they are located mainly in the north and northwest, distant from some of the great industrial centres. Comparisons between the energy situations of China and Japan are especially instructive.

China and Japan

China and Japan dominate the Western Pacific as consumers of energy as well as in most other respects. They provide a sharp and worrying contrast. One is struggling to bring the world's most populous country to a modest level of development. The other, with its own problems of population density, has achieved world industrial leadership. The income level of the average Japanese is now undreamed of outside North America and some Western European countries.

Table 5.3 shows the estimated primary energy demand of Japan and China in 1987. The combined total of these two countries amounted to 75 per cent of the total energy demand of the countries of the Western Pacific. (If South Korea, Taiwan and Hong Kong are included, the percentage goes up to eighty-five.) If Japanese forecasts of future demand are taken as a guide, China and Japan will continue to consume over 75 per cent of available energy.

Table 5.3. China and Japan: primary energy demand—1987 (million tonnes of oil equivalent)

	Coal	Oil	Gas	Hydro	Nuclear	Total
Japan	73.5	230.0	40.9	22.9	42.2	409.5
China	448.2	109.2	13.8	22.4	-	593.6

Source: *Energy Demand Forecast for the Pacific Basin in 2000, 2030*, Institute of Energy Economics, Japan.

Table 5.4. China and Japan: future primary energy demand

	Coal	Oil	Gas	Hydro	Nuclear	Total
Year 2000						
Japan	93.1	322.3	64.3	29.5	68.0	577.2
China	592.8	168.9	22.8	53.2	6.8	844.5
Year 2010						
Japan	96.4	351.9	80.9	34.7	67.2	631.1
China	776.3	219.1	36.3	94.2	9.1	1135.0
Year 2030						
Japan	88.8	358.2	120.0	65.3	125.6	757.9
China	1197.7	331.5	93.9	267.7	14.9	1905.7

Source: *Energy Demand Forecast for the Pacific Basin in 2000, 2030*, Institute Energy Economics: Japan.

In 2000 the energy situation in these two countries should not have changed greatly but by 2030, if present trends are anything to go by, China could be producing about three times as much primary energy as its neighbour, and more than half of that would come from coal. To achieve this level of output there will have to be big increases in just about every aspect of production, including, oil, gas, hydroelectricity and nuclear power. The estimates might be within the bounds of possibility in the case of Japan, but China's future situation remains obscure.

It is acknowledged in Beijing that energy development, especially electric power, is fundamental to future economic strategy. Nevertheless capital and technology are likely to be insufficient to achieve the proposed increases in coal production and utilization which would meet the target for output of between 1.3 to 1.5 billion tonnes by 2000. The investment requirements are thought to be of the order of one trillion yuan (Liu (ed.), 1987, pp. 176-93).

Because domestic industry cannot hope to make a major contribution to the sophisticated equipment required for safe nuclear generation, and because the foreign capital requirement would be very large for even a few nuclear plants, that programme is in doubt. There will be difficulties also in meeting targets for the production of oil and natural gas.

Further development of hydro-electric resources is acknowledged by the Chinese Government to be an important priority. Chinese technology may be adequate in this area but there are other problems associated with interference with river flows, inundation of land and displacement of people (Xin, 1988, pp. 43-54).

Some of the problems China is facing in its energy sector stem from the illogical price structures which are the legacy of the central planning system. Compromises are continually being made between technical proposals, resource constraints and the visions of party ideologues. This has resulted, for example, in production of coal for production's sake, deficiencies in transport and inattention to the need for efficiencies at all points in the system. Frequently lack of concern for the precise requirements of industry has occasioned great waste (Garnaut, 1989, p. 191). In addition the planning system seems to have been unable to get many basic priorities more or less right. In the 1980s energy supply became a bottle-neck. This caused a great deal of idle capacity in industry because of power shortages. This situation does not seem to have much improved. Coastal regions, where many export industries are located, continue to face interruptions of supply. Chinese analysts have not tried to gloss over the serious nature of these problems. They pointed out that in the mid-1980s these shortages caused 30 per cent of China's productive capacity to lie idle (Liu (ed.), 1987, p. 181).

Taken as a whole, the Chinese system is wasteful in production of fuel, generation of power, provision of transport and other aspects of the distribution of goods. The planning system has proved inadequate. The irrational price system for fossil fuels works against efficient use throughout the economy. There are no fixed norms for energy consumption in many important industries, usually no means for measurement, and few systems which enable responsibility for use to be attributed to particular management. In agriculture, where nearly 70 per cent of the energy needed comes from timber and plant stalks, there is great inefficiency (Liu (ed.), 1987, p. 187).

The disadvantages inherent in planning for further vast increases in production of fossil fuels are understood by sophisticated people in China. As some of their economists pointed out several years ago:

> ... we must ensure an adequate supply of energy to attain the objective of quadrupling the gross value of industrial and agricultural production by 2000. If we take the increase coefficient of energy consumption as 1, then energy supply must be quadrupled if the industrial and agricultural production is to be quadrupled. In 1980, China produced 637.21 million tons of standard fuel. Quadrupling, this figure gives us 2.5 billion tons. Can this much energy be produced by 2000? The answer is no, because in exploiting energy resources, tremendous investments must be made at one time ... In this situation, we must attach equal importance to broadening the range of energy sources and reducing energy consumption with the latter claiming precedence in the near future. If we can double the energy supply and increase the efficiency of energy utilization, we will be able to quadruple industrial and agricultural production (Liu (ed.), p. 181).

These were sobering considerations for a country which needed, but failed, to get its energy planning on to a soundly-conceived base in the 1980s. China seems likely to reach the mid-1990s without the capacity to plan this vital sector in the efficient manner needed. That is indeed ironic for a socialist system, and may mean that China will not be able to attain its growth objectives because of the continuing inefficiencies which dog its energy sector.

Vaclav Smil suggested in 1988 that Chinese policy-makers have access to sensible critical evaluations which put long-term energy planning on much the same basis as other countries. It was not beyond the bounds of possibility, he suggested, for the government to draw up and implement sound, sustainable policies. But there is a need for caution in assessing developments in this crucial sector because:

> The Chinese decision to continue with coal as the main energizer of their economic development is inevitable given the country's huge deposits of five bituminous coals as well as of lignites extractable in giant surface mines. Many complications, however, ranging from the necessity of large scale, long-distance transfers of northern coal to the risks of acid deposition caused by combustion in new large thermal stations, will make both the planned doubling of coal output (especially if the quality is to increase considerably) and largely coal-based quadrupling of power generation taxing challenges. Much greater attention to environmental consequences of coal-fired generation will be necessary: costly but essential, it will prevent large-scale environmental degradation (Smil, 1988, p. 225).

China is enduring a prolonged political crisis, during which the very philosophy of state practice continues to be under challenge. The problem is that developing a modern, efficient energy system suited to China's needs is a severely practical matter, requiring the solution of a massive set of problems given the nature of the country and, obviously, some clear-headed undogmatic political bargaining so as to ensure a reasonable balance in allocations of capital and technical expertise between provinces and between industrial, urban and agricultural needs. It is also an area where external assistance and investment could bring relatively rapid benefit. It is doubtful whether China's relations with Japan and other countries which are capable of and interested in supplying what is needed are yet good enough to encourage them to make the necessary long-term commitments.

No country is more aware of China's problems than Japan. It has established a working relationship with China but has not been able to overcome the suspicion about its motivation which is the legacy of the violence it perpetrated on China during the first half of this century. The Japanese Government and business share the universal scepticism about the future of the Communist Party in China, and notably about its capacity to effect industrial modernization of the eastern seaboard on the South Korean and Taiwanese models without leaving inland provinces greatly disadvantaged.

Japan is, of course, almost an exact economic opposite of China. Its highly efficient and technically advanced economy requires large quantities of imported fuels and its energy industries are carefully balanced. They are very efficient, even by comparison with other advanced industrial countries. No country appreciates better than Japan the virtues of economic use of imported fuels.

Japan has been working on systems designed to maximize efficiency and to reduce pollution in the production of most sources of energy since atmospheric pollution was first recognized as a potentially serious problem three decades ago. The process was stepped up after the first of the oil price rises in the 1970s. Japanese energy economists and engineers are now examining in extraordinary detail the possible consequences of having substantially to reduce emissions of CO_2 and other greenhouse gases, as well as ways of bringing about even greater efficiencies throughout the entire economy (Yuasa, 1990, pp. 55-75).

Unlike China, Japan has been able to slow down growth in demand for energy to a rate rather lower than growth of GDP — a reduction in the energy intensity of GDP. In 1988 energy demand was only 12.2 per cent higher than in 1973. That year the economy was using about the equivalent of 300 million tonnes of oil equivalent compared with just over 400 million tonnes fifteen years later. Since that time GDP about quadrupled (Institute of Energy Economics, Japan, 1990). Big gains have been made in the conservation of energy, but many power plants are approaching ceilings in the thermal efficiency of their present technology. There has been a decline in demand for energy from the industrial sector per unit of added value in manufacturing. A prime example is in the iron and steel industry but improvements have been made throughout most sectors of the industrial economy. Likewise the energy efficiency of transport improved as more efficient less polluting engines were introduced but growth in the number of vehicles and increasing traffic congestion are eroding the gains which were made earlier. In this area, too, limits are being reached in achieving efficiency in the use of piston engines.

Demand for energy for commercial and residential use has increased absolutely and proportionately (16.4 per cent in 1970, 24.5 per cent in 1988). There are several reasons for this: a big increase in the working population in tertiary industry, increasing per capita floor area, the growth of office accommodation and air conditioning, inadequate temperature control of cooling/heating systems and the enormous proliferation of appliances and electronic devices (Sagawa, 1990, pp. 47-54).

The Japanese Government and its agencies, including the Ministry of International Trade (MITI), are actively examining all these issues in the context of what is regarded as an increasing imperative to reduce imports of fuel, to limit emissions of greenhouse gases and further to improve the quality of the environment in Japan (Environment Agency of Japan, 1990; MITI, 1990b). At this stage the thrust is broadly based, with the primary emphasis on achieving further efficiency in the use of fuels and in the distribution of electricity. A major expansion of nuclear generation is being planned, as well as much more extensive use of liquefied natural gas. Some of the effort being put into research is focusing on using alternative and new energy sources such as exploiting temperature differentials in rivers and sea waters, exhaust heat which is presently wasted, photovoltaic generation, solar water heating, conversion to methanol as a source of fuel, and introduction of co-generation systems which reduce wastage of heat to a minimum (MITI, 1990c).

The motivation behind this programme is clear. Japan's long-term interests necessitate that it remain at the forefront of research into and the development of efficient energy systems, especially those using fossil fuels, and continue to seek to achieve technological superiority in the production, distribution and utilization of energy. The target is a further improvement in energy conservation between 1988 and 2010 of as much as 36 per cent expressed in energy consumption per unit of GDP. Behind this lies an assessment that mastery of energy engineering will contribute significantly to Japan's objective of consolidating its position as the world's most advanced economy. The strategy being developed in Tokyo rests on the eminently sensible assumption that, if Japan develops a technological lead in a broad range of energy-efficient and pollution-control systems, it cannot fail further to enhance its position as a leader, if not the leader, among the great industrial powers.

Japan seems already to be forging ahead in both the intellectual quality of its analysis of current problems and the capacity of its science and industry to develop technical solutions which may not solve but could reduce the severity of many problems associated with the massive use of fossil fuels by modern industrial societies. It has already opened up a big gap in technological terms with its neighbours in the Western Pacific, even South Korea and Taiwan. China cannot hope to make up much ground in the foreseeable future. Its system militates against the sort of reform that is necessary. It would take considerable time for any country to create the educational and research facilities, as well as the modern industries, needed to mount a coordinated programme which is now well within the capacity of the Japanese technological giant.

Not long ago the assumption was that the provision of abundant and cheap energy was among the fundamental planks of a successful policy of development. That seems no longer to be the case, because of the environmentally adverse effects of such policies, especially in a huge coal-dependent economy like China. During recent decades it has become evident that successful societies will develop very high levels of efficiency in the production and use of all forms of energy, and will ensure that distribution systems match efficiencies at the production end. China must achieve that not only for its own purposes, but also because of the impact deterioration of its energy systems will have on neighbouring countries which will be adversely affected by the continuing degradation of its environment.

From this perspective the future relationship between China and Japan takes on an overwhelming importance for the Western Pacific. Japan and its smaller industrialized neighbours are now well placed to contribute to the improvements needed to transform China from a grossly energy-wasteful to a more energy-efficient country. The immediate priority seems to be, however, not so much for Japan, South Korea and Taiwan to provide the technology and some of the capital required as for China's Government to demonstrate that it is effectively responding to both an intellectual and a technological challenge by continuing with basic reforms and notably the rational pricing of fuels.

Although the Chinese leadership has had an opportunity to reflect on what has happened to industry in Eastern Europe and the Soviet Union, where wasteful processes and excessive dependence on coal have contributed to industrial decay and environmental disasters, so far they seem barely capable of responding effectively to the pleas of their own experts to begin the process of putting their house into order step by step. There is great irony in this because all societies must plan their energy systems to a relatively high degree. It has always been the boast of the socialist systems that rational planning is the key to the successful achievement of a fair, classless and efficient society. In fact, however, the socialist systems have failed spectacularly in this key area of central planning. A future government in China will have the opportunity to give real impetus to the remedial process. It remains to be seen whether it will be able, in the era after the gerontocracy of the Long March has passed away, to implement rational planning of its crucial energy sector and make effective use of the assistance it may be able to get from Japan and other countries.

Sustainable energy systems, which are intrinsic to the survival of large-scale industrial/agricultural and other societies, should reflect decreasing not increasing demand for energy by the people which comprise them. Their utilization of energy, especially when their numbers are growing, deserves close analysis because it enables judgements to be made about the capacity of their share of the biosphere to continue to support them over the long haul.

In the Western Pacific five countries, Japan, South Korea, Taiwan, Australia and New Zealand, and two city-states, Hong Kong and Singapore, have reached high or very high income levels through mastery of the use of energy in its industrial and domestic applications. Two more countries, Thailand and Malaysia, are in the process of becoming high-energy societies. Seven others, China, Indonesia, the Philippines, Vietnam, Laos, Cambodia and Papua New Guinea are endeavouring to increase the availability of energy as an essential concomitant of their further development. The larger countries in this grouping each encompass regions which can be described as high-energy intensity urban/industrial pockets. Examples in Southeast Asia are Jakarta, Bangkok and Manila. There are numerous others such as Tokyo and Osaka in Japan, Seoul in Korea, Shanghai, Beijing and other great cities of China, Singapore, and Sydney and Melbourne in Australia. They bring people, raw materials and energy together in fulfilment of development on the twentieth-century model. They symbolize a process which has been changing the nature of society in Asia since Japan embarked over a century ago on its programme for catching up with the European powers and the United States.

It is uncertain whether the countries of the Western Pacific, whose combined populations will probably be about 2.2 billion in 2010, will be able to manage their societies on a sustainable basis. The reason for this uncertainty is the still substantial if conjectural effects of the sum of the activities of a population of this size on the environment. One indication of the likely growth of economic activity is the present and likely future utilization of the major sources of energy. At present nearly 1.8 billion people consume about 1.3 billion tonnes of oil equivalent. In 2010 a larger population could consume something like 2.5 million tonnes, of which coal will be a very large proportion.

In practical terms that could mean that the intensification of industries and the increased numbers of vehicles in use could so increase the pollution load as to endanger the societies themselves. It will add very significantly to the present burden on the land, water and atmosphere caused by the combustion of fossil fuels and the proliferation of wastes.

Already evidence of the burden of pollution directly attributable to the use of fossil fuels is increasing. Even if resources and technology were available, it is especially difficult to limit its impact when numbers are still increasing so rapidly. Regrettably the necessary resources and technology do not exist outside the developed economies and some of them, notably South Korea and Taiwan, have to remedy serious problems of degradation. If numbers are increasing and utilization of fossil fuels is rising as an accompaniment of economic development, and if there is, at the same time, widespread loss of vegetation and degradation of soils and water, then, as the next chapter seeks to substantiate, the foundations of economies, whatever their level of development, could actually be undermined.

At present all the countries of the Western Pacific are following the conventional model of development through attempting to keep up the fastest possible rate of economic growth (Garnaut, 1989, pp. 106-23). An enormous momentum has been generated which can be likened to the forward movement of a supertanker. Such is the momentum of this kind of vessel that its crew must be very careful to avoid situations where the ship needs to avoid an obstacle without adequate warning or to slow down and reverse course. The size of the ship ensures that such manoeuvres are conducted slowly and deliberately. Consider then what might be needed fundamentally to change the direction of the Japanese or South Korean economies from their present pattern of very high, even if relatively efficient, consumption of energy, to a situation over several decades where their demand for energy from fossil fuels, especially coal and oil, is about one-quarter of their consumption in the early 1990s. Consider also what would be needed to change China from an energy-wasteful society to an efficient one.

For Japan this would require an exceptionally profound trans-formation. At present the Japanese are importing big quantities of fossil fuel to generate electricity, to fuel their steel, cement and other industries and to keep their motor vehicles and other engines running and, among other things, air conditioners operating. The concept of sustainable growth must involve industrial societies gradually finding ways of greatly reducing demand for energy by heavy and light indus-tries, by transport and by commercial and domestic users. At this stage governments in Japan, Australia and New Zealand have begun to think that this might be inescapable. Elsewhere awareness of longer-term problems associated with the present direction and energy intensity of development does not seem to extend very far.

Energy planners have taken the view that conservation is a luxury which only rich countries can afford. They seem, however, increas-ingly to be confronted with circumstances which are forcing them to radically revise this judgement. The *Far Eastern Economic Review* reported in 1991 that:

> Asia is in the midst of an electricity crisis brought on by booming growth and the profligate use of energy. Virtually every country in the region is facing a potential capacity crunch. Cheap, dependable electricity is vital for continued economic expansion, yet the cost of new power stations is staggering.

> If the region's utilities keep building power stations without the promotion of more efficient use of electricity, the amount of capital invested will result in the economic growth they are seeking to sustain being aborted. Providing the electrical power for an increasingly rich region is likely to require a revolution in its conservative utility world (Clifford, 1991, p. 50).

The important institutions have been possessed by the create mate-rial wealth now, consider efficiency and clean up later philosophy which has only recently been abandoned in Japan. At least it is gradu-ally being perceived, because of what has been done in Japan and because of the direction of energy technology there, that it is possible to snap the link between economic growth and increasing use of elec-tricity. The fact that it is cheaper to save energy than to build new plants is becoming apparent but still requires an ideological revolution in the most important of all industries, especially in such an energy inefficient and such an important country as China.

Energy production is just one aspect of the complex set of problems economists are attempting to elucidate as they develop a valid conceptual framework for sustainable economic activity. It is an immense task because they are trying to develop concepts, methodologies and statistical techniques which will enable a better understanding of the relationships between economic activity and the biosphere, and which have been neglected in conventional economic analysis. In the end, however, the concepts and the methodologies derived from them have to be translated into terms which ordinary mortals, especially politicians and their advisers, business executives, financiers, engineers and architects can understand. Eventually the analysis will have to be given effect through the implementation of policies which will limit the dangers for the biosphere of current modes of economic activity.

The conceptual task in the Western Pacific (and elsewhere) is to encompass the consequences of the activities, especially the use of energy, of the more than two billion people who will comprise its population within two decades. It is challenging conceptually because there needs to be a synthesis of ecologic and economic thinking. It is also fundamental because it is virtually certain that any set of prescriptions for the future will necessitate a shift away from economic activity based on increasing use of fossil fuels.

A major problem at this stage is that analysis of what this could actually involve is exceptionally complex. Nevertheless the governments of the countries of the Western Pacific will have to give careful thought to whether big increases in the provision of energy will bring greater disadvantages by contributing to the deterioration of environments than the advantages they confer. It is a new and now persistent nightmare which troubles increasingly the highly industrialized, fuel-deficient, countries of Northeast Asia. They are also coming to understand other problems which are the consequence of increasing economic activity in China and other developing countries of the Western Pacific. They cannot ignore these problems on the grounds that they will have little impact on their own interests.

The trilemma of energy, growth and the environment will have to be resolved during the next century otherwise the improvements to the human condition achieved during the past two hundred years will be squandered. When the consequences of growth are accepted as including the relentless pressures that increasing and more economically active populations are likely to impose on natural vegetation, soils and water systems it is possible that optimistic predictions about the consolidation of economic progress in the developing countries of East Asia may eventually prove to be an academic and journalistic illusion.

The following chapters describe many of these pressures and the ways in which governments are attempting to respond. Their purpose is to attempt to further elucidate the question of whether or not the great surge of development and material progress in the Western Pacific which has commanded world attention is capable of being sustained.

6. The Changing Environment of the Western Pacific

Imagine the Western Pacific without national boundaries. The long-term health of this part of the world, its sustainability, depends on the balance between its vegetation, its water systems and its human and animal populations. It also depends on the preservation of the health of the forests, river systems and agricultural land which, together, provide the basis for the societies which have developed, or are developing, in Asia and Oceania.

The Western Pacific, like other parts of the earth, is experiencing problems of degradation and pollution. They are part of existence. Never before, however, have these manifestations of human activity become global in their scope and potentially dangerous to the long-term survival of many, if not all, human societies. The word 'degradation' is used to refer to the processes which lead to the loss of fertility in soils and to the decline of surface and underground storages and flows of water. It is a slow but extremely dangerous process which insidiously reduces the fertility of land and the capacity of fresh water systems to support life. Pollution involves contamination of air, water and soil by human activity. It complicates and worsens the deterioration of two of the primary resources which support life—soil and water.

Although the pace of economic development has only recently begun to accelerate outside Japan, Taiwan, South Korea and Australia and New Zealand, vast changes have been wrought within a few decades. Before many more have passed, such changes may be seen to have worked to undermine the capacity of many of the countries in this part of the world to support their populations. Some assessments are alarmist. Others confine themselves to expressions of serious concern partly because of the lack of widespread awareness of the consequences of present and future activities. Rapid development could conceivably undermine the basis of agricultural productivity—organically

133

rich soil. Further industrialization, tragically, may create more problems than it is capable of solving.

Whatever one's views about the consequences of twentieth-century
economic development, if one wants to grasp the scale of problems
with which Western Pacific governments will have to cope in the next
century, it is important to understand what is happening to the river
systems—great and small—of the Western Pacific.

If one were to follow the course of one of the great rivers which
drain down from Central Asia to the Pacific, it would be possible to
collect evidence of how the processes of degradation and pollution are
threatening societies in this and other parts of the world. There has
been an assault on the mountain and sub-mountain forests because of
excessive demand for wood. This has increased the processes of
erosion. Further downstream, as farmers have pressed into steeper
country to develop more farmland or have their animals graze more
intensively on whatever grass is available, erosion has also become
more threatening. Use of chemical fertilizers and pesticides has
contributed to increasing production, but has also led to excessive
concentrations of nitrates and pesticide residues in water systems.
Upstream erosion has increased the silt load of the river, creating
problems for the irrigation systems on which ultimately the people of
the lower lands are exceptionally dependent. When the river reaches
the areas where cities and their industries have developed, it has to
carry growing amounts of human and industrial waste, some of it
biologically dangerous and toxic, as well as providing drinking and
industrial water. This burden increases as the river approaches its
mouth where, inevitably, great concentrations of people are striving to
increase their economic activities. While the river may be able to
discharge great quantities of silt and wastes into the ocean during
periods of peak flows, during dry seasons and droughts its capacity to
sustain this vital task may be greatly diminished. The estuarine areas
and off-shore waters also bear the burden of human activities along the
river. Their capacity to support fisheries of all kinds, as well as other
creatures which are part of the food chain, are bound to be impaired as
the quantity of wastes harmful to life that are poured out by the river
continues to increase.

Some of these systems, notably the great rivers of China and the
Mekong and Chao Phraya to their south, have global significance

because of their historic capacity to support great numbers through the highly productive systems of agriculture which have developed over several millenia. What has happened and is continuing in their basins has been duplicated along many of the shorter rivers of the continent and its archipelagoes.

Are these river systems capable of supporting increasing numbers of more economically active people and their domestic animals? Indeed, are they capable of sustaining existing numbers indefinitely as human beings engage in increasingly sophisticated economic activity which inevitably places greater demands on land and water?

For the most part, shortage of water is not a serious problem, although in some areas ground water is becoming seriously depleted (ESCAP, 1990, pp. 44-6). Silting seems however to be an increasingly serious problem especially in China. This problem is well known in the Huang He, which drains the loess plateau of northwestern China. The siltation of the Sanmenxia dam on that river was more rapid than the engineers had calculated. Upstream water levels were higher than anticipated. In order to alleviate environmental and other problems it was necessary to pierce the dam and lower the head of water. Inevitably its capacity for the generation of power was greatly reduced. While what happened might have been expected of a river which has always carried a great burden of silt, the problem has become aggravated in other rivers in China. Vaclav Smil, from whose work the foregoing has been drawn, remarks:

> ... Danjiangkou, so far China's most voluminous reservoir in the Han Shui in Hubei, lost one-seventh of its capacity in just a decade, silt content of seven major rivers in the Chiang Jiang basin rose by about 25 percent during the past three decades, and the Yangzi itself now carries nearly 650 million tons of silt a year as it leaves Sichuan and before it enters the gorges, almost 25 percent above the value of the 525 million tons used in the original design (for dams in the gorges) ... in the 1960s (Smil, 1988, p. 222).

The future of all the river systems, without exception, depends on what is happening in the areas where they and their tributaries rise. It also depends on their capacity to provide water for irrigation and to accept discharges from the human settlements in their basins. The major rivers of China and Indochina originate in the eastern part of the great Himalayan chain, others originate in lesser ranges such as the borderland between Vietnam and Laos, and in the mountain spines

which dominate the geology of most of the islands of the archipelagoes.

Processes of degradation have clearly accelerated during this
century. As World Bank consultants have pointed out:

> About 65% of Asia's rural populations of 1.6 billion live and earn their
> livelihood in rain-fed watershed areas. Despite the existence of soil conservation
> agencies and watershed management authorities in Asian countries, the real
> managers of these lands are local farmers and villagers. Constrained by poverty
> and lack of technology, their pursuit of arable land, food and fodder has
> profound effects on the land and water resources of both upland and lowland
> areas. Throughout the region mounting pressure on scarce land forest resources
> stemming from rising human and animal populations is leading to severe
> environmental degradation.
>
> The extent of watershed degradation has not been exactly measured, but it is
> manifest in numerous ways, including high rates of soil erosion and declining
> yields on large areas of agricultural land, reduced livestock-carrying capacity,
> sedimentation of dams, reservoirs and irrigation systems, and clearance of
> forests with consequent loss of biological diversity and forest products. Together
> these trends threaten the ability of upland people to sustain an already precarious
> existence (Magrath and Doolette, 1990, p. 185).

Degradation of watersheds can be attributed to a combination of the
sheer necessity for marginal farmers and shifting cultivators to survive
and of commercial and non-commercial demand for wood. There
seems to be no doubt that in combination they are creating excessive
demand for wood. This has already had a severe effect on forests
throughout the Western Pacific. The consequences of these factors for
tropical, sub-tropical, temperate and mountain forests seem to be
becoming better understood. As an ESCAP Report puts it:

> The loss of trees also means that soils are impoverished of essential nutrients to
> the extent that the level of organic matter in the soil is reduced and nutrients are
> lost by leaching. This further curtails any attempt at renewing growth by the self-
> healing and equilibriating forces found in nature. In many cases the re-growth
> that does take place is altered. It is smaller, slower and less well formed, leading
> to a reduced density and height of the tree strata. These factors also alter the
> carbon cycle, the radiation balance and contribute to climate change (ESCAP,
> 1990, p. 13).

It is well understood that erosion is a consequence of the loss of
vegetation, and that the steeper the slope the worse the effects are
likely to be. What may not be so well understood are the adverse

consequences for fresh water systems inevitably associated with large increases in populations and improvements in the material wealth of people. There seems to be a distinct danger for the countries of the Western Pacific that the processes of development will progressively degrade most of the river systems which support large numbers of people because (1) the balance between forested and agricultural land has been disturbed to the point where degradation will proceed too rapidly for a sufficiently high level of agricultural productivity to be maintained over the long run, and (2) the systems cannot adequately cope with increasing loads of silt, wastes and industrial pollutants.

It is quite unrealistic to expect poor people at or just above the margin of existence to relent in their search for energy materials. Vaclav Smil, writing a decade ago, described the situation in parts of China thus:

Trees in protected forests and along roads are cut illegally: bark is stripped off the living trunks; stumps and roots are dug out; branches are lopped off; pieces of sod are carved out; animal dung is collected—and when all other possibilities have vanished, peasants in the warmer regions grow sweet potatoes on odd patches of land and use dried tubers for fuel. And even so, most of China's peasants are acutely short of fuel. Official sources acknowledge that of 800 million rural inhabitants, 500 million suffer from a *serious* shortage of fuel for at least three to five months a year, and in the worst-off provinces, 70 percent of the peasants lack fuel for up to half a year every year ...

Here is human suffering and an environmental crisis of truly immense proportions: serious recurrent shortages of even minimum quantities of fuel needed for cooking and heating afflicts every three out of five rural families, about half of the inadequate supply coming from crop residues and dung which should not be burned but rather recycled to maintain soil tilth and fertility and to protect against erosion, and the other half secured at an even heavier environmental cost of stripping soils of their protective cover, fostering rapid erosion and nutrient loss, and rendering the sites unfit for eventual regeneration (Smil, 1984, p. 151).

Considerations such as these are largely ignored by economists whose judgements are often based largely on analysis of the components of GDP, notably production of goods and services and foreign trade data. They measure important aspects of development, but ignore or underestimate what is occurring in those sectors of the economy for which reliable data may be more difficult to obtain —especially biological and hydrological information.

Evidence is nevertheless accumulating that the pressures created by great and growing concentrations of people are becoming so intense as to render doubtful any assumption that the future economic prosperity of the countries of the Western Pacific is assured. On one hand industrial progress, led by Japan, has been exceptionally impressive. On the other, the demands made on the environment to fulfil the imperative to increase production have also been exceptional.

Perhaps the best way of capturing present trends in a balanced way is first to consider the situation in China; subsequently to describe the situation in the countries to China's south which border the Mekong River; then to provide an outline of circumstances in Southeast Asia, especially the Philippines and Indonesia; to examine what is happening in the developed economies of Northeast Asia and Australia, and briefly to describe the state of the seas between Japan and Indonesia. The objective is to summarize acknowledged problems, and to examine in the chapter which follows whether governments, especially those of China and other developing countries, are likely to manage effectively the consequences of the increasing economic activities of their people.

China

China has engaged in the great and perilous experiment of Marxist-Leninist socialism, a system grafted on to Chinese institutions when the communist armies of Mao Zedong prevailed in 1949. Since then the Communist Party of China (CPC) has endeavoured to socialize the means of production, distribution and exchange, in order to lift living standards and enhance the status of a gravely impoverished country which had been brutalized by domestic conflict and foreign aggression.

Despite the self-administered set-backs of 'the great leap forward' of the late 1950s, and the nihilistic nightmare of 'the cultural revolution', from the late 1960s to the mid-1970s, China's achievements have been impressive (Gittings, 1990). At a time when the communist regimes of Europe have collapsed, China has succeeded in improving the living situation of a population which has doubled since the CPC gained control. Food shortages have been overcome. Industrial production has reached the point where China has a heavy industrial and production machinery capacity, some high-technology capability and capacity to produce and, in contrast to the Soviet Union, export a wide range of goods.

On one reading of the situation China seems to have avoided the disaster that central planning is now seen to have perpetrated in the Soviet Union and its former satellite economies in Central Europe. China too faces great difficulties, as is only to be expected in a country of such size, density of population and extraordinary complexity. But, despite the political turmoil of the late 1980s, it does not seem to be threatened with economic and political collapse (Cheung, Cheng and Hendry, 1991, pp. 25, 28 and 29).

Nevertheless, while the survivors of the revolutionary era live out their last decade of power, the clouds are gathering. Politically they were evident in the events of 1988-89 which culminated in the massacre of students in Beijing in June 1989. Economic evidence is also accumulating that the achievements of the past forty years in China have been bought at considerable price. That price at the very minimum may be the forfeiture of any chance of achieving even half the target set over ten years ago, of a per capita GDP equivalent to $US1,000 by 2000.

There is no need to reiterate the problems which rapid population growth has brought to China. They are better understood in China than elsewhere, and the Government of China has made more strenuous efforts than any other to address the problem. What follows is a summary of the way some informed Chinese and competent foreign observers view the environmental consequences of economic development since 1950. To its credit, the Chinese Government has not, for more than a decade now, attempted to disguise growing problems. With its great population, and the dependence of about three quarters of the people on agriculture, the balances in China are very fine. There seems always to have been an awareness of potential disaster. This is attributable to historical experience of the fragility over time of the irrigation and other systems which have made the favoured lands of China sufficiently productive to feed one-fifth of the world's population. The labour of millions, with pick, shovel, basket and wheel-barrow, has kept these systems going for centuries, and can be very effective when flood damage and the consequences of other calamities have to be repaired (Cheung, 1991, p. 18). Nowadays a great deficit caused by decades of progressively more serious damage to almost every aspect of the environment seems to be building up.

Chinese commentators on the state of the country's natural resources and its environment have pointed out that since 1958 the emphasis has been on rapid development. This involved intensifying the exploitation of natural resources as they were the basis for fulfilling production targets. As in other socialist countries this type of exploitation was predatory, because there was little or no concern to protect, replenish and regenerate resources. The Chinese ceased to think of soil and forests as primary resources which need to be carefully conserved.

There are several examples in the primary production sector. Forest reserves have been severely depleted. Trees were cut down in order to meet targets for the production of timber, for domestic use and to create more arable land. Reafforestation, even though approved by planning authorities, was largely neglected. Forests were increasingly damaged by fires as a result of unsound management practices. Official data indicates that forest cover in China is 12 per cent, somewhat less than when the Communists took over government in 1949. The actual figure may be less than 10 per cent. This compares with 66 per cent in Japan, 33 per cent in the United States and 29 per cent in West Germany. Consumption of timber for fuel, building and paper, according to Chinese sources, is running at an annual rate of 300 million cubic metres, while forest growth is estimated at only 200 million cubic metres. Although there is great emphasis on reafforestation, the success rate of planting seems insufficient to offset exploitation (Forestier, 1989, p. 24).

Degradation of land has occurred as a result of excessive utilization of grasslands through over-grazing or attempts to farm in marginal areas. The consequence has been the extension of deserts and loss of soils through water and wind erosion. Environmental damage in the open country of northwest China and Tibet has been serious.

As far as basic agricultural policy is concerned, it is acknowledged in China that excessive emphasis was placed on production of grain, and insufficient attention paid to other crops. Land sown to cash crops diminished, forests and pastures were destroyed, and embankments were built around lakes to bring in more land to increase grain. The outcome has been siltation, loss of essential water, even climate change as a result of disturbing the ecological equilibrium.

The conversion of land where mixed cropping had been practised to monocultures such as cotton has gradually deflected fertility. The substitution of chemical fertilizers for traditional organic manures has also contributed to a decline in the quality of soils. This has been exacerbated by a system where many peasants, deprived of a sense of ownership of land they worked, ceased to care about the maintenance of fertility (Liu (ed.), 1987, Chapters 5, 18 and 19).

Loss of farmland is a growing problem. The causes extend beyond erosion, salinization and acidification and decline in water supply systems. There is great tension between the need to improve housing in villages, the growth of towns and cities and the necessity to increase food and fodder production through conserving and, if possible, extending and improving highly productive land. It appears that each year as much as one per cent of farmland is lost because of degradation or conversion to other uses. One estimate puts the amount of land diverted at 8.5 million hectares each year. A significant proportion of the loss is attributable to the encouragement of village industry and house building in the countryside and towns. This process seems irreversible. As has been pointed out, it is inevitable that people will flow from rural areas to towns and cities. They have to be housed and industries have to develop to employ them in their millions (Forestier, 1989, pp. 24-6).

Coal

The massive dependence of the Chinese economy on coal as its major source of energy brings in another dimension of basic economic activity which is causing immense problems in all the socialist countries. Chinese economists have summarized the significance of reliance on coal in this way:

- China's coal resources are distributed mainly over the northern and northwestern parts of the country. The reserves can meet the needs of the metallurgical, chemical and power industries. These factors plus the rich experience gained in coal mining, make coal a conventional form of energy to be counted on in China's economic construction.

- If coal output increases at the estimated rate of 30 million tons per year, then in twenty years time, the amount of coal produced will reach 1.2 billion tons ... This increase in output will call for an annual rise in production capacity of about 35 million tons if allowance is made for the closing down of mines which have become exhausted. So as to ensure that supplies will meet demand, allowing for a construction cycle of six years, projects capable of producing 200 million tons will have to be under constant construction. That is recognized to be a formidable task.

• Urban atmospheric pollution is largely attributable to the extensive use of coal as fuel in addition to the burning of some 400 million tons of plant stalks by rural people.

• City air is heavily laden with dust, noxious gases and sulphur dioxide. Acid rain has become a severe threat in many areas. Industrial use of coal is exacerbated by the use of coal as fuel by city people both for cooking and heating. The smoke, with its high content of ash and sulphur, has become a bane of existence in most cities (Liu (ed.), 1987, Chapters 6 and 19).

The problems caused by acidification are clearly serious although their effects are hard to assess in a country as large as China with limited resources for collecting and analysing data. Chinese reports are unequivocal that damage caused to forests, fresh water, fish, buildings and materials is severe. Grain production has been adversely affected. One report suggests that the loss could be as high as ten million tonnes. Pollution by inorganic materials such as salt, cadmium and phenol has damaged soils and polluted water, as have petroleum products and cinders. Industrial waste and unmanaged urban sewage have also taken their toll (Vermeer, 1990, pp. 44-6).

The picture which emerges from the industrial centres of China is in a sense a replica of what happened in Europe as the industrial revolution produced those dark, satanic, coal-burning mills. The amount of coal burned crudely is excessive. This problem is basic. As Vaclav Smil has pointed out:

A high dependence on coal will always be a major source of emissions, but the situation is made worse by the poor preparation of Chinese coals before combustion and by the very inefficient conversion technologies. In general, Chinese coals are of reasonably good quality ... However, unlike in the other large coal-producing countries where most of the extracted coal is sorted, washed, and sized to remove impurities and prepare fairly uniform fuel, only 17 percent of Chinese coal output is cleaned or otherwise prepared before conversion. Naturally, combustion of mostly raw coal adds greatly to the generation of airborne emissions, ashes, and slag (Smil, 1984, p. 115-6).

Industries have been unable to afford, because of the prevailing price structures, equipment to clean smoke-stack gases or the exhausts from coke ovens. Energy is wasted at every point. The process of bringing about improvements at all levels will be slow. The present emphasis is on increasing production of coal, rather than making better use of what is already available. There are, however, doubts about the transport system's capacity to handle vastly increased quantities even if production targets are achieved. What is certain is that a gradual shift to high efficiency is unlikely in the foreseeable future. It would require a major shift of priorities, a big increase in the numbers of energy engineers and technicians, and a change in industrial priorities to produce the necessary equipment. Like the other developing and, particularly, socialist countries, China is dependent on technology which should have been replaced years ago.

Water

The Government is faced with the consequences of loss of forest, desertification and the inefficient use of coal for the rivers on which Chinese civilization has always depended. In ancient times irrigation systems were perfected and canals built which enabled this great country to become by far the world's most populous.

Nowadays water control and water quality are threatened. The problem is not simply lack of water, although that problem is becoming acute in the drier north, but progressive deterioration in quality because silt loads are increasing and growing quantities of human and industrial wastes are discharged untreated into streams, canals and rivers.

Siltation is a major threat to irrigation systems. Whether ancient or recent they have to be continuously maintained. Some built in the 1950s and 1960s are already deteriorating because construction standards are less than optimum. The problem becomes more acute as the silt burden of the rivers increases. The loss of vegetation in the head-waters and downstream degradation of the basin of the Chiang Jiang poses especially serious long-term problems. This river is one of the world's most important. It rises in the mountainous western areas of Sichuan and Yunnan and flows down through central Sichuan and the great gorges to Hubei, where Wuhan and other cities form an industrial complex. It then drains the plain of central northeastern China, most of which is shared by the provinces of Anhui and Jiangsu. In 1990 the population of these provinces, Hunan and Jiangxi, which lie in the basin south of Hubei, and that of Shanghai, just south of the mouth of the river, was 433 million. About a quarter of these people live in Sichuan (*Beijing Review*, 17-23 December 1990, pp. 21-2).

For this population there is a danger that much of their collective economic capacity will have to be devoted to ensuring that flood control and irrigation systems do rot become degraded. As silt burdens increase river beds rise. This necessitates raising the height of levies and embankments. In China, as a whole, water control is a major task. It has been estimated that the equivalent of over $US26 billion (about 4 per cent of government revenue) has been spent during the past two decades in this area. Some 200,000 dikes and embankments, over 80,000 dams and about six million small reservoirs have to be maintained. Work is usually carried out by requisitioning farm labour during the off-season. This is similar to the feudal system of forced labour which has kept China's water management going for centuries (Delfs, 1990, p. 22).

The same is true of all the other rivers which support irrigation agriculture. The destruction of the balance between forest, grasslands and terrace and lowland cropping systems poses a serious long-term threat. The burden of maintaining the systems could eventually be too much for even a well mobilized and well motivated labour force (Fewsmith, 1988, p. 82).

Towns and cities in China are now having to cope with two other great problems—decline of supplies of ground water and severe deterioration of the quality of water in rivers, lakes and reservoirs. Only small percentages of human and industrial wastes are treated. The industrial waste problem has become more acute as industries, especially those using metals and chemicals, like electroplating, have been encouraged in towns and villages. The following comment by a European expert is based on reports from China:

> 27 per cent of the discharged industrial water is treated, over one-half of which is brought up to standard. This leaves an annual 14 million tons of industrial wastewater which does not conform to State standards ... The target for 1992 is to hold down discharge of industrial wastewater to 31bn tons and urban sewage to 12 bn tons; by then, 33 percent of industrial wastewater, and 6 per cent of the urban sewage should be treated.

> According to scientists, only 2 to 3 per cent of the 18 billion cu. m. of waste water released by China's 75 largest cities is adequately treated. There are 5,300 kilometres of rivers with 'dead' water, 47 per cent of all navigable rivers cannot be used for either drinking or fishing, and half of China's lakes are seriously

polluted. 152 of China's 232 cities suffer from water shortages. Nitrification of rural drinking water, and eutrophication of surface water, both resulting from chemical fertilizer use, is most serious; in a survey of the Taihu region, a third of all drinking water wells contained more nitrates than the official health standard ... and 40 times as much nitrates as the WHO (World Health Organization) standard. The vegetables cultivated in the suburbs of Tianjin were found to contain, on average, half the permissible maximum of heavy metals (Vermeer, 1990, p. 44).

Wastes

The sheer numbers of people and their efforts to industrialize have created a massive problem of waste disposal. The rivers have been expected to carry the load. They are now reaching the stage where they could become dangerous to the people who rely on them. Pollution laws are strict but there is little evidence of effective compliance. Sulphur oxides, fly ash, cyanides, phenol, oil, mercury, chromates, smelting and chemical sludge are all discharged into water systems, because capacity for treatment of industrial waste (about 27 per cent) is so limited (Vermeer, 1990, pp. 45-6).

This problem is made worse because of the growing difficulties in disposal of urban sewage. Six per cent may be treated in 1992. Handling the growing quantities of garbage is another major problem. Only about 5 per cent of the latter seems to be treated. Little can be incinerated because of its high moisture content. The inorganic content is high because much of it is coal ash from stoves and heating systems. Although little is known about the extent to which garbage dumps contribute to pollution of water, there seem to be few doubts that this is a big problem especially in the vicinity of great low-lying cities like Shanghai (Vermeer, 1990, p. 46).

An international environmental conference was held in Beijing in 1990. A British journalist reported:

> ... nobody, least of all the Chinese officials concerned, denies that China is on the brink of an ecological catastrophe as bad or worse as Eastern Europe. Many, however, doubt the sincerity of the authorities' protestations that they intend to tackle it (*The Guardian*, 9 March 1990, cited in Vermeer, 1990, p. 34).

The question of whether the Chinese Government has the will and the capacity to deal with growing environmental problems is considered in the next chapter. Suffice it to suggest at this stage that environmental problems could become intractable in many areas unless there is a profound shift in priorities.

Another problem facing the Chinese Government is rooted in its current doctrine. Theoretically socialist development is the product of a wise, all-seeing, all-knowing system of rational allocation of resources through 'scientific' central planning. In 1987 the wisdom of the Chinese Communist Party on environmental protection was expressed in this way:

> In a socialist country such as ours, the basic aim of economic development is to meet the ever-growing needs of people, material as well as cultural. No clash of interest of a fundamental nature exists between economic expansion and environmental protection; both of them are indispensable components of a high level of material and spiritual civilization. Environmental problems do exist in this country, and some of them are even serious. However, such problems cannot be attributed to China's social system; they are due to a lack of understanding of the importance of environmental protection and, to a greater extent, to the failure to map out sound economic policies suited to the social system.
>
> Socialist public ownership of the means of production and a planned economy afford favourable conditions for providing environmental protection and maintaining ecological balance. What we should do now, is to take full advantage of these conditions to build a prosperous economy and create a favourable environment (Liu (ed.), 1987, p. 420).

The evidence seems to indicate that socialist public ownership and a planned economy based on production targets may actually contribute to severe environmental damage. In fact concepts of ecological balance have only recently come to be considered important. The Academy of Sciences in China established an Environmental and Ecological Warning Team only a few years ago. It has submitted an *Analytical Report on the National Condition* which, according to press reports, has engaged the attention of the intellectual community. Its basic contention is that the strategy of future social and economic development policy should be changed from a pursuit of further growth of GDP to the protection of people's lives and the sustainable development of living space (*Inside China Mainland*, March 1991, p. 24). But the Ten Year Plan which came before the Plenum of the CPC in 1990 reaffirmed that the most important goal for China should be to continue to seek to double the level of GDP per capita reached in 1980. The route proposed is increasing production of coal, even greater use of raw materials and an inevitable increase in the burden of pollution.

The Academy of Sciences appears to be challenging this by expressing the view that the most serious threat to national security and the people's existence will come from the combination of a sharp increase in the country's population, the exhaustion of natural resources, an energy crisis, ecological destruction and environmental pollution. These problems are in the process of translating themselves into formidable political and economic pressures. The possibility cannot be excluded that they will intensify the problems of distributing limited resources among different interest groups and regions in ways which might not be easy to resolve politically.

Countries of the Mekong

The Mekong River rises in China, skirts eastern Burma, descends through Laos then delineates the border between that country and Thailand. It flows down through Cambodia where its system connects with the great central lake of that country—Tonle Sap. Finally it forms the delta country of the south of Vietnam, one of East Asia's most productive areas. The Mekong delta is one of a series which add enormous character to the coast of the Western Pacific from northern China to Thailand.

The valley of the Mekong is underpopulated by comparison with those of the major rivers in China. It drains the southeastern extension of the Himalayan system and what used to be uniformly densely forested country in the great ranges and valleys of the marches between Burma, China, Laos, Thailand and Cambodia. It does not support a string of major cities along its middle and lower reaches. Its waters have only recently been exploited for major irrigation schemes upstream from Vietnam and Cambodia.

The development of its hydroelectric and irrigation potential has inevitably been hindered by decades of conflict in Indochina. An international plan was first developed in outline by the United Nations Economic Commission for Asia and the Far East (since renamed Economic and Social Commission for Asia and the Pacific) over thirty years ago. It established a Committee for the Coordination of the Lower Mekong Basin which arranged for proposals to be drawn up to construct seven dams on the mainstream and tributaries, capable of irrigating 4.3 million hectares and producing over 24,000 megawatts of electricity. That in itself gives some indication of the size and potential of the Mekong. Some work has been carried out in Laos and Thailand, but the conflicts which have devastated Vietnam and Cambodia have prevented construction on the mainstream and all but a few of the tributaries. Such work as ESCAP has been able to organize has been largely confined to collecting hydrological and water quality information and studies of the impact of dam construction on water flows and the environment (Heibert, 1991, pp. 24-8).

If this gives the impression that the years of conflict in Indochina have left the middle and upper Mekong relatively pristine, that would be wrong. The river is largely untouched by major development projects but its valley has suffered the impact of increasing population expressed in the activities of the hill farmers of the Golden Triangle where the opium poppy is the principal cash crop, of slash-and-burn farming, of charcoal makers and of logging operations. The invasion of watershed country has progressively reduced the vegetative cover, and triggered as elsewhere the processes of rapid erosion, excessive flooding and siltation. The steep upper hillsides of the Mekong system provide another example of what is happening even in hitherto very remote areas. Exploitation of timber and fuel steadily increases (Magrath and Doolette, 1990, p. 186). Tree cover alone does not necessarily prevent erosion. Although trees may survive and areas look densely forested from the air the understory of shrubs, herbs and forest litter may have deteriorated, allowing greater penetration of heavy rains.

It has been estimated that forest cover in the Mekong basin has declined from about 50 per cent of the land area in 1970 to about 27 per cent in 1985. The limited amount of development which has taken place has brought with it some stern lessons. Irrigation projects in northeastern Thailand, for example, have increased the area of irrigated land, provided greater scope for fish production and made much needed hydroelectricity available. But many of the people displaced from flooded river valleys have been left with no alternative but slash-and-burn agriculture on the hillsides. This form of survival agriculture necessarily leads to deforestation, erosion and silting.

While no major dam has been constructed on the Mekong itself, it is now well understood that the benefits of a project must be balanced against attendant disadvantages. Interference with the flow of major rivers poses great problems for those displaced by the waters which are impounded and often for people downstream, even if the hinterland remains in pristine condition. The Aswan Dam on the Nile is perhaps the foremost example. Interference with the flow of any river can threaten the livelihood as well as conferring benefits on the people living downstream. In this case whatever happens in Thailand and Laos will affect the vital interests of Cambodia and Vietnam. Tonle Sap in Cambodia acts as a flood overflow from the Mekong. Its viability and that of the people around its shores depend on the Mekong. The same is true of the people of the delta in Vietnam. Even now dry season flows are sometimes insufficient to flush out the sluggish waters of the delta. As a result acidic waters tend to accumulate in some areas, while in others the fertility of the land is threatened by salt water intrusion when fresh water flows are low. Over three million hectares are estimated to be adversely affected by these conditions (Heibert, 1991, pp. 24-31).

Construction of a barrage on the Mekong could alleviate some of these problems. It depends on how the project is managed, and that has necessarily to involve all the riparian countries.

There are attractive prospects for development. Full exploitation of the river could do much to relieve the acute shortage of energy in the countries of the Mekong. But it poses enormous challenges if it is to enhance rather than diminish the sustainability of the Mekong Basin. Destruction of vegetation is already interfering with the natural flow of the river. It could prejudice hydroelectric and irrigation projects which seem essential if the energy is to be provided for soundly-based future development and water made available for the further extension of cropland. To be successful such a scheme would require effective long-term international cooperation among the governments concerned. The distressing legacy of recent decades provides few grounds for confidence. In the meantime the hinterland continues to deteriorate.

Of the countries which share the Mekong, Vietnam is of particular importance. At present it makes greater use of Mekong waters than all the others combined, yet it is distant from the areas where damage is being done to the watersheds. It must look to China, Laos, Thailand

and Cambodia for understanding of its concerns about the future viability of the delta. Antagonism among its neighbours towards Vietnam has not diminished. Suspicion and hostility characterize relationships between the countries of Indochina and between them and Thailand.

Apart from the consequences of war, which damaged about two million hectares of forest, other factors have caused excessive loss of forest cover throughout Vietnam. In 1989 about two-thirds of the land area was considered to be degraded. As elsewhere the rate of land clearance for agriculture and the extent of shifting cultivation have increased. There has been much uncontrolled exploitation of timber. Topsoil has been lost to run-off, former forested areas have degraded as unexploitable vegetation has taken over, or have become denuded. The most serious problems are in upland areas where soils were not especially fertile. In 1981 the Council of Ministers in Vietnam was sufficiently alarmed by scientific assessments to endorse a national programme for the rational utilization of natural resources and environmental protection (Cuc, 1990, pp. 2-3).

Vietnam, like China, is going though a philosophic and economic time of trouble. Its environment has been devastated by a war where herbicides were used as a weapon, as well as by the necessity for a big and still growing population to survive in circumstances that most people elsewhere would have found unendurable. It is trying to make good the loss of forest cover and to remedy other problems, which in densely populated areas match those of China, but the scale of the task is immense. With foreign aid now greatly diminished, the development of the Mekong and the Red River, which it shares with China, takes on even greater significance for Vietnam. At present, however, it is the prisoner both of its recent history and of a system of government which is clearly hindering its recovery from decades of war. These factors still impede the rapid development of collaboration with countries, now that the Soviet Union has backed away, which could provide some of the financial and other assistance which is urgently needed. Effective collaboration with Thailand, Laos and Cambodia on the energy and other projects which are vital to its future may be very difficult to achieve.

If environmental problems are serious in socialist Vietnam, they are no less concerning in Thailand. The problems facing Bangkok have been described in Chapter 4. The situation in the hinterland is equally grave. There is now only about 18 per cent forest cover in a country whose resources of teak were once a source of special pride. In order to keep an appropriate balance, forest cover should be close to 40 per cent of the land area (Handley, 1991, p. 44). Thai companies are now encroaching on forests in neighbouring Burma. The loss of forest and the vegetation which thrives below the canopies has led to an increase in surface run-off. The capacity of the land to absorb water has been reduced. This has caused the siltation of dams and more extensive flooding. The authorities acknowledged that the severe flooding of 1987 was largely due to deforestation. Drought is another hazard of the process of devegetation. When forest microclimates are disturbed and the earth exposed to the full force of the tropical sun, drought conditions appear over areas which were once characterized by an abundance of moisture (McDowell, 1990, p. 311).

Other problems include the pollution of lower reaches of rivers, estuaries and coastal waters, notably along the southern coastline where industrial development is proceeding apace, and in the vicinity of tourist resorts like Pattaya and Phuket.

The Developing Archipelagic Countries

It is both permissible and convenient in a survey of this kind to include the Malaysian peninsula among the developing archipelagic countries of the Western Pacific. Two of the states of Malaysia, Sarawak and Sabah, share the island of Borneo with Indonesia. The other countries in this grouping are the Philippines and Papua New Guinea. There have been enormous changes in this exceptionally diverse area of peninsula and islands during this century, especially since 1945. Colonial regimes have disappeared. Nations have however been formed from ethnic groupings on a basis which probably reflects the European incursions into Southeast Asia rather than ethnic and historic links between them. The primary characteristic of the countries which have emerged during the past fifty years is diversity, but they have developed more cohesion than might have been expected, and some of the elements of national identity.

These countries dominate the archipelagoes in both land area and population. It is easy to discern the places where the growth and increasing economic activity of populations is creating excessive, pressures and where there is serious deterioration of the environment on the pattern described in China and the Mekong countries. They include some heavily populated islands like Luzon in the Philippines, Java in Indonesia, many smaller islands and areas like the highlands of Papua New Guinea where a relatively small but rapidly growing population is exceeding the capacity of the land to sustain it. In Borneo (Kalimantan in Indonesian) the depredations on the tropical rain forest have been extensively publicized. The ecology of a vast, lightly populated island is being transformed by chainsaws, heavy equipment and fire (*Asiaweek*, 25 November 1988, p. 52-60). There is concern that what is happening in Borneo will be repeated in West Irian, the western half of the island which Indonesia shares with Papua New Guinea. The latter only emerged from colonial rule in the 1970s and is politically very fragile. Its government may be tempted by the timber companies of Northeast Asia to compromise its present policies and allow excessive exploitation of its rainforests.

The future of the Philippines and Indonesia is inseparable from the future of the two major islands of the northern archipelago, Luzon and Mindanao, and of Java and Sumatra in the southern one. These islands support big populations, exceptionally large in the case of Java. Their prosperity is ultimately based on the careful husbanding of their fertile areas and of their coastal seas. The need to bring in more agricultural land, to implement construction projects, to manage the growth of cities like Manila, Jakarta and Surabaya with their commercial and industrial sectors has, as elsewhere, increased environmental pressures. Even islands with agricultural environments legendary for their productivity and resilience must eventually reach limits beyond which they can no longer adequately support growing populations. If foreign exchange were available, a solution would be to emulate Japan and draw massively on external sources of supply, but the resources available are unlikely to be remotely sufficient.

As I have pointed out in Chapters 4 and 5 the growth of population and the increasing demand for energy as societies proceed towards the goals of twentieth-century development inevitably involve increasing pressures on the land, water and air. Eventually these assaults can become so extensive as to undermine, or threaten to undermine, the processes of economic development. Nowhere is this more evident than on many of the islands of Southeast Asia which, along with Brazil and Central Africa, support the broken ring of equatorial rain forest (Poore, 1989). Southeast Asia is becoming an area of rapid industrial development, spurred by availability of labour, growing pools of technically qualified people, rapidly accumulating business skills, significant reserves of industrial and energy raw materials, and access to some capital and technical assistance from Northeast Asia, North America and Europe.

The city-state of Singapore is used as an example of the bright industrial and commercial future which will further change the face of the Western Pacific. With its strategic position on the Straits of Malacca it has shown what can be done by a population with a passion for education and advancement. It is the great modern high-technology city of Southeast Asia with communication and transport links radiating from it throughout the region and to the rest of the world (Balakrishnan 1991, pp. 55-7). It seems to herald an assured future, as its dynamic development extends to the southern tip of the Malaysian peninsula and neighbouring Indonesian islands in the straits.

But that may be an illusion. The emergence of pockets of prosperity based on a city-state or a special economic zone may obscure fundamentally much more important trends in basically more important places where much larger populations are concentrated. What we may see if we look more critically is the development of profound social inequalities, as well as material advancement, as growth proceeds rapidly in some places, while less favoured areas degrade and deteriorate. It seems prudent therefore to question assumptions that the big countries of Southeast Asia are going to emulate their predecessors—Korea and Taiwan—as newly industrialized countries. That may be true of Malaysia. Its population is small. Its resources are extensive. But population growth and environmental pressures cloud the outlook for the two big archipelagic countries, the Philippines and Indonesia.

The example of the Philippines has been used in previous chapters to suggest that there is already cause for serious concern, primarily because of the enormous loss of forest cover. The present circumstances of the Philippines illustrate how the combination of a growing population, a market economy system and corrupt and ineffective government can contribute to the degradation of the environment of a once fertile country.

What is happening in the Philippines however provides another example of the consequences of circumstances where increasing numbers of poor struggle somehow to survive. A World Bank report has described what may be the core of the problem.

- The people seeking to make a living in the uplands have no option but to use extensive, basically subsistence, farming practices. Lack of anything even approximating secure tenure in these areas, as well as the absence of surplus income for investment, necessarily involves deterioration rather than improvement of land. Severe erosion is often a consequence.

- Downhill, damage is done to schemes designed to consume water for terrace and lowland fields, which, as things slowly get worse, causes people to migrate in one direction or another, to the uplands or to the cities.

- Along the coasts pressures to survive mean that poor people engage in unsustainable fishing practices and invade mangrove forests in search of fuel and timber for other uses. Where the people have capital to invest bays are converted to aquaculture. This can cause deterioration of traditional fisheries as the loss of coastal vegetation can contribute to the deterioration of breeding grounds.

- Extraction of coral from reefs for use as a raw material for cement and for construction purposes can open up coasts to the forces of sea erosion as well as to the exhaustion of reef fisheries (World Bank, 1989, p. x and 33-46).

There is a possibility that the fabric of the productive environment of Luzon and Mindanao and other islands is beginning to unravel. There is a continuing assault on the land, while at the same time people are flowing into the cities, especially the capital. The national and provincial administrations lack the resources to provide the infrastructure which will ensure a safe and reasonably harmonious existence in the growing cities.

A now familiar pattern has emerged. Rivers and streams have become polluted, shanty towns have sprawled over land on the perimeter of cities and the lack of adequate waste disposal facilities threatens the maintenance of adequate standards of public health (United Nations, 1986). There seems little prospect of industrial and other forms of development in cities and towns proving sufficient to absorb the present surplus labour, let alone future inflows from the countryside.

Indonesia faces similar problems, especially in Java. The forests of Kalimantan continue to be ravaged and the situation of Sumatra is worsening as land clearance proceeds and cities grow. By comparison with the Philippines, Indonesia has some advantages. Resources of hydrocarbons, coal and other minerals are much more extensive. It now has the capacity to attract foreign capital. An educated workforce has developed and will continue to expand. Nevertheless, there is a danger that the balances which have sustained an exceptionally productive rice-based agriculture in Java are being seriously disturbed primarily by the growth of population. Java might not be adequately able to support its population if the environmental situation should continue to deteriorate.

A study of the Brantas River system, which enters the sea at Surabaya in western Java, documents the way in which the pressures of population growth, and more intense economic activity in the countryside, can threaten the breakdown of crucial balances between forest cover and agriculture which have enabled Java to be so extraordinarily productive.

The Brantas basin has the following characteristics:

* It is one of the most densely populated agricultural areas of an island which ranks among the world's most populated places.

* An area of some 12,000 square kilometres supports 14 million people, an average density of 1200 per square kilometre. Using present rates of growth the population could reach 19 million by 2001.

* About 22 percent of the land is forested.

* There is excess labour in the rural areas. Scope for bringing in additional land is now very limited. Improvements in agricultural practices tend to reduce demand for labour. Educated youth are drifting to the cities.

* Six of the nine hydroelectric stations in east Java are located in the Brantas basin

* Demand is rapidly increasing for both industrial and domestic water in response to the continuing industrialization and urbanization of the Brantas basin (Balasubramaniam, 1987).

Surabaya, on the delta of the river, is the second largest city in Indonesia and the centre of a major industrial area. The river basin on which it depends seems slowly to be deteriorating under the combined pressures of an increasing population and urban and industrial development. This repeats, albeit on a smaller scale, what is happening all along the great rivers of the Asian mainland.

Forests are being depleted in the highlands. As elsewhere there is a desperate need for firewood. This, together with some logging of timber and attempts by farmers to bring steeper slopes under cultivation, is causing serious erosion.

The problems facing the farming communities in this area of Java have been summarized in an expert's report:

> Agricultural practices in many areas tend to ignore long-term management of the land. This is partly due to lack of incentive on the part of small farmers to increase productivity because land ownership patterns do not furnish any incentives. Most of the excess yield tends to get appropriated by rich landowners. Secondly, they are unable to control terracing where drainage tends to flow down the slope rather than ridges across the slope. This militates against soil conservation practices. Nor are crops designed to promote conservation strategies ... attempts to deal with the problem have met with little success. The problem has fundamentally to do with the low income of the farmers, their lack of awareness of the problems, their lack of access to technical expertise, their resistance to changing well-tried traditions, the pattern of land ownership which does not encourage local initiative, and population pressures that tend to promote cultivation in excess of the carrying capacity of the land (Balasubramaniam, 1987, pp. 50 and 53).

Downstream there are growing problems of sedimentation and flood control. In the Surabaya region of the delta familiar difficulties are occurring in addition to flooding. Waterways are polluted through industrial development and by chemical fertilizers and pesticides used by farmers. Industries pour large quantities of dangerous chemicals into waterways along which there are pumping stations for urban water supply. Groundwater resources have been excessively exploited causing, as in Jakarta, intrusion of salt water. This brings with it both a threat to supplies of fresh water and the loss of valuable coastal agricultural land.

Can Indonesia survive as a coherent nation-state if the environment of Java deteriorates to the point where more people slip down to or below subsistence levels? In the urban areas there are already the accumulating problems which characterize most cities of Asia and which do not need to be enumerated again here. In Indonesia everything radiates from Java, and from Jakarta in particular. The same fundamental problem persists as in the Philippines. Rural people have to try to cultivate unsuitably steep land or move to towns and cities where the infrastructure is inadequate even for the present population.

Underemployment is a serious problem throughout Indonesia, especially in Java. The Indonesian Government has been struggling for years to deal with a problem which is more likely to worsen than improve because of the burden of a still rapidly growing population. One of the consequences has been an inevitable concentration of available resources in Jakarta and other major cities, in an effort to avoid an excessive gap developing between the needs of their increasing populations and essential services.

Despite much investment, the rapid growth of Jakarta poses enormous problems for the country as a whole. The situation is described in a United Nations' report:

> ... less than one quarter of Jakarta's population currently has access to clean piped water. A large proportion of the population in the city's poorer areas purchase water from vendors at inflated costs. Moreover, the water supply situation is likely to become critical in the future because of sea water intrusion, which has created a zone of salinated groundwater reaching the central city ... In addition, the city lacks a water-borne sewerage system, and uncollected waste has traditionally been dumped into the canals and drains, which serve as the principal sewers (United Nations, 1989, p. 1).

This serves again to illustrate the dilemma facing governments of the developing countries of the Western Pacific. Progress is bought at a relatively high price. The solution of current problems necessitates mobilizing vast amounts of capital both to provide employment and the infrastructure needed for people, industry and commerce. It is unlikely that this can be found in the heavily populated countries themselves, especially the Philippines and Indonesia. Yet it must if those countries are to avoid the dangers of instability.

Developed Countries

Japan, South Korea and Taiwan are the advanced sector of an industrial area in Asia which extends into China.

The three Asian advanced countries all provide examples of the environmental problems which are an inescapable consequence of development. What has happened in Japan is being repeated elsewhere. It has tackled its problems with considerable success in some areas but with less in others. The history is provided in the annual reports of the Japanese Environmental Protection Agency, which record the struggle to bring and keep air pollution under control, to preserve the quality of water and to deal with wastes of all kinds.

Constant effort is needed to maintain air quality in the face of a high volume of emissions from industry and the increasing number of vehicles which clog the roads of the crowded islands of Honshu and Kyushu. In such a densely populated country it has not been easy to prevent levels of air and water pollution which would pose a threat to the health and well-being of the people.

Regulation of emissions, which began in earnest some twenty years ago, brought about a great improvement in the quality of air in Tokyo and other major centres, but the problem is reccurring in what is now one of the most heavily motorized and industrialized societies on earth. Emission control equipment has brought real benefits but there is a limit to what can be achieved when traffic congestion becomes very severe.

There is probably even greater concern in Japan about the risk that the authorities may not be able to maintain adequate quality of water in many areas. One source of this threat is the heavy use of nitrogenous fertilizers in agriculture. The farming industry is heavily protected and it has been an objective of government to make Japan self-sufficient in the production of rice. This has been achieved through an intensive system of cultivation dependent on chemical fertilizers. Inevitably undesirable chemicals get into ground water. The short, fast-flowing rivers of Japan carry most of the residues away but the problem appears as they take their inevitable toll of estuarine and of coastal waters (Sakiyama, 1979, pp. 20-39). While river water may still meet quality standards, less than 50 per cent of lakes and reservoirs do. This seems attributable to the still high level of acidic gases discharged into the atmosphere in Japan and neighbouring countries which precipitate as acid rain and snow. A still undesirably large volume of waste water finds its way untreated into water systems (Environment Agency of Japan, 1990, pp. 8-12).

The extent to which the coastline of Japan has been modified as the country has become industrialized and urbanized deserves attention. One of the prices has been the loss of pristine shore as land has been reclaimed for industrial and residential use and for aquaculture. Tokyo

Bay is virtually biologically dead. The Inland Sea has been extraordinarily degraded as a result of developments around its celebrated shores. Red tide caused by blooms of undesirable algae is a phenomenon which the Japanese have reluctantly accepted as one of the costs of progress. Other problems arise from the flushing of industrial wastes into the coastal seas. The consequences of the dumping of mercury wastes made the town of Minimata infamous in Japan, and wakened concern about industrial pollution (Sasaki, 1991, pp. 33-4). While efforts have been made to clean up that area, the problem of build-up of heavy metals in coastal sediments has not been addressed, let alone solved. The consequences for coastal fishing have been severe in some areas.

The other major problem is part of the process of Japan's emergence as a great industrial and consumer society—domestic, commercial and industrial waste. Although some of the most serious problems caused by the dumping or discharge of industrial waste into water systems have been dealt with since Japan seriously began the task of cleaning-up in the early 1970s, it shares with other industrial countries the continuing tasks of dealing with a consumer society which is inherently wasteful. It may not be as wasteful as the United States, but the problem may become acute because of the very limited land area available for residential and industrial use. About one kilogram of waste is generated daily by each Japanese, about half the level of the United States and much the same as Germany or Britain. The doubling of the total waste burden since the 1960s reflects the growth of the consumer society and of a commercial environment which produces vast amounts of waste paper and other garbage. Added to this are the worn out or obsolescent machines, packaging and appliances which are not being recycled (Tanaka, 1990, p. 29).

Local authorities attempt to deal with waste disposal through a combination of incineration and landfill. So great are the quantities, so small the land areas, that each approach has serious drawbacks. Incineration adds to air pollution although it reduces large quantities by volume. It is more hygienic than landfill. Heat from the incinerators can be put to other use. But many toxic substances are not eliminated, and the gases add to the burden of air pollution. Ash which goes to landfills often contains heavy metals. Finding sites for landfills is becoming more and more difficult. It is virtually impossible in a high-rainfall country like Japan to prevent the leaching of undesirable elements into water systems (Murata, 1989, pp. 68-72).

Problems of this kind now affect nearly everyone in Japan. Judging from the now frequent commentaries on them which appear in English language publications sponsored by the Japanese Government, there is a growing awareness that in combination they pose a threat to national well-being. The issues are not glossed over. Indeed they are described with brutal frankness.

It is to Japan's credit that it is not faced with serious problems of erosion which might threaten the farms and gardens in the valleys and on what is left of the plains as the cities and towns gradually expand. The steeper hills and mountains of the archipelago are densely forested. Human incursion into these mountains, perhaps surprisingly given the depredations in most other parts of the Western Pacific, seems effectively to have been limited.

The rivers run fast and clear at least until they reach closely farmed and densely populated areas. It is on the narrow coastal plains where the impact of the great industrial society of the Western Pacific is placing great burdens on its environment. There are few who doubt the capacity of the Japanese people to prevent environmental degradation from reducing these regions to an intolerable state. They have the technology and the capital to keep their problems under control, and an understanding of what is involved.

There is a perception that Japan is facing a second environmental crisis. This time the culprits are not so much industries as consumers. They are responsible for the growing burden of waste and for growth of demand for energy which is partly attributable to the phenomenal growth of appliances. In addition, the rise in emissions of nitrous oxides has been traced to the increase in the growing number of diesel-powered vehicles. Increases in deliveries to homes and convenience stores has brought what has been described as an armada of small trucks on to the already crowded roads of Japan (Johnstone, 1991, p. 37).

This state of affairs is shared by South Korea. It has modelled itself on Japan and is on the way to sharing with it all the characteristics of industrialized consumer society. It is endeavouring again to double its production within another two decades. The situation of the two countries is similar. The mountains are well protected by forests which are not over-exploited. But agriculture has become highly dependent on chemical fertilizers. Land available for habitation and industries is limited. The number of vehicles has increased rapidly. The use of oil and coal is forecast to about double during the next decade. Although the Government of Korea can now enforce strict emission standards for industry and vehicles, it runs the danger of unacceptably high levels of sulphur and nitrogen oxides in its atmosphere as well as the consequences of heavy use by farmers of chemical fertilizers and pesticides. Increasing discharges of industrial gases bring the added danger of a deterioration of forests, lakes and reservoirs from acid rain. There is also the familiar problem of deterioration of coastal waters as they take the burden of waste disposal from industrial areas, especially in the vicinity of Seoul in the northwest and Pusan in the southeast.

Of the three advanced Asian industrial economies of the Western Pacific, Taiwan seems most clearly to demonstrate the environmental price of rapid industrial development. The Kuomintang Governments have managed a programme of industrial development at least as remarkable as that of Korea. They have transformed a small, very densely populated island into an important industrial country through a programme of capitalist development which is in absolute contrast to that of mainland China except in one respect. It has come at immense cost to the environment of a once tranquil island of legendary beauty.

Little attempt has been made to control pollution from industries large and small. Indeed plastics, chemicals, pesticide, electroplating, tanning and other industries have flourished in Taiwan, partly because they have not, at least until recently, had to budget for the usually heavy cost of controlling discharges into the atmosphere and into water systems. The consequences have been excessively high urban air pollution, contamination of land and coastal waters by heavy metals, deterioration of water systems because of very limited capacity to treat sewage, and the problems of finding places safely to dispose garbage and industrial waste.

The advent of heavy industries and the growth of a motor vehicle-owning society in a densely populated island has added to the overall burden. The Government in Taiwan, like Korea, is just beginning to acknowledge the need to clean-up now that it has attained a high level of industrial development although the situation is becoming close to intolerable in many areas. It shares a problem with newly industrializing countries further south in that it has accepted highly polluting industries from Japan. Moreover many of its factories are small. They are largely indifferent to environmental concerns and are unlikely to be responsive when attempts are made to enforce regulations after decades of toleration of what now may be regarded as unacceptable practices.

For example, there is widespread indifference to the pollution of rivers and steams. Companies are reported to have rerouted effluent pipes up to three kilometres so as to escape detection. Pig farmers ignore regulations and dump raw animal waste directly into rivers. Consequently, half the population is drinking water from heavily polluted sources (Savadove, 1991, p. 42).

The Government of Taiwan expects to spend the equivalent of $US33 billion on the control of pollution during this decade. That in itself is a measure of its now very substantial economic capacity.

Australia is the other significant industrially advanced country in the Western Pacific. For two hundred years its ecology has been modified by agricultural, forestry and mining practices derived from Europe and North America. At this stage in its development there are two large urban/industrial areas based in Sydney and Melbourne with combined populations close to half Australia's total of seventeen million. These two cities exhibit all the environmental characteristics of major modern industrial and commercial centres. Their administrations are concerned with problems of atmospheric pollution during calm weather, waste management, degradation of some local rivers, bays and estuaries.

While such problems are becoming progressively more difficult to manage, the most serious environmental threat to the continent is the consequences of more than 150 years of timber cutting, of extensive grazing and farming and horticulture in a land where rainfall is often sparse except along the eastern seaboard. The introduction of cloven-hoofed animals, which now graze in vast numbers, and the extensive cultivation of wheat and other grains on land where the native vegetation has been excessively diminished, has opened up intrinsically fragile soils to the processes of erosion by wind and water. Desertification is a great threat to inland Australia.

Government agencies acknowledge that the degradation of land due to the loss of vegetation, desertification, salinity and acidification has had adverse consequences for more than half the land area

(Commission for the Future, 1990, p. 38). It has been estimated that about 30 per cent of rain-fed croplands have been degraded to some extent by overcultivation. As a result of this and overgrazing, water systems, especially the vitally important Murray-Darling system which drains the eastern inland of the continent, are at risk especially from salinization. Interference with water tables through unsound irrigation practices and as a result of changes in and losses of vegetation has flushed salt from ancient seabeds to the surface. Some land has become degraded beyond recovery (Grainger, 1990, p. 131). This has led to questioning of the sustainability of agriculture and a growing appreciation of the imperative to implement agricultural practices which enhance the quality and integrity of the rural environment (Australian Government, 1991, p. 1).

Australia can be used as an example of the way in which inappropriate agricultural practices, which may have yielded great wealth over the years, have gradually used up too much of the most valuable of capital—fertility of soils. The problem has been exacerbated in some areas where productivity has been achieved through the development of extensive irrigation systems. Lack of appreciation of the geology and hydrology of some areas and policies which led to excessive use of water by most farmers has caused perturbations in local hydrology which have potentially disastrous consequences for Australian agriculture.

Such problems as these have to be effectively addressed. It will prove very costly to solve or at least arrest problems which originated when colonist farmers moved on to virgin frontier country during the nineteenth century and which have been exacerbated in some areas by agricultural and horticultural practices that proved to be unsound.

Coastal Seas

The coastal seas which lie between Japan and northern Australia are being stressed as a result of the growing amounts of sediments and wastes carried by rivers, by the increasing intensity of sea traffic, by the development of fisheries of all kinds, by changes to microscopic plant and animal life and by the modification by people of coasts and reefs.

Sedimentation comes from agriculture, logging, mining and construction as well as from normal geomorphological processes. In some places it is damaging underwater plants, with consequent adverse effects on stocks of fish. Mention has been made of the effects of the residues from agricultural fertilizers in the seas around Japan. This is a common phenomenon. Algal blooms are happening in many other areas. Detritus from mining is also degrading coastal waters especially where it contains significant amounts of heavy metals. This problem has been identified in the waters of coastal Malaysia, the Philippines, Indonesia and Papua New Guinea (ESCAP, 1990, pp. 73-6).

Sea traffic is particularly intense in Southeast-Asian waters. In the 1980s it was estimated that about 150 ships passed through the Straits of Malacca each day, carrying some 3 million tonnes of cargo, of which about 10 per cent was oil. Pollution of the seas by oil slicks from shipping, from refineries and from discharges from off-shore wells is increasing (Gourlay, 1988, p. 114). The highest concentrations of hydrocarbons have been detected off the coast of Vietnam and in the Makassar Strait near the outfields of Kalimantan and Brunei.

It is difficult to exaggerate the importance of fisheries to the countries of the Western Pacific. They have traditionally been very productive, and have provided about 11 per cent of the world catch. While there is scope for expansion in some places, two important areas have been overfished—the Gulf of Thailand and the Straits of Malacca. Other areas are being degraded by the continuing and increasing flows of dangerous organic and inorganic wastes. The algal blooms encouraged by residues of fertilizers mentioned above are often toxic capable of killing some organisms and contaminating many food species. Increases in concentrations of faecal coliforms from untreated sewage are occurring everywhere. Shellfish in particular can easily become contaminated. Pathogens are now common in many species of fish.

The destruction of mangrove forest because of the need to gather timber for construction and fuel, and to clear areas for fish farms, housing and industrial use, has diminished the extent of important estuarine areas where fish breed, and has opened up coasts to the forces of erosion. The mining of coral reefs has also contributed both to the decrease of stocks of fish and to increasing damage from tides and storms (ESCAP, 1990, pp. 78 and 81-4).

The state of the coastal seas of the Western Pacific naturally reflects the economic development which has taken place this century, especially during the past four decades. The outlook for these waters is not particularly good as marine traffic, exploitation of underwater minerals—notably oil, gas and tin—will continue, maritime traffic will increase, greater quantities of detritus from mines will flow into the seas, the volume of sewage and industrial wastes will increase, coastal vegetation will diminish and coral formations will be mined. Beyond that many species are threatened because of over-fishing, or because their habitats are being degraded. ESCAP notes that in East Asia five million people are dependent on fishing. As populations further increase the fishermen will try to increase catches, so the number of areas which are overfished is bound to increase. The problems of the coastal waters cannot simply be dismissed as transient. They are a function of what is happening on land, and are becoming increasingly serious.

No inhabited part of the world is exempt from environmental problems. They differ only in their degree of severity. In Europe and North America the most serious threats seem to be those associated with forest death and eutrophication of water caused by acid rain and snow, pollution of water systems from industrial and agricultural activity and the deterioration of inland seas like the Black, Baltic, Mediterranean and Caspian. It is now widely appreciated that the consequences of these problems are especially severe in Eastern Europe and the Soviet Union. Those societies are now counting the cost of the despoliation caused by decades of industrial development which largely disregarded consequences for the environment.

There is however a significant difference between the circumstances of the countries of Europe and North America and the Asian countries of the Western Pacific. Although some parts of all these areas are densely populated there is a remarkably different ratio between rural and urban populations. The transition to largely urban living has taken place in Europe and North America, even in the Soviet Union. The decline of the agricultural population in many Western European countries since 1950 has been remarkable.

Throughout Asia, and as much along its part of the Pacific Rim as elsewhere, most of the major countries have large agricultural populations, especially China. Although cities and towns are growing and ratios between rural and urban people are changing everywhere, the sheer numbers of people engaged in agriculture broadly defined have for some time contributed to pressures on their environments which over the long haul could prove to be threatening to their futures.

The pattern which has emerged this century is one of sharp contrasts. There are great concentrations of industrial and commercial activity ranging from the very efficient high-technology areas of Korea and Japan to the relatively inefficient but still large industrial areas of northeast and central and southern China. Elsewhere there are smaller pockets of concentrated economic activity like Taiwan, southeastern Australia and the big cities such as Hong Kong, Singapore and those of Thailand, the Philippines and Indonesia. Nearly everywhere in the developing countries, however, millions are struggling to make a living from the land and small rural industries.

The evidence suggests that many of these people have changed gradually from living in harmony with the land in accordance with their long traditions, to what amounts virtually and unavoidably to being at war with the land. They are abetted in this war by the excessive commercial demand for timber for both domestic and foreign use which is so rapidly diminishing forest cover everywhere except Japan and Korea, and excessive use of chemical fertilizers.

There is another serious problem which can best be described as the deteriorating hydrological state of the river basins. It is no exaggeration to suggest that if they continue to deteriorate, the future of the countries of the Western Pacific is at risk. The United Nations has issued warnings for many years. They were reiterated by ESCAP in 1990:

> Increasing numbers of people mean more sewage, more erosion, more agricultural runoff, and more industrial wastes all of which degrade supplies of fresh water and increase health risks. Although not nearly enough research has been done to assess the quality of water resources in the region, there is sufficient evidence to show that serious problems are developing in terms of growing loads of pathogens, BOD (biochemical oxygen demand), nutrients and silt. The rivers of the Asian and Pacific region are among the rivers with the heaviest silt loads in the world. Further, toxic chemicals and trace element pollution are new hazards that have emerged in the wake of rapid industrialization.

> More than half the people on the planet live in the ESCAP region, but it is estimated that clean water is available to only 60 per cent of the region's

population. In future, if water supplies and water quality continue to decline, many millions will be deprived of a basic human need (ESCAP, 1990, p. 66).

Does this really matter? The accumulating evidence suggests that it does. There are two major threats. The first stems from the stripping of the vegetation of vast areas of land, especially in the head-waters of the rivers which have supported the great agricultural civilizations of Asia with their sophisticated systems of irrigation. The second is the complex environmental consequences of the wastes of agricultural, urban and industrial development. A set of problems is confronting authorities in every country especially in the heavily populated areas of the developing countries of the Western Pacific. They may need far more resources to correct than conceivably could be made available. Unless one takes the view that the preservation of an essential minimum of forest cover, fertile soils and clean water are not basic to a sound economic future for any country, then the countries of the Western Pacific are running a risk which could have severe repercussions for them in the course of the twenty-first century.

The evidence should not be brushed aside. Gushing forecasts about the bright industrial future of the Western Pacific need to be considered along with the discouraging facts of destruction of natural environments and actual and threatened deterioration of agricultural land, river systems and coastal environments. It would be naive to suggest that technology can solve all or most of these problems. They are related to the circumstances of people after many decades of rapid population growth, and in some cases industrial growth. Unless attitudes and present practices change, it is possible that the fertility of soils will decline over large areas, and problems of acute, very widespread rural poverty will emerge once again.

The rise of a powerful industrial region in Northeast Asia has changed the global balance. Industrial predominance is no longer the preserve of the Europeans and North Americans. But for all their achievements the governments of the countries of the Western Pacific must successfully deal with complex interrelated problems if they are to avoid a situation where the insidious processes of environmental decline offset the undoubted benefits of much industrial and commercial development. It could contribute to such acute social and political problems that the precarious stability of the past two decades could be threatened.

7. Government Responses to Population and Environmental Problems

In the late 1970s Asia was singled out as a demographic success story with many countries, including some of the world's largest, registering major declines in fertility and mortality. It seemed that prospects were reasonably good 'for the cessation of population growth in the foreseeable, if still distant future' (Hull and Larson, 1987).

While growth of populations is slowing down in most countries of the Western Pacific, the actual cessation of their increase still seems very distant. In some instances the slowing down has involved positive government action which seems to have helped to change the attitudes of many people at various levels of societies to that most fundamental of human concerns, the size and composition of families. This is in sharp contrast to Europe and North America where it has generally been left to individuals. Changing attitudes to the size of families is as touchy in a political sense in East-Asian countries as elsewhere. In most cases much importance is attached to inheritance through male lines of descent and well-founded traditional concepts of children being useful in the fields and in family businesses from what would be regarded since the last century in western countries as a very tender age.

There is an increasing and surprisingly widespread understanding of the problems of rapid population growth in many countries of the Western Pacific. Most of the countries have experienced population explosions. Japan and Korea are prime examples. While they are a long way from 'standing room only' situations their relatively small non-mountainous land areas have become exceptionally heavily populated during the past century. However, like other high, or relatively high, income economies, the rate of growth has tended to slow down. In nearby China, where the relentless march of technological civilization began somewhat later, there is acute awareness of the sheer problem of growing numbers. It is regarded as a threat to Chinese society. That perception seems also to have gained ground in Vietnam, Thailand and in Indonesia where the pressure of increasing numbers is especially manifest on Java and some of the smaller islands of that archipelago.

In Malaysia and the Philippines, by contrast, the influence of Islam in the first case and Roman Catholicism in the second have either encouraged population growth or hindered the effective articulation of family planning programmes.

A glance at the population statistics reveals that the overwhelming problem is the continuing growth of population in China. When the populations of Japan, the two Koreas, Vietnam, the Philippines, Thailand and Indonesia are added to that of China, it is evident that the greater proportion of the population of the Western Pacific is nurtured by the exceptionally fertile belt which runs from the island of Honshu along the Western Pacific perimeter to Java, Bali and Lombok. Perhaps the most important element of social policy in all the major countries of this belt is the acceptance that population growth should be slowed down and, in China's case, reversed if at all possible. Otherwise there could be great difficulties in the way of continuing to bring about material improvements to peoples' lives. It is self-evident that targets for improvements in per capita GDP are much more difficult to achieve unless there is a decline in rates of population growth.

This chapter first reviews the population policies of the major developing countries of the Western Pacific. That is not meant to imply that the policies, or in some cases, lack of them, in the industrially advanced countries are not important. But, the population of Japan is relatively stable and it seems to be so in Taiwan. Such increases as are occurring in Australia and New Zealand seem to be largely due to immigration into the larger of the two. Only in South Korea is population growth rather higher than would seem to be the norm for a relatively affluent country.

The second and third parts of this chapter review government and intergovernmental responses to environmental problems. It seems important to reiterate at this point that, in so far as environmental degradation is a function of human activity, there is the closest linkage between the activities of populations, especially growing populations, and the land and waters that support them. Perhaps one of the reasons why the Asian countries of the Western Pacific are now so significant in global terms is not just that they comprise collectively an important if rather dispersed industrial area, but that several of the larger developing nations among them are trying to deal with excessive growth of population. Whether or not they will be successful is another matter. The global significance of their population programmes should not be underestimated.

While the advanced industrial countries of the Western Pacific, Japan, South Korea and Taiwan, dominate because of their great and growing industrial power, it is unwise not to measure their present and future roles against the social and economic circumstances of China and the other four big developing countries, Indonesia, Vietnam, Thailand and the Philippines. There is now an interesting basis for comparison and contrast between the situations in the Asian countries of the Western Pacific and greater Europe. The advanced economies have a vast, developing, or perhaps deteriorating, neighbourhood, just as the countries of Western Europe must now concern themselves with the deteriorating economies to their east. The difference is that there is no country other than India which can match the circumstances and complexity of contemporary China.

Population Policies

China

Articles in Chinese government publications often use the word 'grim' to describe the consequences of continuing population growth. It seems to be widely understood in China that, if the population should increase to 1.5 billion, there is a grave risk that the majority of the people will be deprived of all but the necessities of existence. It seems also to be understood that one of Mao's many serious errors of judgement was to encourage the growth of population despite the articulation of a family planning programme in the 1950s. As Chinese writers have put it:

> Too many people; too little arable land; a poor foundation; a large rural population; backwardness in the modes of production; low educational level; remnants of feudal thinking ... are all basic characteristics of China ... The doctrine of a large population and the backward concept of human reproduction jointly added fuel to the flames of unchecked population growth (Liu (ed.), 1987, p. 293).

Current population policies have their origin in programmes which began to be articulated in 1977. The Constitution promulgated in 1978 mentions family planning in Article 25:

> The state promotes family planning so that population growth may fit the plan for economic and social development.

In 1979 the one-child-per-family programme was initiated with some local authorities and then, in the 1980s, developed into a full-scale national programme. During that decade the Chinese Communist Party was able to demonstrate the extent to which it was able to use both rewards and penalties to achieve a clearly defined national goal (Liu (ed.), 1987, p. 305). There were serious repercussions. Accounts of forced abortions and also of female infanticide, especially in peasant communities where so much importance is attached to having an heir to the family name and assets, seem to be accurate.

The demographic approach which was adopted was based on the achievement of a total fertility rate of 1.5 and holding it at about that level for no less than fifty years. It was considered that it might then be possible to raise it to 2.16 after 2040. By the end of the twenty-first century China's population might be stabilized at about 700 million. Chinese social scientists argued that it would be a level which would enable the nutritional requirements of the people to be met adequately, and would be consistent with fresh water resources and the preservation of overall environmental balance (Song and Yu, 1984, pp. 517, 520, 524). This policy was also regarded as conforming with eugenic principles. In other words it would contribute to an improvement in the quality of the population (Liu (ed.), 1987, p. 299).

The authorities in China have not pursued these policies with unrelenting rigour. Criteria allowing a second birth have been relaxed and minorities have not been fully required to conform. The target of containing the total population within 1.2 billion seems no longer capable of achievement. Prospects of reduction seem very remote. The realities of trying to regulate the lives of families, especially those of peasants, seem to be understood fully but the inevitability of further growth, given the present numbers of fertile and potentially fertile people, is well understood and not glossed over by the current leadership.

Premier Li Peng linked family planning and environmental protection in his lengthy report to the 1991 National People's Congress on the outline of the ten-year programme and the eighth five-year plan for economic and social development. It is worth noting that he too used the word 'grim' to convey the leadership's view of the population problem:

- China has a large population base but it has grown by an average of 16 million annually.

- A baby boom will occur during the eighth five-year plan (because of the sheer numbers of fertile people).

- Average natural population increase is to be held below 1.25 percent over the next ten years.

- About one-fourth of increasing national income will be consumed by the growth in population.

- In the coming decade the population problem will have a still greater bearing on China's overall economic and social development.

- It is essential to continue widely and extensively to publicise basic state policy for family planning.

- Current policies will continue to be implemented: encouraging late marriage and late birth; preventing more children than the plan allows; cracking down on criminal violations; focusing attention on rural areas by speeding up service networks for family planning in counties, townships and villages (*Beijing Review*, 15-21 April 1991, p. xv).

What are the prospects of success for these policies? That is the great unknown in the Western Pacific. Success may depend on the Chinese Communist Party, or a successor organization, maintaining sufficient coherence throughout the country for many decades to secure compliance. The difficulties are acknowledged in English-language official publications:

... the implementation of family planning policies across China has been uneven. In many places, particularly culturally and economically backward rural areas, deep-rooted traditional ideas remain stubbornly entrenched—especially the notion that 'the more sons, the more blessings'. Some local authorities have also failed to take their family planning responsibilities sufficiently seriously, and others have even adopted a 'laissez-faire' attitude.

Furthermore, since China began invigorating its economy, the floating population has risen to around 50 million. And with the difficulties of monitoring this group and effectively implementing family planning, they have produced a large number of over-large families (Yang, 1989, p. 4).

In the time which has passed since this was written there is no evidence to suggest that the morale of local authorities, who are responsible for the success or failure of the programme, has improved. Nor does it seem that the problem of the floating population will easily or indeed ever be brought under control (*China News Analysis*, 1991, pp. 1-3). A radical population policy designed to reduce a large population is without precedent. It has both profound global and regional as well as national implications. So far only the rate of growth has been slowed down. The population could reach 1.5 billion with consequences which must involve intensification of pressures on an already stressed environment. Although one cannot do other than admire the way the Chinese Government has attempted to cope with a problem which threatens to undermine much of what the Chinese people, however misguided some might think their governments, have sought to achieve since 1949, it must be acknowledged that problems occasioned by even greater numbers will impose more difficulties for all levels of government. They could also have adverse repercussions for the stability of East Asia because large numbers may seek to leave China for a better life elsewhere. That is already happening in the important country to China's immediate south.

Vietnam

The history of population policy in Communist Vietnam bears some resemblance to China's, although the Government has been much slower to grasp the nettle of excessive growth. A family planning programme was developed in the 1960s but, perhaps surprisingly, growth of population did not slow down appreciably during the long war in that country. It was not until 1985 that a target of getting the growth rate to 1.7 per cent was incorporated in a five-year plan. It had been estimated to be 3.2 per cent in 1976 and 2.2 per cent in 1981. In this case couples were encouraged to limit their families to two children. The problems in the way of this programme are enormous regardless of whether local authorities have their hearts in the task of persuading people of the need for compliance with the policy. Children are still regarded as an asset in the countryside, contraceptives are in desperately short supply, medical services are limited and, as in China, the people of fertile age are increasing (Hull and Larson, 1987, p. 54).

The situation which has developed in Vietnam is illustrative of the tragic consequences of conflict and the unyielding attitude of the United States and other countries which have sought since the 1970s to persuade Vietnam to relinquish its hold on Cambodia. Vietnam has been described as a country which has become trapped by constraints in addition to poverty. International trade embargoes and exclusion from sources of capital, among other things, have made it virtually impossible to create the essential structure of a family planning programme. Even if contraceptives could be made available, internal distribution problems and the lack of clinics would be a severe handicap. The two-children policy was codified by the Council of Ministers in 1989, but the problem remains, for a government beset on every side, of making it possible for people to cooperate (Hull, 1990).

Indonesia

Indonesia's destiny was in the hands of the erratic and brilliant President Sukarno until the second half of the 1960s . During the first decades of independence official policies were pronatalist. Population in an inherently productive and resource rich-country grew rapidly. One approach to the problem of the great population imbalance between Java and many other islands in the archipelago was for the Government to sponsor transmigration from Java to other islands. It proved incapable of making any impression on the growth of population there.

Shortly after President Suharto assumed power following the crisis of the mid-1960s, the Government was persuaded of the need to reduce rates of fertility. In 1970 a National Family Coordinating Board (BKKBN) was established. The objective of the population programme in Indonesia was to achieve a consensus among the people that family size should be reduced with the long-term objective of stabilizing the population. The programme acknowledged the great differences, regional, cultural and social, between the thousands of elements which make up the population of Indonesia. It is the Indonesian way to seek to pursue national objectives through patient efforts to achieve consensus. It scarcely bears emphasizing that this was crucially important in an Islamic country.

A decline in fertility has been achieved, although it is insufficient to prevent the population from further doubling. That has been attributed to programmes which enabled contraceptives to be efficiently distributed and for family planning services to be available throughout the country. By the late 1980s over half the married women were recorded as users of effective forms of contraception (Hull and Larson, 1987, pp. 46-7). Nowadays children are increasingly regarded less as bringing practical assistance to a family in day-to-day work and more as involving responsibility for upbringing and education.

BKKBN continues to sponsor the national programme for achieving fertility control in Indonesia. Its symbol and its slogans are known throughout the country. But responsibility for population policy has been transferred to a Ministry for Population and Environment, an interesting combination which may prove to be a precedent which other countries may follow. It is too early to tell whether it will become influential. The process of decision-making in Indonesia seems to involve a process of reaching understandings by individual power brokers with their constituencies, or between groups of them, rather than through transparent consultative procedures (Hull, 1989). Indonesia is reaching into the difficult areas of effectively linking issues of population growth and protection of the environment with the overall process of policy formulation but it is hard to tell whether the senior people concerned will be genuinely influential.

Thailand

The evolution of population policy in Thailand has some similarities with that of Indonesia. Its political history has been peppered by military coups but there is an underlying continuity which may have something to do with the institution of a revered monarchy and the gradual development of civilian expertise in government. The origins of the population programme trace back to a visit in the 1950s by a team of advisers from the World Bank. They argued the disadvantages of rapid population growth from a national development perspective (Tirasawat, 1984, p. 111). That view ran counter to the traditional notion that a large population of presumably contented subjects was a sign of benevolent and benign government. The programme seems to have been more successful than was expected. New generations have come to see that control of their fertility was actually the key to being able to enjoy the material benefits economic development was bringing (Hull and Larson, 1987, p. 53).

Governments in Thailand have avoided any suggestion of compulsion. They have used the consensus approach as they worked at changing traditional attitudes. Family planning services have been extended as well as the essential information programmes. Laws conflicting with the objectives of the programme have been revised. The two-child family has been encouraged as the norm and small families have been made eligible for special benefits.

The rate of population growth has been reduced but is still sufficiently high for the population further to double. There are other problems which Thailand shares with neighbouring countries, notably the maldistribution of population caused by the enormous growth of Bangkok. That seems to be almost intractable.

Malaysia and the Philippines

These two countries contrast with their partners in ASEAN because they have decided against attempting to limit the growth of their populations. Policies based on a high growth rate in population were adopted when Malaysia became independent some three decades ago. Subsequently, on the pattern of Thailand and Indonesia, this policy was reexamined and a National Family Planning Board was established in 1966. The First Malaysia Plan (1966-1970) included three objectives in the areas of population and income policy:

- To reduce the annual rate of growth from three per cent to two per cent by 1985;

- To enhance efforts to raise per capita income from $M950 to $M1,500 over a twenty year period;

- To improve the welfare of families through the extension of family planning programmes.

In the Fourth Malaysia Plan (1981-1985) an explicit objective was adopted of bringing the crude birth rate down from thirty per 1,000 to twenty-six (Tan, 1984, p. 83). Not long afterwards the Prime Minister, to the surprise of his demographic advisers, announced that there was to be a basic change in policy. The new objective would be for the population of Malaysia to increase towards a target of 70 million by the end of the twenty-first century. The rationale behind this change was, it seems, to ensure that there would be a population sufficiently large to support major manufacturing capacity. There was a deliberate shift therefore in the Government's approach to manpower planning and ways designed to increase numbers and improve the quality of the labour force. Although the growth rate was expected gradually to diminish, the rate of decline would be slowed down and the population would, in the course of time, more than triple (Hull and Larson, 1987, p. 49).

What has happened in Malaysia is not surprising given the strength of Islam among the Malay community, and the imperatives of an industrial development programme which had contributed substantially to the achievement of per capita income targets. Nevertheless there is widespread scepticism about whether the still relatively abundant resources of the Malayan peninsula and the states of the federation on the island of Borneo, Sabah and Sarawak, are in fact capable of supporting a population as large as 70 million at the equivalent of present living standards.

The situation in the Philippines provides another interesting contrast with Indonesia and Thailand. In this case the dominant religion is not Islam, although it reached the southern islands from what is now Indonesia, but Roman Catholicism. It dates back to the beginnings of Spanish colonization. Understandably the story in this country is one of resolute opposition from that church to family planning based on the use of contraceptives. All the evidence points to the probability that rapid population growth, especially on the island of Luzon with more than 50 per cent of the total population, and its city of Manila (over 12 per cent), is contributing to a situation where the islands of the archipelago are being denuded of forest cover and increasingly exposed to the forces of erosion.

The disadvantages of rapid population growth have been acknowledged by governments since the early 1970s. In 1977 a presidential decree authorized the distribution of contraceptives through both commercial channels and paramedical personnel. It also articulated policy on internal migration and the spatial distribution of the population. In the 1980s the development plan for the years 1982-1987 stressed the need to bring the population growth rate down from the 2.4 per cent of 1982 to 2.0 in 1987. The official approach was to advocate the regulation of the size of families through voluntary means avoiding any suggestion of coercion (Zablan, 1984, p. 241).

Since the fall of the Marcos regime in 1986 there has been little progress with population control programmes. It is interesting to note the wording of Article II, Section 12 of the Constitution adopted in 1987:

> The state recognizes the sanctity of family life and shall protect and strengthen the family as a basic autonomous social institution. It shall equally protect the life of the mother and the life of the unborn from conception.

As one commentator has put it 'there is still a national family planning programme in the Philippines, but its enemies have developed a powerful constitutional weapon which can be used in the bureaucratic politics of setting the agenda for government' (Hull, 1990). In this country the political struggle goes on. Advocates of population control through family planning have managed to get their objectives, albeit expressed in terms of objectives related to maternal and child health, included in the development plan for 1987-1992 but opposition to the extension of contraception is powerful and persistent. The present situation seems to be one of drift in a nation whose future is probably the most precarious, along with China and Vietnam, of any of the countries of the Western Pacific.

The overall picture among the Asian countries of the Western Pacific is a remarkable one by comparison with other parts of the world. Governments in most of the large countries recognize the dangers inherent in the growth of populations and are devising programmes to limit rates of growth which would be suited to their circumstances. No country has reached a desperate situation but the Chinese can foresee it in their more densely populated regions and so too, probably, do the Vietnamese and the people who live on Java, Luzon or Taiwan.

Areas where over-population is posing difficult problems or becoming potentially threatening to the stability of societies are clearly growing. Sichuan province and the environs of Shanghai, to mention only two areas of China, as well as many other places, provide their own warnings. The affluence of Japan and the improving situation in

South Korea masks a situation where pressures on individuals, because of the sheer density of population and the intensity of economic activity, are evident despite the fact that Asians generally enjoy the propinquity of close-density life in cities large and small.

The present era, if it is anything, is a time of growth of both populations and motor vehicles throughout the world. City environments in particular have been invaded by motor vehicles of all shapes and sizes. The Western Pacific now leads in vehicle technology, maybe because industry in Japan responded to the world demand for vehicles of all types and descriptions. They range from the farm bikes and four-wheel drives which have increased farm productivity in Australia and New Zealand, the two- and three-wheeled vehicles which augment the pressures created by conventional cars, vans and buses in Bangkok and elsewhere, to big trucks which clutter highways everywhere. The crowded towns and cities of the Western Pacific are polluted both by the noise and fumes of these vehicles. They have compounded the pressures of daily life whether in high-income modern cities like Tokyo and Hong Kong or in less affluent places where the background noise is provided by the scream of mopeds and motor bikes and the harsh roar of diesel-powered buses and trucks. The problem may be not so much providing more than standing room as providing space for a reasonable amount of tranquillity. Scope for enjoying that is diminishing in most cities of the countries of the Western Pacific as well as in other parts of the world.

Population policies need to be integrated with other major areas of policy, to be regarded as part of a whole. They should be considered in the context of transport, forestry, agricultural, housing and industrial and other policies which together create the circumstances which have their inevitable impact for good or for ill on the environment. While governments in the Western Pacific are aware of this, it is questionable whether many of them have the capacity to achieve the necessary integration of population with other policies as they grope their way towards less unsustainable economic activity.

Environmental Policies

It would be tedious to approach the way governments of Western Pacific countries are responding to environmental problems by describing their legislation, the ministries, departments, commissions and agencies they have established with responsibility for environmental problems. The approach ESCAP takes in its 1990 *State of the Environment in Asia and the Pacific* is to comment on constitutional provisions, environmental framework legislation, pollution-prevention legislation and resource-conservation legislation in that order. Pollution prevention includes air and water pollution and controls on the disposal of hazardous wastes and toxic chemicals. Land use, forestry, coastal management and fisheries and national parks come under the heading of resource conservation (ESCAP, 1990, p. 159).

Most governments have set up institutions for the formulation of environmental policy, although the emphasis seems largely and understandably on the control of sources of pollution. Legislation has been enacted or decrees promulgated in a majority of countries aimed at penalizing polluters and establishing environmental standards. It is necessary however to distinguish between the formulation of policy, its expression in law, the establishment of institutions and effective implementation and enforcement. Government action, or inaction, in environmental policy-making and implementation, reflects the division between rich and relatively rich and the relatively poor and poor countries in the Western Pacific. Japan, South Korea, Taiwan, Singapore, Australia and New Zealand have the overall capacity to give effect to environmental protection. Whether they are fully committed is another question. They can, however, establish effective agencies of government, enact and enforce laws because they have the resources to deploy the equipment, skilled people and the law enforcement officers which are needed.

It is often overlooked that the protection of the environment requires the collection and analysis of data on an enormous scale. If the necessary studies are not done, and updated, if instrumentation is not available, if computers cannot be utilized in data analysis and if the responsible senior people are incapable of undertaking the analysis required as part of the process of advising governments, then it is understandable that environmental precept is not translated into practice. That is the dilemma of the poor countries. Their governments may have the best of intentions, but actually be incapable of making policies effective. The people who are required and the facilities they would need simply cannot be conjured out of thin air.

Before using several examples to illustrate the differences in capability between wealthy and poor in the Western Pacific, it is important to stress several points relevant to the effective protection of the environment in the area generally. The dynamic industrial development which has spun off from Japan has involved the shift of many heavily polluting industries from that country to others. It has happened partly as a consequence of the need in Japan to reduce the pollution of its environment and partly because of a conscious policy there to reduce demand for energy. Heavily polluting industries are often both exceptionally demanding of energy and relatively inefficient.

One way to view the Western Pacific is to portray Japan as the core, Korea and Taiwan in its immediate semiperiphery, Australia and New Zealand the wider semiperiphery, and the ASEAN countries in the periphery. A process of the transfer of the more polluting industries from the Asian developed economies to the developing economies has been pin-pointed. As the economy in Japan has evolved it has been able to escape the heavy industrial pollution which was characteristic of its phase of heavy industrial development from the 1950s to the 1960s. It seems to have passed much of that burden on to its neighbours who have made industrial breakthroughs and more recently to countries of its periphery. Japan has been accused of managing to reduce the pollution of its own environment by exporting much of its heavily polluting industry (McDowell, 1990, p. 325). Now Korea and Taiwan, which accepted this process as a necessary price for becoming advanced industrial countries, are having to clean up. Thailand, Malaysia, Indonesia and the Philippines seem now prepared to have polluting industries transferred to them.

Leaving China aside, the process of the creation of a great industrial area in the Western Pacific has inevitably involved investments which have been heavily polluting as well as grossly destructive of forests. This has been one of the consequences of the development of a dynamic industrial culture. It can be traced to the extension overseas of the great companies of Japan and the extraordinarily complex pattern of business activity which has transformed the Western Pacific. It has brought with it unparalleled prosperity for millions. They may still be a relatively small proportion of the total population, but they have been sufficiently numerous to excite not so much envy as a conviction among the less fortunate that they too can become rich or at least relatively affluent by the standards of their country.

The business communities involved, Japanese, Korean, Chinese from Taiwan, Hong Kong and Singapore, Southeast-Asian and Australasian, have been caught up in the extraordinary dynamism of a period during which development has exceeded most expectations. Networks have developed. Many of them are characterized by the patron-client relationships which distinguish Asian ways of doing things. It has not quite been unvarnished, exploitative capitalism but the business leaders who have emerged have not, with few exceptions, been given to thinking about wider considerations. They have pursued expansion to meet the demands of markets that they have substantially created and of governments who have been able to fund big infrastructural projects. It has been, and still is, a tough competitive environment characterized in many cases by favours given and received. If laws could be broken with impunity or evaded through appropriate disbursements or more subtle favours to government ministers and officials, then that would be regarded as understandable if not acceptable business practice.

The deterioration of the environment in China seems largely to be attributable to the fantastic growth of population since the 1950s and to the consequence of the command system of economic planning with its obsessive emphasis on production for production's sake and excessive investment in heavy industry, especially steel production (Smil, 1988, pp. 203-28). As with other countries whose development was based on Marxist-Leninist prescriptions, the potential conflict between the pursuit of growth through planning of production, the potential conflict between production objectives and the environment was disregarded. In the meantime China is clearly among the countries which could worsen its existing situation by accepting the transfer of polluting industries from other places.

The developed countries

In Japan the Government has acted firmly since the 1960s to deal with air and water pollution and with problems caused by hazardous discharges of elements such as mercury, cadmium and lead. The Environment Agency is a competent, well-staffed organization. Since the late 1960s the industrial sector has been encouraged largely through financial and tax incentives to abate pollution. Examples are pollution controls on motor vehicles, smoke and soot removal facilities, flue gas desulphurization and denitrification, waste water and noise-control facilities and encouragement of recycling. Research is well funded and the overall effort is buttressed by continuing attention to more efficient use of energy (MITI, 1990b).

It is a constant battle given the sheer scale of industrial development in Japan, the number of vehicles on the roads and the amount of waste generated. Nevertheless a national consensus was forged some time ago that there must be an unrelenting battle against pollution. There will be no opportunity to relax. To give just one example, the support of intensive rice production requires vast amounts of chemical fertilizers, the consequences for fresh water systems are serious and the coasts are blighted with algal blooms as the chemical nutrients find their way to the tidal areas (Sakiyama, 1979).

Recently the Japanese Government has recognized that the threat of the degradation of the environment is not simply a national problem. The international ramifications of environmental problems have not affected the islands of Japan directly, apart from a possible increase in the incidence of acid rain and snow. Nowadays the Japanese political/ commercial system appears increasingly to understand that these problems have a direct bearing on both its national and its now very extensive international interests. The Japanese seem to be gradually coming to appreciate that the substantial loss of tropical forests and other environmental problems, for which Japanese demand is partly responsible, will cause an indirect loss to Japan through damage to trading partners especially in Southeast Asia. Japanese interests will not be served by declining and environmentally impaired, as distinct from vigorous and soundly-based economies, in the Western Pacific. In the longer term, the threat of a rise in sea levels through global warming, is alarming given the amount of low-lying and reclaimed land in Japan.

The Japanese Government has established a Council of Ministers for Global Environment Conservation. In 1990 it agreed to formulate:

• An 'Action Programme to Arrest Global Warming' which will include near-term measures for global warming so that Japan can act appropriately within international developments in this field;

- Appropriate concrete targets for the stabilization of greenhouse gas emissions at their lowest possible levels by the year 2000, and

- A global and long-term strategy entitled 'The New Earth 21' (MITI, 1990a).

The elements of this latter concept are summarized later in this chapter. It seems sufficient to note at this stage that by 1990 the Japanese Government was articulating a philosophy based on acceptance of the dangers of global industrial development for the biosphere which would involve a further massive adaptation of the Japanese economy. While there might be an element of altruism in this, there was also a perception of what might be required to further Japan's interests as a power with global economic objectives and vast overseas assets. A shift to more environmentally benign modes of production, at whatever level of technology, is now seen in a positive light by the Japanese. They have made so many advances, especially in areas of energy saving and propulsion, that they perceive that research into environmentally sound processes and products will provide a basis for their country to retain its industrial leadership throughout the coming century.

Korea is about an industrial generation behind Japan and heavily dependent on its connections with Japanese industry. It is attempting to redress the problems Japan began seriously to tackle over twenty years ago. Although an Environment Administration was established in the 1980s and regulations enacted, it was not until early 1990 that a Ministry of the Environment was established under a cabinet minister. This ministry consists of two principal offices, Planning Management and Policy Coordination. There are also bureaux dealing with air, water, solid waste management and engineering and technology. Following the Japanese pattern, the ministry has a National Institute for Environmental Research attached to it as well as Resource Recovery and Reutilization and Environmental Management corporations (ESCAP, 1990, p. 162).

Taiwan is now faced with a situation where it has no alternative but to follow where Japan and Korea are leading. Its neglect of the environmental consequences of its headlong rush into industrialization parallels that of mainland China although the economic philosophies of the two Chinese states are in complete opposition (Mindich, 1991, pp. 5-18). In the Southern Hemisphere, Australia and New Zealand are responding to the environmental challenge. Despite their small populations they are not exempt from problems. Australia's big cities reflect the environmental problems of cities elsewhere, but the great problem in that continent is land degradation through desertification and salinization. A minister responsible for the environment is in the inner cabinet but has other responsibilities. The federal environmental bureaucracy is small and lacks influence with the powerful departments of state. Measures for the protection of the environment must be negotiated with state governments in a country where historical rivalries between states have frequently prevented the articulation and execution of national policies.

In Australia at least some progress has been made in articulating principles of ecologically sustainable development for agriculture, forestry, energy, manufacturing, mining and transport (Australian Government, 1991). Special working groups have identified the most important problem areas, suggested some priorities for achieving change, and have tentatively explored solutions which would meet both environmental and economic goals and proposed time frames during which change could be implemented. The value of this exercise is that it brings out the extreme complexity of the task, especially achieving integration between sectors, and the difficulty of changing prevailing attitudes and practices.

While problems of air pollution and disposal of hazardous wastes are not unknown in remote, lightly populated New Zealand, land degradation through the forces of erosion has been known and feared since European settlers first cut into rain forest and let their farm animals overgraze both native and introduced grasslands. While much has been done to repair the damage, it is a constant struggle as so much steep country is grazed throughout the islands.

Environmental policy is articulated in the Environment Act 1986 which established a Ministry responsible for legislation relating to water, soil and river conservation and control and to town and country planning. The 1986 legislation created an office of parliamentary commissioner for the environment. That officer reviews the systems and agencies established by government to manage the allocation, use and preservation of natural and physical resources. He also investigates the effectiveness of environmental planning and management carried out by public authorities and is required to suggest improvements (New Zealand Government, 1988-89, pp. 79 and 505).

Developing countries

ESCAP has commented that environmental institutions in its region have proved inadequate. A study has shown that the ratio of expenditure on environmental administration in some countries was very low in relation to GNP compared with developed countries. Developing countries in Asia and the Pacific lack funds, environmental expertise and infrastructure. The task of achieving effective protection of the environment is of unprecedented difficulty. In ESCAP's view the traditional command and enforcement model for policing regulations designed to protect the environment is inadequate without strong public support. That seems exceptionally difficult to bring about amid widespread ignorance of the causes of problems of even those impinging on the daily lives of people. Without greater public education, a huge task in itself, compliance with environmental law cannot be expected (ESCAP, 1990, p. 163).

These difficulties can be illustrated by taking the examples of two market economies, the Philippines and Malaysia, and of the perhaps disintegrating command economy, China.

In the Philippines, as in other developing countries of the Western Pacific, the law and institutions of environmental protection and administration are relatively well developed. The 1987 constitution deals explicitly with protection and enhancement of the environment. Article II, Section 16 provides that 'the State shall protect and advance the right of the people to a balanced and healthful ecology in accord with the rhythm and harmony of nature'. Subsequently, Congress is also enjoined 'to take into account the requirements of conservation, ecology and development'. In Article XII, Section 3, it is provided that 'forest lands and natural parks shall be conserved and may not be increased or diminished, except by law'. The following section speaks about 'measures to prohibit logging in endangered forests and watershed areas'.

A Department of Environment and Natural Resources was established in 1987. It is responsible for the conservation, management, development and use of forest and grazing lands, mineral resources and other lands in the public domain. It has six bureaux including forest management, land management, mines and geo-science, environmental management and ecosystem research and development. Several agencies or corporations are attached including a Pollution Adjudication Board, a National Mapping and Resource Information Authority and a National Resources Development Corporation and the National Electrification Agency. The department itself has to work in conjunction with other departments notably agriculture, agrarian reform, national irrigation administration and the national economic development authority as well as local governments and non-governmental organizations (World Bank, 1989, pp. 47-59).

According to the World Bank, the Department of Environment and National Resources has to transform its image from that of a corrupt regulator to an enlightened developer. In addition to an image problem, which is not exclusive to the Philippines, the development and implementation of environmental policies is desperately constrained by lack of resources of all kinds. Staff have been appointed but their average level of skill is low. Data collection is limited, there are few vehicles and communication systems are poor or non-existent. Staff are understandably reluctant to go into the field without vehicles or communication equipment because they know their security could be at risk. There is the added difficulty of achieving the cooperation of local governments whose agencies are also understaffed, undertrained and underequipped. The World Bank seems to have captured the essence of the problem when it used these words in a study of environment and natural resource management in the Philippines:

> The reliance on rules and administrative discretion, rather than a proper pricing system for access rights to valuable resources, creates opportunities for financial abuse at almost every step in the resource management process from inventory, to extraction, transport, processing and export. The sums involved can be significantly more valuable than government salaries and allowances ... The current Government, in general, and the incumbent DENR Secretary in particular, have made an issue of the need to maintain high standards of integrity. Recent senior appointments drawing on people from outside the system, increased salaries, enhanced public awareness of the problem and greater transparency in operations, all contribute to this objective. However, the potential rewards to corrupt behaviour are still very high and staffing and procedures in field operations have undergone few changes. Unless the system for allocation, management and regulation of resource use is first changed to reduce scope for administrative discretion and increase mandatory resource use fees to levels commensurate with economic rents, current programs of decentralization within those

bureaus may simply decentralize the locus of corruption (World Bank, 1989, p. 58).

The Government of Malaysia is not confronted with insurgency nor the complexity of economic and social problems which has all but overwhelmed the administration of Corazon Aquino in the Philippines. Nevertheless, Malaysia exhibits the same understandable discrepancies between precept and practice which are the rule, not the exception, in all the major countries of the Western Pacific.

Malaysia is an excellent case study because of the importance to its economy of five industries which, given the way they are generally managed, are environmentally damaging: forestry, rubber, palm oil, tin and chemical fertilizer-based agriculture. As in Japan it seems that a disaster wakened government to the need for protection of the environment. The Jaru River was poisoned in the 1970s by the spillage of chemicals. An Environmental Quality Act was passed in 1974 and a Division of Environment established in the Ministry of Science and Technology. It was acknowledged in the third Malaysia plan of the mid-1970s that 'it is vital that the objectives of development and environmental conservation be kept in balance so that the benefits of development are not outweighed by the costs of environmental damage' (McDowell, 1990, p. 319). In subsequent plans environmental impact assessments have been made mandatory for significant development projects. Progress has also been made in handling the effluents of factories which process the products of plantation agriculture. There are still serious problems with the quality of water in rivers which will require more determined efforts by national and state governments to redress.

Malaysia is a country which has the capacity to attack many of its environmental problems, and especially the enforcement of laws. It is clearly going to be less difficult there than in the Philippines or Indonesia to build up gradually the necessary groups of skilled and dedicated people and to get on top of problems of data collection and analysis, of transport and communication. Serious problems still persist, however, especially in the forest sector.

In the peninsular states there has been a concerted effort to codify and make effective the selective management of forests (Burgess, 1989, p. 144). But in Sabah and Sarawak, where the problem of carrying out a forest inventory is formidable, logging has been going on at an exceptionally destructive rate. It matches the excessive extraction of rainforest timber in the neighbouring Indonesian part of Borneo. It is on this island that one finds a concerning example of the difficult choices facing governments in Southeast Asia because of the realities of life in developing countries. Companies dominated by Chinese interests are working hand in glove with politicians to meet the voracious demand for timber from Japan, Korea, Taiwan and elsewhere. It is known that a Minister for the Environment in Sarawak was greatly advantaged by making forest concessions available to business interests in which fellow Chinese were prominent. The argument deployed was that the exploitation of the rainforests was inescapable if these states of Malaysia were to progress economically. Because of direct action by local tribespeople and environmental groups, which seem to be far from toothless in Malaysia, the Malay-dominated National Government was caught between its professed concern for the long-term interests of the indigenous peoples and the business interests of the immigrant Chinese. They are notorious throughout Southeast Asia for their unswerving attachment to profiting from business (McDowell, 1990, p. 322). Corruption is pervasive. Government-appointed guardians of forests on low salaries have faint prospect of ensuring enforcement of law relating to forestry concessions (Burgess, 1989, p. 145). They cannot be expected to turn aside bribes which might enable them to live in comfort.

The Government of China has come round to acknowledging the need to enact laws and create administrative structures which will help to ensure adequate protection of the environment. It has at least escaped from one of Marxist-Leninist delusions. The orthodox view was that capitalism as an inherently exploitative system involved degradation of the environment. Socialist development, being inherently rational and equitable in concept and execution, would be in harmony with the environment (Smil, 1976, p. 163). Nothing could be further from the truth. The disastrous record of recent decades illustrates the incontestable fact that rapid development of any kind, drawing on vast quantities of energy and other materials, is at odds with the health of local environments and ultimately with that of the biosphere.

An implicit recognition that Marxist-Leninist nostrums could be dangerous to the future of China seems gradually to have taken hold in government in the late 1970s. In 1979 the Standing Committee of the National People's Congress adopted a Law for Environmental Protection. Two years later the State Council issued a decision on environmental protection during the period of economic readjustment. An elaboration of environmental law has continued following consideration of three alternatives: let pollution remain at the current levels; attempt to control pollution at key places; controlling pollution effectively. It was decided that that was the most desirable objective but that it could not be afforded. The strategy which emerged was based on bringing environmental pollution and destruction under control in the first decade through enforcement of appropriate policies. In the next decade, assuming continuing rapid economic development, the focus would shift to implementing technology which would fit into a comprehensive and planned approach to improvement of environmental quality. Beyond measures for control of pollution, especially that occasioned by the use of energy, the strategy envisaged protection of water resources, forests, the agro-ecological environment, the urban environment and of rare wild animals and plants (Liu (ed.), 1987, pp. 419-36).

China now has a National Environment Protection Agency. There are more than 200 institutes carrying on studies in aspects of environmental protection with, according to Chinese sources, more than 17,000 scientists and technicians involved. The director of the Agency admitted in 1991 that China lacks the resources to implement effective anti-pollution techniques. Although the State Council has drafted a series of policy statements on the protection of the environment, implementation is an enormous problem (*Beijing Review*, 1991, p. 8).

The environmental situation in China further illustrates the nature of the dilemma facing developing countries everywhere. It is not just a matter of effectively controlling pollution. Rather the fact has to be faced that the process of development has brought with it deterioration of the environment and no quick or even slow fix, or series of fixes over time, will address the fundamental set of problems. What is needed in China is a profound reorientation of policy involving the abandonment of emphasis by the planners on quantitative production goals.

Two examples may suffice. The setting of production goals for timber expressed in cubic metres has done untold harm to forests. As long as production targets were met no one got into trouble with the authorities. Who cared that the consequence could be erosion of sloping land and destruction of the capacity of that forest to revive naturally? That has been serious enough, but may be less significant than the consequences of the totality of energy policy with its inevitable primary focus on the utilization of coal. The present intention is to plan for further increases in output with coal production perhaps going up to at least 1.2 billion tonnes annually. This is regarded as inescapable given the current shortages of energy in China. It seems to overlook the very substantial cost of mining the additional coal and transporting it to wherever it is needed in a country where utilization of energy materials is very inefficient and polluting.

The basic problems of energy shortages and damage to the environment from burning coal could be more effectively dealt with by concentrating on improving energy efficiency at all stages. Again, it is the human as much as the economic dimension which means that it is unrealistic to expect that progress could be other than very gradual. Price structures are irrational and do not help. The people involved both in planning and in management are too few in number and in many cases incapable of handling the problems which beset them. Three decades of rigid central planning, working environments which do not provide incentives, and a philosophy which seems to offend those charged with dealing with practical problems, have done untold damage. On top of that there are simply too few adequately educated and experienced people (Smil, 1988).

The problems afflicting other countries are shared by China. Laws have been enacted, bureaucracies set up. But it seems that nowadays everyone has his or her price. On top of that there is the problem of the enforcement of law by a state which owns the polluting industries.

It is in China, as has been stressed, that the totality of the environmental problem has been exposed. It is not simply a matter of attacking pollution, although it is very serious; there is increasingly a pressing need for the system to change to use effectively whatever resources are available to prevent further deterioration of forests, water, the agroecological and urban environments. There has to be a shift away from brute production to efficiency at every level. Even more important, the loss of vegetation has somehow to be made good. The present leadership acknowledges the problem. The scientific community points out that everything is interlinked, and the fundamental issue is growth of population in an age when economic activity is steadily increasing. The present leadership seems however to be intellectually and morally bankrupt. China needs all the help it can get from the international community. The political situation is so uncertain that such help China gets will be limited and grudging. That will limit what can be done to remedy environmental damage.

International Cooperation

The United Nations Economic and Social Commission for Asia and the Pacific has for some forty years provided a meeting ground in Bangkok for representatives from countries throughout Asia and the Pacific. While it cannot be portrayed as having a significant influence on inter-governmental relationships in the vast area it is required to cover, it has performed a useful role in providing impartial analysis of population, agricultural, industrial, energy, transport, water resources, human development and environmental problems.

The quality of ESCAP's work on environmental problems is reflected in its two reports *State of the Environment in Asia and the Pacific* which appeared in 1985 and 1990. They reveal the range of the ESCAP Secretariat's responsibilities, the seriousness of environmental problems in Asia and the Pacific, and the extent to which the Commission can over time influence the formulation of national and international policies. The United Nations Environmental Programme, which has its headquarters in Kenya, maintains an office in the United Nations' building in Bangkok. The ESCAP secretariat is able to coordinate its environmental work with that of UNEP through this link.

ESCAP established an Environmental Co-ordinating Unit in 1978. It attempts to encourage the integration of environmental considerations into the national development plans of member countries. That is a task of monumental proportions beyond the capacity of any international secretariat let alone the relatively small one in Bangkok. Nevertheless, ESCAP takes the long view and presses on with such resources as are available. It has designated four major areas:

(a) environmental awareness with special attention to policy planners and the media;

(b) institutional and legislative aspects of environmental management with emphasis on promotion of environmentally sound and sustainable development;

(c) protection of marine and coastal resources with emphasis on coastal environmental management planning;

(d) management of terrestrial ecosystems with attention to desertification and deforestation (ESCAP, 1989).

The ministerial-level conference on environment and development which was arranged by ESCAP in Bangkok in 1990 did not make a major impact but it served the purpose of requiring the responsible ministers to review the status of the implementation of the recommendations of WCED (ESCAP Secretariat, Abstract for Conference, 10-16 October 1990). They must have returned home understanding that very little progress has been made. The communique they issued on 16 October 1990 is platitudinous even by the standards of United Nations' conferences. Among other things they:

• Committed themselves to adopting an integrated approach to environment and development, and wherever possible and in accordance with their priorities and capabilities, to incorporating environmental considerations into economic planning with a view to effecting the co-ordinated development of their economies and environment;

• Urged countries in the region to adopt effective and sound population policies and accompanying measures for that purpose;

• Emphasized the need for all countries and relevant international agencies to intensify their cooperation to support and assist the developing countries of the region (*ASEAN Economic Bulletin* 7 (2), November 1990, pp. 226-8).

ESCAP is not a decision-making organization. Its area of coverage is too large and that role has not been expected of the regional organizations of the United Nations. Little coherent action can be expected until problems are analysed and action programmes devised on a subregional basis by countries which share resources, are capable of damaging each other's environments and conclude that they can more effectively deal with intractable problems through collective action.

The only regions where there are some signs of progress in this respect among the countries of the Western Pacific are Southeast Asia, the Southwest Pacific and the lower Mekong Basin.

The ASEAN countries, which share the seas of Southeast Asia, recognized in 1977 the need to cooperate in solving environmental problems. A whole series of statements and declarations on the environment have been issued by them since that time. The most recent came from the fourth ASEAN ministerial meeting on the environment in mid-1990. It noted the launching of the ASEAN Senior Officials on the Environment (ASOEN), the adoption of what is known as the Kuala Lumpur Accord on Environment and Development (annexed to this chapter) and the adoption of a common ASEAN stand on major global environmental issues. This covers the international protocol on substances that deplete the ozone layer, the convention on the control of transboundary movements of hazardous wastes and their disposal, the proposed climate change convention and biological diversity (*ASEAN Economic Bulletin*, 1990, pp. 222-4).

Six working groups have been established: nature conservation, ASEAN seas and marine environment, transboundary pollution, environmental management, environmental economics and environmental information, public awareness and education. An important initiative whose task overlaps that of these working groups is the Coordinating Body on the Seas of East Asia (COBSEA). It is the outcome of an intergovernmental exercise in which UNEP was involved. China, Vietnam and Cambodia participate as well as the ASEAN countries. Problems in this important area include oil spills along exceptionally busy sea lanes taking traffic from the Persian Gulf and Indonesia to Northeast Asia, as well as pollution from human, industrial, and mining wastes, and the sedimentation which is accelerated by deforestation. Other tasks on the COBSEA agenda include compilation, evaluation and systematic analysis of data on the seas, assessment of oceanographic phenomena, oil pollution, non-oil pollutants, the impact of pollution on coral and other ecosystems and information and data exchange (ESCAP, 1990, p. 76). It is not difficult to imagine the political and other complexities given the number of countries involved, the extent of the seas, the richness of their ecosystems, the density of maritime traffic, the growth of mining and industrial development on and offshore and the lack of skilled people and physical resources to deal with such an immense set of problems.

Further to the east a beginning has been made in international cooperation to ensure the protection and management of the marine environment of the island countries of the South Pacific. A South Pacific Regional Environment Programme was established in 1982. It involves countries from Papua New Guinea in the west to French Polynesia in the east, from Guam in the north to New Caledonia on the line of islands running towards New Zealand. In this case, ESCAP, UNEP and the South Pacific Commission, a sub-regional body outside the United Nations' system, were involved as well as Australia and New Zealand. The objectives of the programme are the enhancement of the shared environment, especially the marine and coastal ecosystems. An Association of South Pacific Environmental Institutions emerged in 1986 which coordinates scientific advice for the programme. Work is being carried out on national conservation strategies, coastal-zone management, the collection of traditional resource knowledge and the possible impact of climate change on island countries (ESCAP, 1990, p. 167). One objective is to build up a regional data base. That is not a simple task for such a vast maritime area.

A beginning in sub-regional cooperation among East Asian countries was initiated many years ago among some of the states which share the waters of the Mekong. Progress was extremely limited during the long years of war in Indochina and terror in Cambodia. ESCAP has however persisted. The Lower Mekong Basin Development Environment Programme is the result of the patient work of an interim committee for the coordination of the investigation of the lower Mekong Basin which was reactivated in 1977. As the participants are Vietnam, Laos, Cambodia and Thailand, the difficulties of getting people around the table, let alone planning coordinated development, scarcely need to be stressed. Some work has been done in two areas, environmental assessment and management and rehabilitation activities with special focus on fisheries. ESCAP reports that changes in water quality and water balance are being assessed as well as the incidence of water-borne diseases. Surveys, aerial photographs and satellite imagery have been used to prepare land use, crop suitability and pedo-geomorphological maps. Some work is being done with the objective of assessing the likely impact of development projects which would involve the generation of power, flood control, intrusion of salt water, upgrading and extending irrigation, improvements to navigation and the augmentation of flows during dry seasons (ESCAP, 1990, p. 170).

Two important international financial institutions are capable of playing an important part in the development of the Western Pacific, the World Bank and the Asian Development Bank. Both institutions can be fairly accused of failing to appreciate the consequences of funding schemes which have contributed to the degradation of land, rivers and shores although they may, among other things, have opened up access to areas with considerable short-term economic potential or funded energy projects where there was a pressing need. In 1980 the two banks, along with UNEP, subscribed to a declaration on environmental policies and procedures relating to economic development which seems to have slowly brought about a change in emphasis (ESCAP, 1990, p. 241). If the World Bank's *Philippines Environment and Natural Resource Management Study* released in 1989 is based on an approach which may become common if not general, assessment teams will take progressively into account the full environmental problems associated with development.

The Asian Development Bank was even slower than the World Bank to change its orientation to take environmental considerations properly into account. It has however established an environmental division which has (a) incorporated an environmental assessment element into the method it uses for the appraisal and implementation of projects; (b) prepared manuals setting out environmental impact guidelines for all its projects; (c) sponsored a number of regional planning projects spanning both economic and environmental issues; and (d) initiated a programme designed to support the development of environmental standards in developing countries (ESCAP, 1990, p. 241).

Another initiative by the Asian Development Bank could prove to have important long-run implications for the Western Pacific given the central role the Japanese play in the direction of its activities. A technical assistance programme is under way apparently as a means of enabling the Bank to demonstrate that it is actually responding to the recommendations of the World Commission on Environment and Development. Its objective is to attempt to translate these recommendations into national programmes which will be implemented in seven countries: Korea, Malaysia, Nepal, Indonesia, Pakistan, the Philippines and Sri Lanka. The focus is on the management of natural resources and the environment through modifications in economic policies and programmes such as budgeting, prices, levies, taxes, subsidies, debt management and trade policies.

The Asian Development Bank should not be regarded as an extension of the financial and economic power of Japan, but that country plays the leading role just as the Americans do at the World Bank. Recently the Japanese have begun to articulate policies which indicate that they, first among the major countries, appreciate the need for the world economic system to adjust over time because of the dangers current modes of production pose for the global environment. As might be expected they are capable of envisaging how more sustainable economic practice could lead to the strengthening rather than the weakening of their economy during the next century.

The Response of the Japanese Government

The Japanese Government, alone among the countries of the Western Pacific, and indeed among the major powers, has articulated a strategy for what it regards as the coming major shift in global economic orientation. Japan has demonstrated how to exploit successfully the combination of efficient production of energy, mastery of metallurgical, electronic and engineering sciences, to name only three, and the development of export industries of extraordinary dynamism and flexibility. It could be said that major Japanese companies have carried on the tradition begun when systems of mass production were devised. They have provided motor vehicles of all kinds for the entire world including vehicles suitable for the Third World. They have also, of course, provided producer and consumer goods in an extraordinary variety and usually good quality.

Now the Japanese seem to be actively shaping a consensus within their country about the industrial strategies they should follow in a century where deterioration of the global environment seems certain and the threat of excessive warming of the atmosphere is more than just a remote possibility. They know at first hand the dangers of burning vast quantities of fossil fuels. They have endeavoured to reduce the emissions of their own industries through technological solutions and through the pursuit of efficiency in the use of energy. It seems to be now understood that they must go far beyond this.

The Japanese Government takes its share of the credit for proposing the establishment of the World Commission on Environment and Development. Since it reported in 1987, a number of steps have been taken beginning with a report from the Environment Agency in 1988 on 'Global Environmental Problems and Japan's Contribution'. The following year a Council of Ministers for Global Environment Conservation was set up. It comprises the Prime Minister, nineteen ministry and agency heads and senior people from the Liberal Democratic Party. This Council adopted six broad guidelines at its first meeting:

1. Japan will lead the international drive to protect the global environment and to cooperate with other nations in solving its problems.

2. Japan's experts will monitor and research the domestic and global environments and share information with foreign experts.

3. Japan will promote the development of technologies which do not harm the environment.

4. Japan will support environmental protection efforts in developing countries.

5. When allocating official development assistance, Japan will take the environmental protection policies of candidate nations into account.

6. Japan will continuously educate its population in ways to lessen the strain their economy places on the environment (Kato, 1991).

An outline of Japan's scientific and industrial strategy for the twenty-first century was released by the Ministry for International Trade and Industry (MITI) in 1990. It is little short of astounding, especially when one contemplates the comparative lack of vision of the Government of the United States and the Governments of the major countries of Western Europe.

MITI's concept is entitled 'The New Earth 21—Action Program for the Twenty-First Century'. It begins with a statement of the need for a progressive and comprehensive strategy in the light of the threat of global warming. In the Japanese view greenhouse gas emissions are growing at rates that exceed the metabolic capacity of the planet. The possibility that their accumulation in the atmosphere could accelerate global warming and other climate changes must be taken seriously because of the extraordinary and adverse impact it could have on human activities. The increase in greenhouse gases is closely linked to the unprecedented growth in production and consumption driven by the use of fossil fuels.

MITI points out that the stabilization of carbon dioxide emissions at current levels by the developed market economies would cause hardship for them and could also have a seriously adverse effect on economic development in both developing and East European countries because of likely decreases in trade, investments and development aid.

The Japanese take the view that, although global warming seems to be a probability, rather than a possibility, it is not going to be easy to create the kind of consensus which will be needed for broad-based, sustained action on a global basis. They suggest that a progressive and comprehensive strategy should be developed which would combine immediate and sustained action on a wide spectrum of fronts, with intensive research to reduce uncertainties and to define the costs of options that governments will eventually have to consider. Any strategy should be flexible so that it can be speeded up or modified as scientific knowledge accumulates.

MITI used a broad brush in writing its Action Program but it deserves serious consideration, so significant are its implications. It is the first expression of a long-term concept so far attempted by one of the governments which is capable of influencing global policy-making:

The Action Plan devotes the next one hundred years to the recovery of this planet from two hundred years of the accumulation of carbon dioxide and other greenhouse gases.

The first fifty years will be the transition period, when environment-friendly technologies are developed and introduced.

The second fifty years are the years in which future generations will draw on the results of the first half to recreate a green planet.

Of the first half century, the first decade, starting now, will be dedicated to intensified scientific research to reduce uncertainties and better energy efficiency through the increased use of available technology, both in developing and developed countries.

In the *second decade,* there will be a reduction in the use of fossil fuels through the introduction of non-fossil fuels, that is safe nuclear power plants, and new or renewable energy sources.

The *third decade* will see the spread of non-greenhouse gas substitutes for chloro-fluorocarbons, carbon dioxide fixation and reutilization technology and revolutionary, low energy production processes

The *fourth decade* will be the decade of big advances in absorption. There will be substantial net gains from reforestation and desertification should be reversed by this time through the use of biotechnology. Ocean sinks will be enhanced.

The *fifth decade* will be the era of future generation technologies, such as fusion, orbiting solar power plants, magma electricity generation, energy applications of superconductive technology and other forms of energy technology which may make fossil fuels unnecessary [author's emphasis].

MITI suggests that an action programme as ambitious as this, which is based on the assumption that it will be possible through international action to reduce emissions and enhance sinks will enable concentrations of greenhouse gases to peak and then decline in the course of the second half of the twenty-first century. It also suggests that this strategy should form the basis of a global partnership in which all countries come together and act in unity. The Ministry notes that the developed market economies can play a decisive role with their collective experience and technological and financial potential. It adds an intriguing proviso if they should maintain the economic strength capable of turning this potential into reality (MITI, 1990a).

This bold thinking was amplified by another short paper released in Tokyo by the Ministry in 1990. It carried the title: *The Global Environmental Challenge: Japanese Initiative for Technological Breakthrough*. The paper stresses that unprecedented levels of economic activity have raised such environmental issues as global warming, depletion of the ozone layer, deforestation. They could pose a major threat to the continued existence and well-being of mankind. It goes on to suggest that current and future efforts to ensure energy efficiency and introduce alternative energy sources will not be enough to combat global environmental problems. 'Sustainable development' will require unprecedented technical breakthroughs in many fields including energy and biotechnology. Accordingly, MITI has initiated a series of research and development projects which will both extend the frontiers of technology and hopefully will lead to new, environmentally friendly industrial technology. This reflects the way the Japanese accept that it is always necessary to acknowledge that circumstances are constantly changing and that an industrial economy will cease to

Conceptual Framework of 'The New Earth 21'

(An illustration)

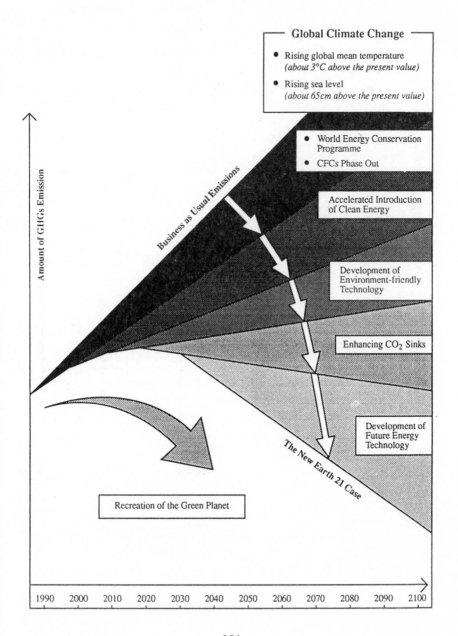

Global Climate Change

- Rising global mean temperature
  (about 3°C above the present value)
- Rising sea level
  (about 65cm above the present value)

- World Energy Conservation Programme
- CFCs Phase Out

Accelerated Introduction of Clean Energy

Development of Environment-friendly Technology

Enhancing CO_2 Sinks

Development of Future Energy Technology

Business as Usual Emissions

The New Earth 21 Case

Recreation of the Green Planet

Amount of GHGs Emission

1990 2000 2010 2020 2030 2040 2050 2060 2070 2080 2090 2100

Action Programme for the 21st Century

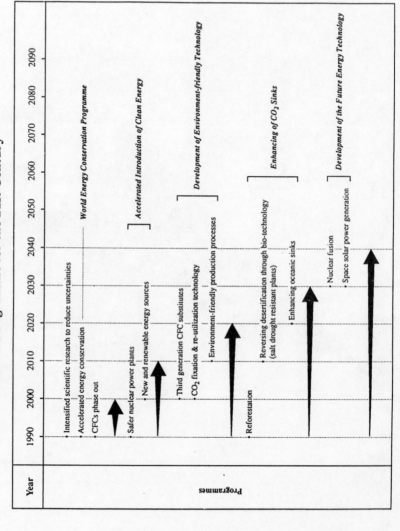

remain dynamic if it loses the capacity to adapt adequately. In an extraordinarily ambitious assertion, MITI suggests that the research programmes will reconcile the apparent dichotomy between economic growth and the protection of the environment by integrating the production and consumption processes into the ageless cycle of energy and matter in the geo-biosphere (MITI, 1990b).

Figures 7.1 and 7.2 illustrate how MITI presents the conceptual framework of 'The New Earth 21'.

A new research and development institute is being established under the acronym RITE—The Research Institute of Innovative Technology for the Earth. It will collaborate with other major research institutions both foreign and in Japan. In 1990 three project areas were identified: development of full carbon-cycle technology, development of environmentally benign materials and the development of environmentally benign production processes. Under the first heading the institute will explore technology for converting carbon dioxide from industrial sources into useful products such as methanol and other hydrocarbon compounds.

In the second category, work will be carried out on CFC substitutes not only to reduce risk of further damage to the ozone layer but also to reduce the potential greenhouse effect of substitutes for that family of gases. Research will also focus on the development of biodegradable plastics.

The third category involves finding ways to achieve significant savings of energy. The initial approach will be to study biological reactions which occur under low temperature and low pressure. That might open up paths to the replacement of energy intensive chemical reactions in present production processes (MITI, 1990c).

How does this seemingly speculative initiative fit into the scheme of things which is unfolding in the Western Pacific? It runs completely counter to the current direction of Japanese industrial policy. Although industry in Japan is relatively energy efficient, it is based on the consumption of enormous quantities of materials and on what amounts at this stage to an addiction to the production of vehicles and all the other paraphernalia regarded as necessities or affordable luxuries by modern medium- and high-income societies. How is it possible to imagine the Japanese economy and the businesses which have extended overseas without the large-scale production at home and abroad of mass-production goods.

The new policies would seem to imply a shift away to environmentally friendly modes of transport, and production of fewer, long-lasting, non-polluting products. It implies that a Japan might emerge in the next century making only a fraction of the petrol- and diesel-engined vehicles which now choke the highways, streets and lanes of the world. There is still virtual silence on this vital issue. Indeed, when the question is asked of the Japanese, there is the characteristic non-committal inclination of the head. That, being interpreted, seems to mean that there is of course a major problem. The foreigner goes away from Japan understanding that time must be allowed to establish a new consensus and then set a new direction. First must come the scientific pathway to the new technology. Then a new balance will be established between public and private transportation and doubtless a less polluting propulsion system for vehicles. This and other fields of industrial endeavour could be transformed if there is a consensus that environmental considerations necessitate fundamental restructuring of the economy and reeducating society to understand the implications that degradation of the biosphere would have for Japan. The process of establishing that consensus is just beginning.

Should the MITI concept be dismissed as window dressing designed largely, with no small measure of cynicism, to show that Japan is responding on paper to the challenge posed by the report of WCED? That may be the case. But it seems more likely that the Japanese are looking for a viable formula which will enable them to consolidate further their industrial leadership during the next century. They are probably more determined about this than their rivals because of the paucity of resources of the islands of Japan. It is in their interests to minimize imports of materials, and to substitute to the greatest extent possible intellectual contributions for materials in the industrial processes which will continue or develop in Japan.

The Government of Japan has made it clear at this stage that an important part of its strategy is the further development of the nuclear-power industry. Despite first-hand and worrying experience with nuclear accidents and the decommissioning of stations, the official

view is that there is no alternative for Japan if environmental considerations necessitate the gradual but substantial reduction of the consumption of fossil fuels. Planning envisages the installation of as many
as forty 1,000 megawatt reactors during the next two decades
(Goldstein, 1991, p. 41). Public opinion in Japan is sufficiently appre-
hensive about the dangers of nuclear accidents that the present and
future governments are not going to find it easy to obtain suitable sites
for nuclear plants. It is probable however that the propaganda machine
will be brought fully into play to establish a substantial consensus that
the further development of the nuclear industry is essential if Japan is
to retain its place among the major powers.

Although the Action Program for the Twenty-First Century is global
in its thrust it is likely primarily to be focused on the neighbouring
countries of the Western Pacific. Until recently Japanese governments
and businesses seem to have based their policies on the view that
deterioration of the environment in other countries, whether the loss of
rainforest in Brazil or Southeast Asia, or the deterioration of land and
river systems in China, or the darks aspects of the mega-cities of
Thailand, Indonesia and the Philippines, would have little direct impact
on Japan. So long as pollution was kept under control in Japan and its
mountain forests preserved, it would be largely unaffected. This
assumption is now understood to have been simplistic. Indeed judging
from the public relations material coming from official sources, a
deliberate attempt is now being made to create a new perception that
the Japanese people, like everybody else, are concerned passengers on
spaceship earth.

There is perhaps excessive faith in new technology coming through
the MITI outline of the Action Program.

MITI's suggestions about the reafforestation of the planet during the
twenty-first century seem to indicate, however, that the Japanese are
aware of the need to redress, for example, through a whole series of
actions—many of them not involving complex technology—the
damage being done to vegetation throughout East Asia. Whether they
are capable of effectively cooperating at all levels of economic activity
with other countries to devise programmes which will assist the transition to more sustainable economic activity, is another question which is
vital to the future of the countries which share the bountiful resources
of the Western Pacific.

Annex: The Kuala Lumpur Accord on Environment and Development

Issued by the ASEAN Ministers for the Environment at the Fourth ASEAN Meeting of Ministers for the Environment, Kuala Lumpur, 19 June 1990

AWARE, that the management of the environment and the pursuit of sustainable development are imperative to secure the well-being of the people of ASEAN today and in the future,

FURTHER AWARE, the management of the environment and the pursuit of sustainable development require close cooperation between the member-countries of ASEAN in particular and global cooperation in general, and that ASEAN should endeavour to strengthen such cooperation,

CONSCIOUS, that the United Nations Conference on Environment and Development, to be held in 1992, provides a forum and an opportunity to further promote such cooperation and for ASEAN to assert its views on environmental management and sustainable development,

RECOGNIZING, that the formulation of such views and practices would require preparatory steps and studies, jointly as well as separately,

ALSO RECOGNIZING, that in such formulation, it would be beneficial to take note of:

the Manila Declaration of 1981

the Bangkok Declaration of 1984

the Jakarta Resolution of 1987

the Manila Summit Declaration of 1987

and the Lankagwi Declaration of 1989

WE THE ASEAN MINISTERS FOR THE ENVIRONMENT
HEREBY AGREE

1. To initiate efforts leading towards concrete steps pertaining to
environmental management, including:

   a. the formulation of an ASEAN strategy for sustainable development and a corresponding action programme,

   b. the harmonisation of environmental quality standards,

   c. the harmonisation of transboundary pollution prevention and
   abatement practices,

   d. the undertaking of research and development and the promotion
   of the use of clean technologies.

2. To initiate efforts leading towards concrete steps pertaining to
natural resource management, including:

   a. the harmonisation of approaches in natural resource assessment,

   b. the development of joint natural resource management
   programmes,

   c. the development and harmonisation of procedures aimed at
   obtaining a better reflection of the state of natural wealth in the
   context of the System of National Accounts.

3. To initiate efforts enabling the inclusion of environmental factors
into economic calculations and thus providing a better base for international economic cooperation.

4. To develop and formulate a common ASEAN position to be
presented to the Ministerial Level Conference on the Environment for
Asia and the Pacific and later to the United Nations Conference on
Environment and Development in 1992, including:

a. affirming ASEAN's commitment to the pursuit of sustainable development,

b. stressing the need to strengthen regional and international cooperation and proposing the principles upon which such cooperation should be based,

c. emphasizing the importance of a global environmental agenda which reflects the priorities and concerns of all countries,

d. calling attention to the patterns of international relations that inhibit the implementation of national environmental efforts in developing countries and their participation in global environmental efforts,

e. reiterating the urgency for a supportive and predictable international economic environment which promotes economic growth and development of all countries,

f. stressing the need for equitable sharing of responsibilities and allocation of liabilities in global environmental efforts,

g. stressing that although global environmental efforts will benefit the common good, such benefits should be shared equitably, including the benefits of Research and Development,

h. underlining the need for substantial additional resources to assist developing countries to pursue their goals of sustainable development as well as access to, and transfer of, environmentally sound technologies at affordable costs and the establishment of appropriate funding mechanisms.

8. The Future of the Western Pacific

The notion of the Western Pacific consolidating its international economic ascendancy is based on bullish estimates of the industrial future of the countries of Northeast Asia including China, and an optimistic reading of the economic future of the countries of Southeast Asia. While much evidence points that way, the outlook is in reality particularly clouded because of continuing population growth and the insidious degradation of the environment. Much depends on the way in which the two great powers, China and Japan, shape their policies and whether the countries of Southeast Asia can surmount the problems which are steadily catching up on them.

There is no escape from making heroic assumptions when attempting to delineate key aspects of the future of an area as vast as the Western Pacific. Enough has been written in Chapter 3 about the character of the governments to establish that political stability in the major countries, other than Japan and the democracies of the Southern Hemisphere, is not assured. There are problems of regime transition in all the other major Asian countries. There is, however, some evidence that such transitions may not be as destabilizing for example as transitions in European countries such as Germany, Italy and Spain during the first half of this century. People throughout Asia value political stability and are much less doctrinaire about the nature of political regimes than Europeans and North Americans. They are also much more inclined instinctively to seek consensus as a way out of the difficulties which may beset them as they endure the inevitable processes of transition from one regime to another.

The key assumption in this chapter is that government in China will not disintegrate. There may be an evolution in the Communist Party of China which will enable it to restore its damaged reputation within the country at large, but the important change in China is likely to be substantial devolution of power from Beijing to provincial governments (Delfs and Cheung, 1991, pp. 21-30). There will inevitably be a shift

209

away from 'old guard' leadership to a new generation which increasingly relies for advice and execution of policy on people who have been educated since the end of the cultural revolution. That could mean that the 'supreme' leadership will pass when Deng Xiaoping dies to someone like Zhu Rongji, the former mayor of Shanghai, who became Vice Premier in April 1991 (Cheung, 1991b, pp. 25-6). Such people may profess adherence to socialist doctrine but in reality they will be pragmatic in their efforts to renew the Chinese economy and repair the devastation caused by adherence, from the 1950s to the 1970s, to economic development on the now totally discredited Soviet model complicated by the nihilism of the period of the cultural revolution.

The principal task of government in China, at both national and provincial levels, will be to preserve stability and a balance between the relatively wealthy provinces along the coast and the less favoured but also heavily populated inland provinces. If China further increases its position in world trade, as seems likely, then the advantages of the coastal provinces are self-evident. The difficulty will be to ensure that there is adequate and effective investment inland as well as in the growing and apparently dynamic industrial concentrations from Jiangsu north of Shanghai to Guangdong. Southeastern China benefits from the activities of the now economically interconnected cities of Hong Kong and Guangzhou, and the zone of rapid industrial develop-ment extends almost to the border with Vietnam.

Nevertheless, there is no reason to be optimistic about the future of China. Its Communist Party may not be in quite such a precarious position as that of the Soviet Union between 1988 and 1991, but it is very difficult for such systems to reform themselves. The Chinese are still unfamiliar with the concept of the rule of law as distinct from imperial rule or the absolute authority of the Communist Party. The ramshackle system that has emerged over the past forty years could collapse. Non-communists, disillusioned by the years of corruption and nepotism, may simply cease to respond to directives from above. The contradiction between the growing market-oriented system in agriculture and light industry, and the decaying state-controlled heavy industrial, energy, transport and other sectors of the economy could contribute to a collapse of the system. There does not seem to be any other political organization which could replace the Communist Party.

Fragmentation of the country, and another period of confusion caused by the disintegration of central control, cannot be ruled out.

Indonesia and the other countries whose regimes are either military or depend on the support of the military for survival may avoid instability because of the relatively high calibre of some of the senior military in most of these countries, and the connections many serving officers have with professionally qualified contemporaries in government and business. Such regimes may become somewhat less authoritative. They will probably err on the side of benevolence rather than resorting to the worst manifestations of preservation of power through the overt use of military authority and of political police to stifle dissent. Lee Kuan Yew of Singapore and President Suharto of Indonesia have provided models which the majority of people seem to understand and, as far as an outsider can judge, respect. Leaders like them provide stability. There is no reason to assume that western democratic systems modified by Asian societies might be successful in that vital respect.

Indeed it is probably unwise to assume that it is likely that the Asian countries of the Western Pacific will remain politically stable. I have shown in Chapter 3 the way in which the governments of most of these countries are in the hands of military regimes or managed somewhat precariously by a combination of military and civilian élites. Corruption is a way of life. The exposure of the ramifications of criminal organizations in Japan has provided added evidence of this dark but pervasive aspect of life in all these countries other than Singapore.

Nevertheless there could be a gradual evolution towards regimes where the military gradually come to accept civilian authority, where the rule of law gradually takes hold and where democratic processes are less threatened by corruption and military coups. For the meantime, however, the best that one can hope for is that present regimes will continue to provide stability and, in the case of the big archipelagic countries, Indonesia and the Philippines, the central governments will continue to be able to prevent disintegration into a semi-anarchy of contending island states.

If assumptions about relatively political stability during the next two to three decades can be accepted for the purpose of this chapter, then one can pose an important question. Do the governments of the major countries of the Western Pacific have the overall capacity to cope with the management of their economies and the development of their societies in the decades immediately ahead?

It seems unlikely that the pace of industrialization will slow down. Technological development may strengthen, especially if the universities of China are able to graduate increasing numbers of well-trained scientists and engineers on the model of Japan. Eventually Vietnam will be assisted to renovate its anachronistic ideology and repair its intellectually devastated and deprived system of tertiary education. Within three decades industrial centres capable of producing high-quality, internationally competitive goods may extend in an almost unbroken sequence from Japan to Surabaya in Java. By that time there will be such large markets in China, Indochina and the ASEAN countries that there will be a much higher proportion of trade within the Western Pacific grouping than at present, although all the countries will continue to trade extensively with other parts of the world, especially North America.

A further question then follows. Will the capital generated by the further development of internationally efficient industry in the islands and along the coasts of the Asian countries of the Western Pacific enable the Governments of China, the Indochinese and ASEAN countries to deal effectively with problems arising from the further growth of populations, notably excessive use of fossil fuels as demand for energy grows, the loss of vegetation in watershed areas, and degradation of water systems and deterioration of soils.

Any answer to this question would depend largely, but not exclusively, on an assessment of the growing power and influence of Japan, its links with the other economies of the Western Pacific as they adapt to changing circumstances, and the prospects for both government and development in China.

A point has now been reached where Japan exercises predominant influence throughout the Western Pacific. There are some countries where the influence of the United States is considerable, but it lacks the networks and the sheer power of the purse which Japan has built up and can deploy. It is puzzling to anyone who lives in the Western Pacific that the Japanese can be accused by Europeans and North Americans of lacking a foreign policy. The reason for this seems to be that they have successfully avoided being drawn into the competition between the powers whose policies have been dominated by strategic considerations. The obliteration of Japan's military machine in the 1941-45 war taught the Japanese that pursuit of military expansion makes one's nation the prisoner of a dangerous illusion. They also learned the dangers of allowing military people to get control of political processes. Since the 1950s the Japanese have followed a foreign policy based on a combination of industrial development with particular emphasis on technological mastery of key areas and the expansion of economic power. They have shown that the latter has dimensions in the age of high technology which were barely perceived by other countries, especially the United States. In pursuing this intelligent and steadfast course, the Japanese have already reached a point where they have achieved an ascendancy in the Western Pacific.

An American commentator has pointed out:

... the Japanese mission is clear. The driving force behind Japan's economic expansion around the world is to create and extract enough wealth to satisfy the demands at home for material progress and to create an economic position that is unbeatable. It's wrong to say the Japanese lack a goal. They do have one: a better and richer Japan. To do that they require a world that is economically efficient, where it is possible and safe to make money.

The Japanese are able to articulate a sense of mission about why they do and what they do. Rather than focusing on the geopolitical and ideological issues that fascinate Americans and Europeans, the Japanese are more interested in creating climates of economic growth.

... As the Japanese attempt to shape the twenty-first century and their innovation spills over into the world, they are bringing their own values, perceptions and systems with them. It is not realistic to expect them to play the power game internally in one fashion and play it in an entirely different way as they emerge on the world stage.

Japan's tools are investment, aid, banking and government lending, trade and technology. This impressive economic complex is managed by bureaucrats, bankers, executives, and intellectuals who are skilled, highly educated and worldly.

... Some pundits say Japan can never be a world leader without being a military superpower, but they are missing an essential point. War is largely obsolete, at least among industrial nations ... In a world that is placing far greater emphasis on economic growth than military or ideological confrontation, Japan's tools could prove even more effective in the coming years (Holstein, 1990, pp. 185 and 187).

There can be little doubt about the perceptiveness of these remarks. The countries of the Western Pacific are no strangers to war. It has been the scene of the two biggest conflicts since 1945. Japan's policies have been tailored to take advantage of its non-involvement in Korea and Vietnam as a means of ensuring its eventual predominance in the Western Pacific.

Japan's economy is dependent on trade. It must import raw materials. It is intimately connected with Australia and the ASEAN countries as it draws so much from them to sustain its industries. It is looking to China for greater quantities of materials which meet its quality standards. It is extending its reach into Vietnam and the other countries of Indochina. While these countries do not in aggregate take an especially high proportion of Japanese exports, they are slowly becoming more important as their industrialization proceeds.

Beyond trade in goods, there is the now extremely important area of non-merchandise trade—transport, travel, insurance and banking to mention the key areas. The major financial centres of the Western Pacific, Seoul, Shanghai, Hong Kong, Taipei, Bangkok, Singapore, Jakarta, Sydney and Melbourne are all closely linked to Tokyo which now ranks with New York and London. In each of the sub-centres of financial activity in the Western Pacific, the representatives from the big Japanese banks play key roles because of the vast amounts of capital available to them and also because of the position several of them have within the *keiretsu* groupings of major companies in Japan. There is constant communication between Japanese trading, industrial and construction firms and their banks, as well as with representatives of government stationed abroad. The networks are extended by the practice of having Japanese nationals seconded to firms in which Japanese companies have shareholdings or with whom they have close contractual arrangements. These people frequently occupy seemingly junior positions and usually avoid being seen to be influencing local management. The reality is that they both carry out strategic analysis and evaluation and make liaison effective with their principals in Japan.

This approach might be described as 'Confucian' or 'inscrutably Asian'. It fact it is pragmatic. Modern Japan understands the sensitivities of the countries with which it is intimately involved in trade and finance. It seems to try to avoid making the mistake of some

American and European international companies which are prone to appoint to head their subsidiaries in other countries people who are sometimes arrogant in their exercise of commercial power and insensitive to the culture of the countries to which they are posted. Japan has made mistakes of this kind in the past and its recent success inevitably breeds arrogance. Nevertheless, wise Japanese work hard to ensure that their country should not repeat its more egregious errors. They are aware of the hubris of economic as well as military power. Most of the people who work outside Japan still appreciate the advantage of exercising the relatively new-found capacity to influence effectively decision-making at most levels with subtlety and discretion.

For all this, Japan can never expect its writ to run completely in the Western Pacific. Other countries may lack economic power but China and the ASEAN grouping, because of sheer numbers and their resource endowments, and their importance as outlets for Japanese products, are forcefully able to negotiate with the Japanese if their leaders have the gumption. Another commentator has suggested:

> Perhaps the biggest challenge Japan faces in East Asia will be political rather than economic or strategic. As Japanese hegemony has deepened, East Asian complaints about Japanese neo-mercantilist practices have become louder. The spectre of a revived 'East Asian Co-Prosperity Sphere' is repeatedly raised by East Asian academics, journalists, businessmen and political leaders. East Asians are demanding that Japan drop its neo-mercantilism, open its markets, extend massive aid to the region, and treat East Asians with respect and equality (Nester, 1990, p. 234).

The point is also made that Japanese companies, especially timber companies, are regarded as particularly destructive of the environment, and their government is condemned by some because of its deliberate policy of encouraging polluting industries to transfer to foreign locations (Nester, 1990, p. 123).

Despite this, Japan is the only country in the Western Pacific with intimate or important connections with all the others and with the capacity to provide capital on the scale required. It is not the hub of the Western Pacific. China eventually might be seen in terms of that image. For the meantime it is the non-strategic power centre of the Western Pacific. It is balanced by the strategic power centre which is clearly the combination of the administration of the day in Washington and the headquarters of the Commander in Chief Pacific, United States Navy at Pearl Harbour in the Hawaiian islands.

Because of the extent and the quality of the networks which Japan has built up in the Western Pacific, its government is uniquely placed to have the work carried out which would enable governments and their advisers in Tokyo to explore the dimensions of the economic-environmental problem of the countries which comprise its neighbourhood and those which are important to the further development of its economy. The first group comprises Korea, China and Taiwan as well as the eastern provinces of the Russian Republic which are not included within the scope of this study. The second group includes Indochina, the ASEAN countries, the Melanesian countries and Australia and New Zealand.

The conventional outlook for the countries of the Western Pacific is based on assumptions about continuing economic growth which largely ignore the mounting bill which has to be paid for the degradation of the environment after decades of furious development. A Japanese economist has summarized the conventional approach suggesting three reasons why East Asia should continue to be one of the world's most economically advanced regions.

> First, because of rising incomes throughout East Asia and the 'demonstration effect' of Japan, South Korea and Taiwan, this area is entering an era of mass consumption and a pattern of growth led by domestic demand;
>
> Second, industrial restructuring will be facilitated by a 'learning effect', with Japan continuing to serve as a model;
>
> Third, the education revolution which has gained momentum in East Asia is such that the skilled labour force will increase both numerically and qualitatively. In addition, relations between management and increasingly better educated workforces are likely generally to improve (Nakatika, 1991, p. 63).

The argument, and it is a compelling one, is that South Korea and Taiwan have reached the stage where growth has become self-sustaining. It is now expected that Thailand and Malaysia, among the Southeast Asian countries, will before long reach that stage. In other words the basis has been laid for an 'Asian economic and cultural renaissance' in the twenty-first century (Nakatika, 1991, p. 80).

If an equally optimistic scenario for coastal China is added to the analysis, this dream seems attainable. Indeed, the Pearl River Basin, with its thriving cities of Hong Kong, Guangzhou and Shenzhen, is increasingly being portrayed as the equivalent of another large, newly industrializing country. The numbers of people who seem to be poised to take advantage of this phase of the development of the Western Pacific is unprecedented. No wonder many Japanese and other analysts are excited about the wonder of it all.

But what about the negative aspects of this great era of expansion and growth? Are they not grossly neglected in conventional economic analysis? Clearly it is inappropriate to develop an optimistic view of the future of the Western Pacific countries without weighing up all the factors which militate against consolidation of the benefits of nearly half a century of high-consumption growth.

It can be forcefully argued that it is only prudent to be pessimistic rather than optimistic about the decades ahead when the complexity of the interconnected problems confronting governments throughout the area are taken properly into account. In the first place, it has to be acknowledged that the population of the Western Pacific countries could reach at least 2.5 billion within three decades. The total number is important but should not be considered in isolation. The activities in both qualitative and quantitative senses of the present and future total population must be included in the reckoning. Although that is exceptionally difficult, it is essential if the analysis is to convey the dimensions of difficulties involved in the management of both national and international economic-environmental problems.

A realistic overview might begin with an analysis of the political and strategic situation in the Western Pacific. It would note that there are profound political differences between Japan and Korea, Japan and China, China and Taiwan, China and Vietnam, the ASEAN countries and Vietnam and, even within ASEAN, between Indonesia and Malaysia and Singapore and Malaysia. This necessitates caution in predicting the political future of the area. International cooperation could be prejudiced if one or more of the major political and ideological fault lines were to send tremors through the Western Pacific. It is too early to tell whether present tensions will diminish and give way to a broader consensus on economic and social policy. What seems to be happening in greater Europe may not necessarily also occur on the other side of the land mass.

As far as the strategic situation is concerned, the first point which might be noted is that there is little evidence of widespread resentment of the series of treaties and arrangements made pursuant to them which has enabled the United States effectively to buttress the physical security of Northeast Asia (Segal, 1990, pp. 235-60). If the *détente* between the countries now emerging from the ruins of the Soviet Union and the United States proceeds, the United States may be able to scale down its forces in the Western Pacific, but the power of its navy, with its air and marine arms, seems unlikely to be diminished.

If the word security is broadly defined then there are grounds for concern because of increasingly complex population, industrial and environmental problems. There are no reasons for complacency about the prospects for the maintenance of stability in several Asian countries of the Western Pacific, especially China, Vietnam and the Philippines. Their political futures are obscure.

In addition, people are already spilling across borders for economic as well as political reasons. These spills might become more difficult to deal with as population further increases.

The analysis might then proceed to examine whether the countries of the Western Pacific will be able to preserve both economic vitality and political stability using a series of sub-headings: collection of data, population, urban development, forestry, agriculture, fresh water resources, marine resources, mineral resources, energy requirements, transport systems and vehicles, heavy industries and capital requirements. There are additional considerations such as communications, education and national planning and international cooperation which help to make up a more complete picture.

Collection of Data

Despite the great progress which has been made in many countries, there is still a serious lack of good quality information. In the economic-environmental context, it is becoming increasingly important to develop systems for gathering scientific information as well as improving the range and reliability of statistical data. This would enable better understanding of basic problems and more informed judgements could be made especially in relation to future industrial development (broadly defined), energy requirements, the state of soils, vegetation and waters, and the provision of infrastructure. External help is clearly needed to enable the developing countries, especially China and Vietnam, to bring about both quantitative and qualitative improvement in the gathering of data and their capacity to analyse what is collected.

Population

Demographic analysis and projections of future population growth are essential to any analysis of the prospects for the Western Pacific. Even cursory analysis of the projections which are presently available would bring out the compelling need for governments to plan for both the benefits of a much larger population in the Western Pacific (more consumers) and attendant drawbacks (excessive demand for some resources and additional pressure on environments which are already stressed). It is important that some attempt be made to assess the processes which are going on apace in China, Indonesia, Vietnam, Thailand and the Philippines where the great majority of the population live. What has been happening in recent times has no precedents. In the case of China, whose population dwarfs the rest, the difficulties in the way of achieving economic objectives have been stressed throughout this book.

What is to be done in the face of the virtual certainty that the Asian countries of the Western Pacific will become much more populous and urbanized during the next three decades? Big investments are needed in industrial and commercial premises, housing, production and distribution of energy and in every aspect of urban infrastructure. Will the capital be found?

Whatever the answers, there can be no evading the probability that populations will peak during the first half of the twenty-first century. Governments will somehow have to manage to avoid the extremes of unemployment and deprivation during what is likely to be a period where sheer numbers will place great strain on essential resources of land and water.

Urban Development

Enough has been said about the circumstances of the great cities of the Western Pacific to substantiate that problems are building up everywhere. The high-income countries, like Japan and Australia, are not exempt from these problems. It would be especially unrealistic for an analysis of the future of this part of the world to rest on an assumption that the processes of economic growth will generate sufficient capital to ensure that the problems of the cities of the developing countries can be solved as tax bases grow. The evidence shows that urban growth is out of control in both developed and developing countries, and that there is a poor prospect of the less wealthy even being able to make up the backlog of essential works that already are needed.

No attempt so far seems to have been made to calculate the amount of capital needed to remedy these deficiencies, especially in key areas such as water supply, housing, sewerage, waste control and urban transport. If the demands of the cities in the high-income countries are growing, it seems more likely that the cities of the developing countries will be severely starved for capital rather than be able gradually to get on top of their problems. In the meantime slums will grow, existing tenements will deteriorate and minimum sanitary standards may be very difficult to maintain even for the high-income residential areas.

Forestry

The consequences of loss of forest and other vegetation now seem to be better understood. There are already many examples of excessive flooding and the problems caused by the siltation of natural and artificial water storages and of rivers, streams and irrigation channels. Clearly the damage which has been done must be arrested and reversed or agricultural productivity will be increasingly difficult to sustain. In addition there is growing evidence of salinization and alkalinization through misuse of irrigation and depletion of flows especially in the delta country of the great rivers.

Hardheaded analysis would demand that this problem be probed before an opinion could be ventured on the prospects for the economies of the Western Pacific. How might it be approached? Reafforestation is a national issue although the consequences of loss of forests, as with the head-water country of the Mekong River, is international. The problem is potentially so serious that it is probably beyond the capacity of any of the developing countries of the Western Pacific to deal with effectively because they lack both skilled human and financial resources. Moreover simply not enough is known about the revegetation of tropical forest land to implement large-scale programmes, even if the financial resources and suitable plant varieties were available.

This is an area where international cooperative action is needed to reinforce national efforts. The International Tropical Timber Organization has its headquarters in Yokohama. Ostensibly Japan is better placed than might otherwise be the case to encourage cooperative arrangements within the Western Pacific both in relation to the better management of existing forests and development of effective planning for the rehabilitation of areas where timber has been extracted. In practice that means developing cooperative scientific programmes and implementing the funding of very large-scale projects especially for China, Vietnam and its smaller neighbours, Thailand, Malaysia, the Philippines and Papua New Guinea.

Agriculture

As far as the agricultural aspects of economic production and development are concerned, there is sufficient information at hand and pouring in to enable qualified people to assess the significance of the loss of vegetation and the processes of acidification and salinization in China, the Philippines, Vietnam and elsewhere for agricultural production and to form relatively soundly-based assessments of the state of major river systems as watersheds progressively become denuded of their vegetation.

Will food supplies be threatened? That is a vital question but it could not at this stage be answered in a categorical way.

One of the great achievements of China and Vietnam during the past half-century has been to provide adequate nutrition for most of their people. Increases in production in less disadvantaged countries have also been impressive. The contrast with the situation in the much less densely populated Soviet Union is probably a measure of this achievement. It is too early even to assess whether the 'green revolution' and the achievements in production brought about by new varieties of plants and the extensive use of chemical fertilizers will prove over a period of several decades to be deleterious for intensive agriculture because of the decline in soil quality and the need to protect the high yielding varieties by using pesticides. These techniques have been utilized throughout Asia. They have brought about the needed increases in production. But they could turn out to be a dubious blessing when organic matter in soil is allowed to decline and pesticide residues accumulate.

In other words, the so-called 'green revolution' may prove incapable of ensuring that agricultural production should continue to increase. Doing things to excess, no matter what the area of economic activity, will have adverse consequences for the environment. Examples in agriculture are misapplication of irrigation waters, too great a dependence on chemical fertilizers, depletion of aquifers and the widespread use of a few varieties of high-yielding plants such as the newer hybrids of rice, maize and wheat.

That takes the analysis back to the relationships between vegetation, including trees and shrubs, grasses, plantation trees and crops, fresh water systems and soils. It simply cannot be argued that forest cover has not declined so severely that much good agricultural land is at risk. United Nations' and other studies of this relationship are soundly based and should not be disregarded. The question now is how fast the process of loss of organic matter in soils is proceeding. Beyond that lies the question whether it is possible to remedy an already serious situation.

A conclusion could well be reached at this stage that effective international cooperation is needed to arrest and reverse the present tendency to deterioration of soil quality. The objective would be to improve the management of fresh water systems and to lay a sound basis for agricultural production from the wet rice agriculture of the tropics to the dry land systems of Australia and the perimeters of China.

Fresh Water Resources

Management of fresh water resources is linked to the sound development of the hydro-electric, irrigation, industrial and human use potential of rivers great and small on both continents and islands as well as ground water resources. Assessment of the health or otherwise of the water systems of the Western Pacific countries are as essential to an evaluation of their economic potential as the development programmes designed to cope with growing populations and further intensification of economic activity. The evidence available already gives cause for concern.

Despite the inherent difficulties involved, an analysis should include an assessment of the state of the major rivers of the Western Pacific, with special attention to the systems of the Asian mainland which support the great proportion of the population. This would doubtless establish the patterns of cause and effect which contribute to the deterioration of the essential support systems of both agricultural and industrial societies. There is abundant evidence of the way bad farming practices, excessive use of chemical fertilizers and pesticides, effluents from intensive animal husbandry and from industry, inadequate sewerage and waste disposal systems contribute to an alarming deterioration of water quality.

As the information from United Nations' sources shows, there are increasing problems caused by the over-utilization of ground water, threats to flood control systems as vegetation is degraded or lost and the inability of many rivers, especially the major ones, to cope with the wastes produced by human beings, their domestic animals and their increasingly intensive economic activities. There is now no doubt that a potentially dangerous situation is developing throughout the Western Pacific. Many rivers are reaching the limits of their capacity to act as conduits for the wastes which have to be carried to the oceans. Until recently that capacity has been largely taken for granted. Their present situation requires careful assessment and effective national and international management if problems of disease and scarcity are to be kept to a minimum.

Marine Resources

If major and minor river systems are being progressively degraded throughout the Western Pacific because they are unable to cope with the combined effects of degradation of their watersheds, the consequent erosion, and the big increases in the amount of wastes they have to carry to the seas, it is axiomatic that coastal waters are also being progressively degraded.

The need to improve the nutrition of increasing numbers of people has meant inevitably that marine food resources are being over-utilized throughout the area. Moreover the damage being done to sea-beds by intensive trawling of coastal seas and eutrophication of sea-water, through the combination of the destruction of aquatic vegetation and increasing discharges of heavily polluted water from rivers, should be regarded as a threat to the capacity of the seas to continue to provide seafood at current levels for very long. Beyond that it would be necessary to assess the increasing threat to seas from discharges from vessels, especially oil tankers. This problem will become more serious in the waters between the Straits of Malacca and Japan as traffic inevitably increases.

Mineral Resources

The prospects for the Western Pacific during the decades immediately ahead are unlikely to be affected adversely because of the depletion of mineral resources. That is a longer-term problem. Some deposits, notably oil, will have a short lifetime. New discoveries are unlikely to be of such significance as to dramatically change the supply situation. Supplies of most other energy and industrial materials would seem to be sufficient to enable industry to continue rapidly to develop well into the next century.

There is no escaping, however, that the rate of utilization of energy materials, especially coal, poses an exceptionally serious problem. The very large annual consumption of coal in the Northeast-Asian countries, including China, is already contributing to the degradation of water, soils and the atmosphere. China alone contributes 18 million tonnes of SO_2 to the atmosphere. It ranks third behind the United States and the Soviet Union in output of this primary source of acid rain. Eighty-five per cent of this comes from burning coal by both domestic (up to 40 per cent) and industrial users. There are no inexpensive, alternative means of providing the energy China needs. The costs of replacing outdated combustion equipment and installing pollution control equipments are reckoned to be prohibitively expensive for the Chinese economy (McCormick, 1989, pp. 197-203).

Yet it is essential for the economic health of the Western Pacific for China somehow to find a way of meeting its energy needs without further increasing the amount of fossil fuel which is consumed.

Whatever happens, this problem must be addressed for national as much as international reasons. The threat to the atmosphere is a primary consideration, but it seems just about matched by the immediate consequences of the combustion of coal for the land and waters of those countries whose energy systems utilize it in such large quantities.

Energy Requirements

Outside China, industrial development so far has not been seriously handicapped by shortages of energy. It would however be romantic nonsense to suggest that, given the processes of development now underway, the energy needed could be supplied in sufficient quantities by sources other than fossil fuels including enriched uranium.

There is an encouraging aspect of the future energy situation in the Western Pacific. Japan, Korea and Taiwan are relatively efficient in their use of energy. It is likely that they will continue to fund major research and development projects which will enable them to become much more efficient and conceivably reduce their demand for imported fuels. Even though prices for the fossil fuels may remain low, other considerations, not least amelioration of environmental problems, may be sufficient to increase the drive to achieve greater efficiencies as well as to exploit alternative sources of energy.

The future energy situation in China, Vietnam and in other countries where wood and other biomass are important, nevertheless poses problems of great magnitude. It seems crucial to the future of China and its neighbours that China should rapidly become energy efficient and that it should reduce its dependence on coal as a primary source of energy. Beyond that, it seems particularly important that China should be able to reduce its dependence on biomass as a source of energy partly to reduce pressure on remaining forests and copses, but also to ensure that more plant material is returned to the soil rather than burned.

China is unlikely to be able to do this without external assistance. But it cannot expect effective assistance from industrial countries unless it develops a coherent plan which will achieve the objective of establishing efficient and balanced sources of energy during the next half century. More efficient use in all sectors will contribute to a reduction in the rate of degradation of the environment. Similar considerations apply to Vietnam and the other Indochinese countries.

It will also be necessary to reduce the demands on biomass in the ASEAN countries, especially wood for producing charcoal. Beyond that there will be rapid depletion of existing deposits of oil and a shift to greater use of natural gas and coal. While the problems of producing energy efficiently are not likely to be as difficult as in China and Vietnam, there are energy-poor areas in the Philippines, Indonesia and Thailand. The big cities create such an enormous demand that energy imbalance has become a major problem which may worsen if present trends continue.

There is another problem. Natural gas may be insufficient to both generate export income from sales to Japan, Korea and Taiwan and to meet anticipated domestic requirements during the twenty-first century. If too much is contracted to the northern tier of countries, as part of the price of servicing debt and generating foreign exchange for other development, then the prospects of achieving balanced energy systems in the ASEAN region will become rather more difficult.

Prospects for new technology, which will diversify sources of efficient energy, are promising, but it is only sensible to be cautious about the possibility of significantly reducing demand for fossil fuels during the next half-century. How could this conceivably be possible when the imperative for governments will be to create industrial employment for growing numbers of people and to enable them to use the vehicles and appliances so many are now able to afford.

Transport Systems and Vehicles

The general irrationality of the transport policies of the countries of the Western Pacific, and the adverse consequences of the rapid growth of motor vehicles of all kinds, are usually ignored in conventional analyses. One would think that proliferation of vehicles is contributing to welfare everywhere. The expansion of motor vehicle industries has contributed greatly to economic growth, but it seems that the congestion and pollution, which has become such a serious problem, should simply be accepted as a small price to pay for material progress. It is not. A situation has developed where people everywhere, even in the communist countries, can now aspire to the ownership of a vehicle even if it is only a scooter or a small motor cycle. The development of cities and towns in many countries has been so influenced by the necessity to house these machines, and to provide the streets and roads on which they roll, that the burden of finding capital for maintenance and further improvements, as well as dealing with the consequences of exhaust pollution, has greatly increased. In addition national road networks have had to be upgraded often at the expense of rail systems. The upshot is roads and streets which are choked by vehicles. Traffic systems cannot cope even in the wealthiest countries. Nobody who has endured a traffic jam in Tokyo or breathed the polluted air of the thoroughfares of Bangkok could fail to grasp the dimensions of the problem.

- The importance of the motor industries of the Western Pacific should not be undestimated. Japan and other countries have come to dominate international trade in vehicles. The contribution this has made to economic growth is substantial. Questions simply must be asked about the future of this great industry in Asia. Notably, can this particular juggernaut be slowed down and all the people involved redirected into other activity? Questions should also be asked about the cost of attempting to remedy problems already caused by traffic congestion, and whether such problems could be dealt with by switching investment into many more energy-efficient public systems than just the subways which help to reduce the traffic problems of some big cities.

Heavy Industries

The problems of the rapid growth of heavy industry, notably iron and steel, cement, pulp and paper, chemicals and plastics need to be considered. The links to problems of excessive waste, too rapid increases in demand for and inefficient use of energy and urban crowding demand critical anlysis.

A balanced appraisal would include an examination of the transfer of polluting industries from Japan and Korea to other countries. This is one of the ugliest aspects of the East Asian 'economic miracle':

Japan has managed to clean up its environment to a great extent by exporting pollution via the export of dirty industry ... Textile factories which discharge harmful acetate dyes have been moved to Thailand, Asahi's mercury-discharging soda plants have been relocated on the Chao Phraya River, and a Kawasaki steel plant, which had gained notoriety because of pollution-caused deaths, was reassembled in Mindanao in the Philippines. Taiwan and South Korea have been the main beneficiaries of this kind of investment. Both have rapidly built up paper industries, partly owing to their high tolerance for pollution. Chromium and mercury chemical plants with questionable worker safety records have been located in Korea. In Taiwan, petrochemical and plastic production have grown rapidly, unhindered by environmental regulations, to the point where Taiwan is now one of the world's most polluted countries (McDowell, 1990, p. 327).

This pattern has a habit of repeating itself. It has already left a disturbing legacy for Taiwan and the Philippines. If the process goes on it will have dire repercussions for the countries of ASEAN. We read now of the Taiwanese studying with great interest Japan's anti-pollution technology with a view to acquiring the most advanced systems for removing airborne pollutants, cleaning up waterways and disposing of wastes (Nakatika, 1991, p. 67). Taiwan may be able to afford sophisticated equipment, but the same cannot be assumed for China and countries further south. Japan stands to gain wherever one looks. If it does not make the equipment now, it is funding research or developing prototypes. What is the outlook for the industries of those countries which are going to be unable to afford the mammoth clean-up which is just beginning in Taiwan? Like population growth in China, the obvious description is 'grim'.

Capital Requirements

Analysis of the likelihood of the developing countries of the Western Pacific being able to attract sufficient capital to redress their current environmental problems, and to provide for those which are anticipated, would be an essential part of a balanced evaluation of the prospects for the countries of the Western Pacific. There needs also to be analysis of the scale and significance of aid which might be made available to the developing countries from both the advanced economies of the Western Pacific and elsewhere.

Table 4.3 is designed to bring out the gross disparities which have developed between the richer and poorer countries of the Western Pacific. The GDP of the richer countries accounts for 86 per cent of the total for the grouping. China's share, although it has 64 per cent of the population is only about 11 per cent even when Hong Kong is included. The countries of Indochina and Southeast Asia have to manage with around 6 per cent between them, although they have nearly one-fifth of the population.

The capital requirements of the developing countries of the Western Pacific are immense. Domestic capital formation has improved significantly during the past two decades, but it is still clearly insufficient. Priority is being given to investment in industries, commercial services and defence and security. Insufficient capital is available for renovation, repair and extension of essential infrastructure, especially projects which will prevent or limit further deterioration of the environment.

Although Japan, Korea and Taiwan have become powerful trading nations and account for close to three-quarters of the GDP of the Western Pacific grouping, it is unrealistic to expect that they would have the capacity to provide most of the additional capital which is needed. All three are major participants in international trade. Their investments are prudently spread across the world, notably in North America. Japanese investment in the United States has helped to compensate for America's persistent balance-of-payments deficits for more than a decade. It has contributed significantly to the preservation of the stability of the international financial system.

Mendicants from around the world are seeking assistance from Japan. They now include the Russian and the other republics which have emerged from the wreck of the Soviet Union and which are trying desperately to find the capital necessary to rebuild their obsolete factories, renovate their infrastructures and repair their damaged environments. What is more, the mismanagement of the economy of the United States during the 1980s can be seen from one perspective to be placing an additional burden on Japan. It cannot opt primarily for a regional role because of the central importance it has assumed with Germany in the maintenance of international economic and financial stability.

Capital will therefore continue to be relatively scarce. Needs are certain to increase, especially in China and Indochina and in the big developing countries of Southeast Asia. Priorities need to be reconsidered to get a better balance between investment in productive ventures on the one hand and essential infrastructure on the other. The chances of achieving an appropriate balance in the disadvantaged countries are not good. The evidence is compelling in that governments in the developing countries lack the capacity and the resources to manage effectively the critical period of transition into which they are moving.

That would, at the minimum, require the planning, both by governments and industries, of a technological leap which will enable the introduction of energy-saving techniques and technology at all levels of production including the crucially important energy industries themselves. It would also necessitate the improvement of infrastructures so that the benefits of changes in productive industries are not dissipated or lost through bottle-necks in supply and distribution or by the further growth of cities which will perpetuate great inefficiencies and degrade the circumstances of the people who are forced to live within their expanding and often chaotic perimeters.

The impressive development of technology, and the likelihood that Japan, at least, will achieve its objective of becoming the most technically advanced economy among the major powers, offers some prospect of an effective response to the problems of unsustainable growth. The Japanese have begun to articulate a new formula which could conceivably foreshadow a change in their industrial orientation of unparalleled magnitude. It may be significant that they would regard a shift over time to sustainable industrial practices not as a threat to their future but precisely the challenge they need to consolidate the scientific and technological lead they have already achieved. They have no difficulty in thinking beyond the mass-production economy they have developed this century, to an era where they will have a mastery of both the products and the processes which will be needed to give some sort of reality to the concepts of sustainable growth.

The extension of radio and television systems throughout the countries of the Western Pacific, as well as improvements in literacy, have laid the basis for effective programmes of communication and propaganda. It is important to distinguish between the two because propaganda should not be thought to be largely the preserve of the authoritarian regimes. It is part of the transmission of information in all societies although some may be more pluralistic than others. It is inescapable in authoritarian regimes. It may be positive in terms of the values of the society concerned and contribute to their stability. It may also be so distorted and remote from current necessities, whether in the Philippines of the Marcos regime, present-day China and Vietnam, or the quasi-military system of South Korea that its effects are likely to be destabilizing over the longer term and cause alienation within the society concerned, especially the alienation of youth. Effective communication, as distinct from propaganda, both within and between education systems will be essential to the transformation of attitudes necessary to achieve widespread understanding of the issues involved in moving away from high consumption growth to more sustainable activities.

Another vital area is the education of scientists, technologists and engineers. Will they be sufficient in both number and quality to make the breakthroughs which are needed and the implementation of new systems which will redress the imbalance between increasing industrial activity and the environment. The present picture in the Western Pacific is very uneven, with a concentration of the better institutes in Japan, South Korea and Taiwan. It is going to take a long time to make up the present deficiencies in the developing countries. The problem is compounded because many of the best people from these countries, including China, are attracted by opportunities in the United States, Canada and elsewhere.

There is no escaping the huge disparities between Japan, South Korea, Taiwan and the countries of Southeast Asia, with the exception of Singapore, and, especially, with China and Vietnam, where the need for scientific people of high calibre, engineers and technicians is particularly pressing. Continuing adherence to outdated philosophies cannot help the generation which will, before long, take over from the current leaderships to deal with the practical problems they are going to inherit. The question whether education in these countries will generally become undoctrinaire cannot yet be answered. That seems essential if they are to adapt and change in ways which will lessen the chances of their heavily populated societies avoiding domestic instability and political upheaval as distinct from evolution.

There is another problem. One of the deficiencies of conventional analysis is that many economists in market economy countries, other than Japan and South Korea, discount the necessity for planning in all modern economies. The word 'planning' is associated primarily with the central planning systems of communist command economies which have discredited themselves during the past decade. Nevertheless all governments are involved in planning to some extent, especially of energy systems, transportation and communications, water supply and urban development. Whether their systems are effective or not is a matter for debate.

If the countries of the Western Pacific are examined in terms of their capacity to implement effectively sensible long-term plans for the supply of energy, for the improvement of infrastructures and for addressing environmental problems, the great disparities within the area are again evident. There is high competence in Japan, South Korea and Australia. It seems to be developing in Taiwan. Elsewhere there are reasons to doubt the effectiveness of much planning both in relation to the philosophies which may underlie the process, the systems of decision-making or the lack of them and, of course, capacity to implement effectively what is decided and funded.

It is important to comprehend the human dimensions of this problem. Planning within relatively circumscribed areas like the generation of power or the coordinated development of a river system depends on the quality of the people involved, and whether or not they can be provided with the resources they need to analyse problems and think through various solutions. It also depends on the ability of political systems at local, regional and national levels to make sensible decisions which will not turn out to be at odds with other decisions in seemingly unrelated but equally critical areas.

At this stage available talent is in short supply. Even some of the wealthier countries are not especially well-endowed with people capable of realizing the consequences of what they may be proposing for other sectors of their economy. While politicians are becoming acquainted with the concept that everything is linked to everything else and that it is crucial for them to work in terms of an overall appreciation of the state of their country, they are not supermen or superwomen. They have to make decisions which disregard a purists' dictum that they should get the whole picture before they do anything important. Moreover, even in the authoritarian countries they have to try and reconcile conflicting views, especially in the technical areas where they may have no competence.

While many governments in the Western Pacific may be improving in terms of their competence to address major problems, and to resolve them logically in the interests of the many rather than the few, their lack of capacity to deal generally with economic-environmental problems at all effectively must be recognized. In other words, to use just one example, it would be unlikely, given the few skilled people and limited resources available, that big countries like China, Vietnam, the Philippines, Thailand and Indonesia will actually be able to slow down the rate of deforestation and then reverse the process.

As for the coordination of key areas of planning through international cooperation, the Western Pacific is thoroughly underdeveloped. ESCAP and the Asian Development Bank have not seriously become involved in solving major problems because member countries so far have not seen the need. Beginnings have been attempted by ASEAN. A need for collective action has been recognized by that group of countries, but the situation has not so far not become sufficiently acute to necessitate effective international action. While the need for development of international cooperation is recognized and may come about, it is easy to generate false expectations about what might be achieved given the inherent complexities of the problems involved. They include the absence of any effective international mechanisms, widespread suspicion of the motivations of the Japanese, and the sheer impetus of present economic policies. Much will depend on the way the relationship between China and Japan might develop. A wide measure of understanding between the two 'great powers' is the essential 'confidence building measure' for collaborative action which might enable the countries of the Western Pacific to change successfully and adapt in the face of greater population pressures and the danger of further serious degradation of environments.

While attempts to discern what the spectra within a crystal ball may mean, there is no question that there are serious imbalances in the Western Pacific. The first is the changing relationship between humans and vegetation; second, sources of fresh water; third, coastal environments and fourth, the atmosphere. Beyond these is imbalance between the rich, the much less rich and the poor countries, exemplified by the vast disparity in wealth between, for example, the Japanese and the Thais, and especially the Chinese and the Vietnamese.

The twenty-first century could be an especially difficult time for the Western Pacific. The economic activity of greater numbers of people is bound to increase. Because of that it is hard to envisage any combination of policies, either national or international, being able effectively to prevent further devegetation, deterioration of waters, decline in the fertility of soils and pollution of the atmosphere especially where industries are concentrated. If average real incomes double in the next twenty to twenty-five years, that would in economic terms mean the equivalent of a doubling of the present population. If the total population of the countries of the Western Pacific should increase to 2.5 billion, economic activity could be the equivalent of much more than a doubling of the present population.

The consequences of such a vast increase in economic activity needs analysis and thought, otherwise the externalities, adverse consequences, of this increase in activity could undermine what has so far been achieved and bring about the destabilization rather than prosperity of the Western Pacific.

What seems to be needed is a new undoctrinaire philosophy which makes economic and environmental sense in the circumstances which countries everywhere now find themselves. What also is needed is a great improvement in international cooperation, putting flesh on the bare bones of the proposals outlined by ASEAN and by the Japanese Government.

9. Sustainable Growth or Limitation of Damage

The use of the word growth in relation to a national economy or to the world economy is a metaphor. The analogy is the growth of a living thing whether plant or animal. Economies inevitably are thought to be similar to living things. Their cessation, their death is seldom considered. The analogy does not go that far. They can decay, as in the Soviet Union and Central Europe, but in this case the metaphor seems to be akin to sickness among human beings. Given the correct remedies, as long as the settings the economists prescribe are entered on the equivalent of life-support equipment, an economy in disarray will recover and begin to grow once more.

There seems to be a failure to appreciate that the systems of thought underlying our various economic systems are wittingly or unwittingly based on assumptions which are not very different from the myth of an achievable utopia. It is evident in derivations of Marxist economics and Fabian socialism. They have a defined objective. It is the achievement of an equitable society which is ever-growing and everlasting because it is the realization of an underlying system of ethics in contrast to systems based on private property and formation of prices through the operation of markets.

A recent variation of the other great stream in economic thinking, economic rationalism, with its stress on private property and the contention that there should be minimum interference with market forces, can also be accused of being utopian. Again, there is an underlying if unstated assumption that market economies are self-adjusting and will provide the greatest good for the greatest number. They will be able to adequately provide for the needs of their citizens, including democratic governments and the rule of law. If the correct prescriptions are followed such societies will be durable, and sustainable over the long haul.

Attitudes based on such assumptions conflict with the understand-ing, which is rapidly increasing, that modern high-consumption soci-eties, regardless of economic philosophy, may in fact be fragile rather than durable because of the adverse consequences of high rates of con-sumption. In other words the last three decades of the twentieth century are a time when many long-held assumptions about the underlying philosophies of the societies in which most of us now live have had to be reconsidered.

For example the assumption that the formation of prices by markets is somehow inherently beneficial needs to be questioned. Free play of market forces evidently contributes to the excessive consumption of many materials and their inefficient rather than efficient use.

This is evident in the case of fossil fuels. Demand has steadily increased. Extraction and conversion technology and specialized trans-port has enabled vast quantities to be delivered inexpensively almost anywhere. This has enabled industries to expand enormously. Yet the fossil fuels, especially oil and natural gas, and all other non-renewable industrial materials are intrinsically valuable. It is now better appreci-ated that they should be used as efficiently and as sparingly as possible. For the most part they are not. Worse, generations of equipment and buildings are wasteful because the energy needed to power, heat or cool them was cheap when they were designed and was expected to so remain.

The world has now moved to a situation where the consequences of market and the other systems, which have provided cheap fuels and other products in response to the growth of demand, can be reckoned. The estimates, being global, cannot be exact, but the quantities of materials used and wastes from energy and production processes can be calculated with sufficient accuracy for sensible assessments to be made of the growing burden on the environment. The word 'environment' in this context means the totality of things; everything in our environs; what surrounds us.

The important point is that for some decades, in the absence of intervention, the price of most materials will continue to remain rela-tively low because of the abundance of supply and the scale and effi-ciency of conversion and transportation facilities. Consideration is being given to remedial measures such as forcing polluters to pay for the pollution they cause and for such devices as carbon taxes to be negotiated internationally to change price structures in the interests of achieving much more efficient use of fossil fuels (Pearce (ed.), 1991, pp. 31-62). Consideration of such measures involves recognition that the consequences of mass production can damage the environment, because the 'free goods', the water systems, the seas and the atmosphere cannot withstand increasing pressures of human activity and cannot absorb the wastes of economic processes without them becoming excessively degraded. That reinforces the argument that mass-production, high-consumption economies are in the long run unsustainable.

Another of the important propositions of economics is that there will always be substitutes. Problems arising from the growing scarcity of resources are not dismissed. They can have serious consequences in some circumstances. But many economists point out, drawing largely on the experience of the past two centuries, that as scarcities of particular materials develop substitutes are found in response to increases in the prices of whatever becomes in short supply. That is hard to deny. One of the great substitutions in economic history was the replacement of coal and coke for charcoal in the iron and steel industries.

We have however to consider whether this concept, which is strongly supported by the historical evidence, should influence policy as supplies of hydrocarbons begin to decline during an era where demand for them is likely to continue to increase. It seems that in the case of the Western Pacific there will not be very much oil in China, Indochina, Southeast Asia and Australasia by 2020. Growing world demand is likely to mean that there will be stiff competition for supplies from the Middle East and other places where deposits will still be worked.

One argument is of course that coal will remain in plentiful supply and other sources of fossil fuels, such as oil shales, will be exploited to make good deficiencies in supplies of once abundant oil. Consequently there is unlikely to be a serious problem. Given the resources of these materials in China and Australia, and the prospect of supplementation from places such as the Russian Far East and the Americas, there should be no reason to be especially concerned about supplies of energy materials. The countries of the Western Pacific are unlikely to suffer from energy starvation during the twenty-first century. Prices may rise. That may be no bad thing. It will provide the spur to greater efficiency. As the case of China demonstrates, that may not be the path of salvation but it would at least avoid proceeding down the present track of trying to solve the problem of shortages of energy by wastefully producing ever greater quantities of fuels and continuing to use them inefficiently.

But the problem is that the world economy is consuming excessive quantities of fossil fuels, especially coal and oil. Utilizing substitutes such as liquid fuels derived from shale, for the latter, is not a solution. The use of such products, which require large amounts of energy to obtain, as well as that of the remaining coal, should be limited, not further expanded, in order to leave something for future generations and to reduce the load of pollutants. Furthermore problems could be compounded because of the probability that biological sources of energy, while renewable, are being excessively exploited.

Forests and soils, neither of which are substitutable, are stores of energy, although they can regrow or be regrown in the first case or replenished in the second. It is probably insufficiently well understood that the organic content of soils is a store of energy for plants. It can be depleted, it can be rebuilt and it can be augmented by chemical fertilizers. The so-called 'green revolution' which has been so important in Asia has come about because of the availability of chemical fertilizers and improved varieties of grains. Governments in all countries have invested or encouraged investment to ensure that these fertilizers could become widely available. Gains in production in those countries, where the fertilizers could be made available at prices farmers could afford, have exceeded the growth of population.

The disadvantage of this is that chemical fertilizers, especially those made from fossil fuels, are just as much a form of energy as a kilogram of coal or a litre of gasoline. Their use can mask a gradual decline in the organic content of soils which relies for its replenishment on organic material from plants and farm animals. If stalks and dung are used for household fuel, if fallowing is rare and crop rotation is discarded for monoculture dependent on chemical fertilizers, the energy content of soils will inevitably deplete and they will slowly but surely become less productive.

This is part of a whole series of processes which contribute to the deterioration of the environment. It should be regarded as diminution of available and important sources of energy. There can hardly be argument against the suggestion that this is potentially serious when populations are growing and their economic activities are also increasing. Loss of energy from forests and soils must be substituted by other forms of energy. If, as seems very likely, fossil fuels provide the substitutes whether in the form of coal, kerosene or gas for cooking and heating, or urea (one of the forms of nitrogenous chemical fertilizer involving the use of much energy in its production), the danger to the environment is redoubled as wastes from the use of such fuels increases.

Previous chapters bring out some salient considerations which should enable the concept of sustainable growth or development to be tested against the realities of the growth of population, increasing demand for energy by the countries of the Western Pacific and the deterioration of their environments.

How does the likely pattern of growth in the Western Pacific compare with the essential requirements of 'sustainable growth'? The short answer seems to be 'not very well'.

Growth will continue. Economies will become larger and could be capable of conferring greater material benefit on growing populations. How can growth be sustainable unless populations and production diminish?

One way of encompassing what could be involved in moving away from present economic activities which are demonstrably unsustainable to more sustainable and, eventually, sustainable activities, is to examine a relatively long list of what I suggest should be on a 'sustainability agenda'.

- There should be fewer people and the intensity of their economic activity should lessen, especially activity measured in their consumption of fossil fuels and timber and other plant material used as fuel.

- The cost of energy materials should rise substantially in real terms so as to encourage their efficient use and diminution rather than increases in the rates of extraction.

- Forests, shrublands and natural grasslands should increase substantially to at least make good the losses of recent times. This would include reversion of land to natural vegetation as well as increases in land covered by plantation crops which serve the purposes of providing crops, regulating run-off, preventing erosion and augmenting the vegetative sink for greenhouse gases.

- The fertility of soils should be rebuilt through the increase of their organic content. The use of chemical fertilizers should be reduced to an absolute minimum so as to decrease demand for the energy which is needed for their manufacture. Use of pesticides should be exceptionally sparing.

- Desertification should be reversed.

- Fresh water systems should be cleaned-up to reduce excessive quantities of silt and other detritus and to limit their use as conduits and sinks for human and industrial wastes. Measures should be taken to prevent salt and alkalis from damaging land and fresh water, especially in lakes and reservoirs.

- Similarly coastal seas, their shores and the estuaries they are capable of invading, should be protected from the damage being caused to them by the burden of silt and wastes being poured into rivers. They need also to be protected from spills at sea, from dumping of wastes. The threat to their ecosystems must be reduced and eliminated in order to ensure that they continue to supply large quantities of fish and other edible things.

- Human habitations need to be redesigned and rebuilt to save energy rather than creating additional demand for it. This applies to all buildings whether isolated or in villages or cities. The habitations must be regarded as integral with the infrastructure of the urban communities, especially the water and power supply, transport and waste disposal.

- Industrial activity should be progressively transformed to be much less energy intensive and prone to churn out large quantities of dangerous and non-biodegradable waste. Products from such industries should be economic of material, especially non-renewable material which is hard to recycle and should be very long lasting. They should not cause demand for energy to increase.

- Commercial activity should similarly be transformed so as to be much more economic in the use of buildings, transport, communications and supplies especially those made from forest products.

- Transportation should change from the present heavy emphasis on the use of motor vehicles, especially for private use, to systems which are much more economic of materials and energy.

- Resources devoted to scientific and other research should be increased with emphasis on devising ways of enabling industrial and commercial activity to continue without making excessive demands on land, water and the atmosphere. Although some solutions will necessarily be complex involving extremely sophisticated science and engineering, there will be considerable scope for simple techniques to be introduced or reintroduced.

- Education programmes need to be revised involving the development of a whole new curriculum of what might be called bio-economics. It would provide a soundly conceived undoctrinaire basis for people to learn from an early age the elements of the ways in which everything which composes the biosphere is connected to everything else and that human activity can have both positive and negative effects on the environment.

- Political ideology should relinquish its present attachment to the concepts of the pursuit of conventional material growth and shift to concepts which would involve the development of a new set of criteria for future investment programmes in every sector of the economy which would limit damage to the environment.

- International cooperation should be greatly strengthened among groups of countries in the Western Pacific, and between them and international agencies, especially financial institutions. Regional planning should be implemented between the countries which share common resources, especially river systems and seas.

The pursuit of goals such as this would involve a profound transformation. But even to fashion policies on the assumption that they could over time be achieved could give rise to yet another utopian paradigm. Behind the word 'sustainable' lies the notion that it will be possible to move to an equilibrium where economic activity will not place excessive demands on the environment, especially soils, water, the atmosphere and non-renewable resources. That is unrealistic when populations are large and growing. Furthermore the pursuit of idealistic objectives is not the way of the world, and there is no reason to assume that it might become the way of the countries along the western border of the Pacific Ocean.

That does not however provide a basis for arguing that events should always be left to take their course. It seems to be the way of the world to attempt to limit damage when situations become very threatening. It is possible that is what governments are beginning to contemplate as they weigh the consequences of two centuries of economic growth.

The ASEAN declarations and the statement of principles and the action plan by the Government of Japan could be of some significance but they are only a beginning. There is a need to proceed to the development of coherent national policies based on the concepts underlying them and for effective international collaboration. The overall purpose should be, as the Japanese Government has suggested, 'to devote the next one hundred years to the recovery of this planet from two hundred years of the accumulation of carbon dioxide and other greenhouse gases'. To this needs to be added words which would reflect a collective determination to reverse the degradation of land and waters which has already taken place as a result of more than 200 years of increasing economic activity.

As far as national policies are concerned, preceding chapters have brought out the difficulties in achieving coherent policy-making in most if not all of the countries of the Western Pacific. In Japan the process of developing a consensus on major issues, let alone this one, is now bedevilled, possibly prejudiced, by venality and the large-scale corruption that comes with great wealth. The reputation of its government has been seriously damaged. In China and Vietnam the situation is especially difficult as those two countries struggle with the philosophic and practical problems they have brought upon themselves through their adaptations of what is essentially an alien ideology. Planning systems are faltering and disintegrating when there is a pressing need for them to be sensible, undoctrinaire, flexible, integrated and effective so as to reduce inefficiency and to make best use of whatever domestic or foreign capital can be deployed for productive and infrastructural purposes.

In Southeast Asia many forms of economic activity seem to be causing so much damage to the land and waters of this part of the Western Pacific that they may eventually be seen to be offsetting the benefits conferred by making available the goods for which foreign and domestic consumers crave. This seems to be acknowledged in the Declaration on Environmentally Sound and Sustainable Development. It is in the interests of the ASEAN countries to collaborate with Japan, and any other country which will help them, to move from the enunciation of principles, and the collection of information, to the implementation of less damaging modes of economic activity. It is also in their interests to support measures which may assist China and Vietnam to reform their economies in ways which will reduce environmental stress.

The longer-term environmental outlook for the countries of the Western Pacific is worrying. While production of goods and services may continue to increase for many decades, the adverse consequences of the economic development which has made greater output possible are gradually catching up with all of them. Many of them do not have the resources to make good the damage which has already been done.

It is easy to proceed from an assessment such as this to predict that the future of the countries of the Western Pacific will be exceptionally troubled because the processes of environmental degradation are insidious and their outcomes capable of undermining the productivity of the land and waters which sustains all of them. Civilizations which have developed sophisticated systems of irrigation have failed in the past. In some cases their decline seems to have been at least partly attributable to the extreme pressures they have placed on vegetation, the increasing rates of erosion after land has been denuded and the inability of the society to rectify the basic problem although it might have considerable engineering skills and the capacity to mobilize a large and competent labour force.

There are no valid grounds however for basing an argument in present circumstances on the generalization that history continually repeats itself. The twentieth century is a technological century. It bears no resemblance to any earlier era. It is also unique in so far as it is the century when, as a consequence of developments in technology, global communications have been perfected. There is also scope for the collection and analysis of data and for consultation and negotiation between and among countries for which there are no earlier precedents. It is now possible for countries everywhere to organize their scientific, engineering and other resources to deal with great and complex problems. In addition to this countries like China retain the capacity developed over thousands of years to organize their people for a common purpose such as limiting the dangers of flooding in river basins or restoring vegetation (Han, 1990, pp. 13-18). In other words there is no reason to assert that during the next century environmental problems will get beyond human remedy and that the global and regional approaches to environmental problems endorsed by the Government of Japan and Ministers of the ASEAN are unrealistic.

Problems could be very serious. Remedial action may take more than a century. But societies are more likely to adjust than collapse. A goal of sustainable growth should be acknowledged to be unattainable for as long as population is counted in billions and most societies use very large quantities of fossil fuels to keep their industries and systems of transport going. The long-term economic objective could be based on the commonsense proposition that it is essential for all societies to be careful about the consequences of their economic activities and especially their use of renewable and non-renewable sources of energy. Moreover it is also likely to be generally acknowledged that it is unrealistic to expect much more than substantial limitation of the amount of damage being done to the environment.

What then are the prospects for effective international cooperation based on a consensus that the countries of the Western Pacific must collaborate to achieve the maximum possible limitation of damage? On the positive side, the nature of the new challenge, what the threat to the environment means for individuals and their communities, is becoming better understood. Questions are being asked in every country about what should be done at both national and international levels.

It is possible that the Asian countries of the Western Pacific are getting close to a stage in their histories where the possibility of severe degradation of the things essential to human existence, air, soils and water might outweigh in political terms all the other things which militate against effective international cooperation. Understanding the extent of degradation and the probability that there will be further serious deterioration of the environment is the factor which is most likely to cause countries to agree that the coordination of national and international action is necessary. In other words, when the stage is reached that it is acknowledged that long-term survival is at stake, then there will be a modification of national attitudes.

The ASEAN ministerial and senior officials' meetings on the environment are the only international model in the Western Pacific. Their regional agenda covers nature conservation, seas and marine environment, transboundary pollution, environmental management, economics, information, public awareness and education. Much more than this is already needed. Realization of the objectives in the ASEAN Declaration of 1990 and the concepts in the Japanese Government's 'The New Earth 21' would necessitate effective consultation, the funding of agreed programmes and the negotiation of international agreements which would commit the contracting parties to effective national and international action.

What seems to be needed to fill the present vacuum is an organization which might be called The Western Pacific Organization for Environmental and Economic Cooperation. Its objective would be to develop a framework of international law and practice which would supplement full international treaties designed to protect the atmosphere and the seas. Because of the complexity of the Western Pacific, most of the work of the organization would probably be carried out mainly in sub-groupings such as: Japan and the Koreas; China, Taiwan and Hong Kong; Vietnam, Cambodia, Laos and Thailand; Malaysia, Singapore, Indonesia and the Philippines; Australia, Papua New Guinea, New Zealand and other Pacific Island countries. Other groupings might be formed specifically to work on the problems of international river basins. Similarly coastal countries would need to come together to negotiate programmes for the management of the regional seas.

An organization such as this should have close links with the Asian Development Bank and with the major national banks of the Western Pacific. It should be different from other international organizations like OECD in that it should both provide a forum for consultation and the negotiation of agreements which would ensure that capital and expertise are provided for agreed programmes.

It is easy to propose. What are the realities? They are, I suggest, reflected in present political and economic philosophies and, more importantly, in present energy-intensive and wasteful economic practices, no matter what the heading is under which they may be listed —forestry, agriculture, fisheries, mining, secondary industry in all its manifestations, transport and commercial, service and government activity. They are also reflected in the ways in which the major countries, China and Japan especially, will pursue their current interests.

To take Japan first, it is very difficult to imagine how Japan will actually find a way to change radically its present industrial direction. Mention has been made of the way in which Japan has chosen to concentrate its efforts in certain well-defined sectors, especially transport equipment. One of the consequences of its industrial success has been that it has helped to unleash much greater demand for energy and stimulated additional economic activity as other countries have built up their secondary and tertiary industries.

How can this momentum be slowed down? How can fundamental change take place unless it does? People everywhere want the wealth expressed in terms of mopeds, cars and trucks, household equipment and stylish clothing, more spacious and convenient dwellings and the inessentials which they know are available if only they can increase their incomes. Why should they be denied when everything is attainable, given a bit of luck and hard work? Emulation of Japan is a powerful motive. If Japan changes course why should others follow?

China seems to be moving towards a more flexible economic system while for the meantime its Government espouses many of the shibboleths and retains the Party organization of Marxism-Leninism. It is handicapped in its efforts to provide modest material circumstances for a population which may before very long exceed one and half billion. The Chinese people cannot be asked to abandon that objective.

The socialist route seems to embody too many contradictions to survive into the next century. It must adapt and evolve into something else: but into what? Unlike Japan, China cannot keeps things going with any confidence. Its situation has become too perilous. Its intelligentsia understands the danger of its present situation. It needs to become efficient, it needs to rehabilitate forests, protect soils, preserve its water systems, manage the transition to a much more urbanized society and to clean up the sources of pollution of the atmosphere which is making life a nightmare in its industrial areas. That is acknowledged. It needs a non-doctrinaire philosophy without losing some of the basic personal morality which Mao's revolution brought to China. It needs to find a way of implementing the rule of law in place of the rule of the Chinese Communist Party. It needs to move to energy efficiency not just in industry but in every aspect of economic activity. It needs to limit successfully population growth and for the population eventually to decline. There is no reason to be optimistic about such changes coming about.

How could China achieve such a transformation? Even allowing for escape from the philosophic prison its Communist Party has fashioned, how could it find the capital, how could it motivate its people? Their disillusion with the present system is profound. The accumulating problems of nearly half a century have to be redressed at a time when it is simply impractical to try to persuade people in China to cease devoting their efforts to improving in material terms the very modest and substandard circumstances facing most of them.

International cooperation is necessary to enable China to change from a very wasteful economy to a reasonably efficient one. There are many obstacles to establishing effective cooperation with China. It may prove impossible for Japan and other countries with the resources to establish a basis for the development of soundly-based relationships because of philosophical, political and organizational differences. Moreover other countries in the Western Pacific have similar problems. They are not going to be altruistic about China. It still could become a bottomless pit, wasting its own and other people's capital. The developed countries in the Western Pacific cannot afford to neglect them no matter how pressing China's needs might become.

That brings us back to an assessment of Japan's ability to define further a new economic agenda and, working according to the modes of international relations among Asian countries, gradually to bring about the consensus which is needed and then to steer future investments in the developing countries towards projects which will limit or rectify damage to the environment.

The Japanese Government appreciates that it should not seek overtly to exercise a leadership role in the Western Pacific. It already has great capacity to influence the course of events and it runs the risk of alienating sensitive neighbours because of that. Its Government is aware of historical animosities and the extent of apprehension about the use of its capacity to deploy economic power in order to achieve its objectives. Japan realizes, however, that its future will be uncertain if it should find itself in thirty years' time an even richer country with China, Indonesia, Vietnam, the Philippines and perhaps other countries unable adequately to house and feed their swollen populations or to repair damaged environments. One comes away from Japan thinking that its élite knows that the future of the Western Pacific depends on the development of effective cooperation between Japan and China. Nevertheless few in Japan would expect anything that Japan could do would erase the underlying hostility and suspicion which the Chinese hold towards their aggressive neighbour. As Allen Whiting has remarked:

Underlying this attitude (a desire to limit dependence on Japan) is a discernible frustration, perceived and acknowledged by the Japanese, over China being the student and Japan the teacher. This reversal of their historical roles was difficult to accept in the last century and was made worse by subsequent conflicts ...

Alleged indicators of reviving militarism were coupled with a recitation of past aggression and seen as a cause for concern. In sum, there was no trust in

Japanese motives, goals and growth in power. Instead Japanese behaviour was repeatedly characterized as 'arrogant' and 'cunning' ...

The conventional cliche about a 'love-hate relationship' does not apply here. There is no 'love' on the Chinese side; at best, there is a grudging admiration for Japanese economic growth and technological modernization ...

Basically, however, it (concern over Japanese ambitions, political as well as economic, in the Asian-Pacific region) will mask an underlying Sino-Japanese rivalry for influence in the area. This in effect rules out any genuine Pacific basin cooperation insofar as that depends on the two countries working together (Whiting, 1989, pp. 192, 196, 198, 199).

But should this last assertion not be challenged given the problems any government in China will have to address? Is cooperation in the Western Pacific totally dependent on a *détente*, an era of amity and cooperation, between China and Japan? China needs assistance from Japan and other industrial countries. A working relationship is needed, not a reconciliation between countries whose relationship was virtually permanently prejudiced during the years of Japan's imperial expansion. China needs expertise and capital from Japan. The Japanese know that the future of their part of the world depends on China managing to get through the next century without descending into anarchy. They appreciate that, should the Chinese political system not become less autocratic, and should its economy deteriorate like that of the Soviet Union, as a consequence of the burden of its population and increasing economic and environmental problems, the mistakes that have been made by the central planners and the degradation of its land and water systems, Japan's interests and even the security of their country could be threatened.

Other countries of the Western Pacific probably share that apprehension. They seem to prefer that other major powers, notably the United States, should provide a counterbalance with China to the capacity of Japan to shape the destiny of its neighbours. Nevertheless it seems to be in their collective interest, as well as that of China, to forge a consensus with Japan which would fill in the detail of 'The Action Program for the Twenty-First Century'. It offers them the prospect of effectively coordinating their efforts in ways which may help them get through a time of perhaps unprecedented difficulty.

Bibliography

Arrhenius, E. and T.W. Waltz (1990), *The Greenhouse Effect*, Discussion Paper No. 78, World Bank, Washington.

ASEAN Economic Bulletin (1990), Institute of Southeast Asian Studies.

Asia Yearbook 1990, *Asia Yearbook 1991*, Review Publishing Company, Hong Kong.

Asian Development Bank (1989), *Energy Indicators of Developing Member Countries*, Asian Development Bank, Manila.

Asiaweek (1988), 'Rape of the Rainforest', Vol. 14, No. 48, Hong Kong.

Australian Financial Review, Sydney.

Australian Government (1991), *Ecologically Sustainable Development, Working Groups*, Australian Government Publishing Service, Canberra.

Balakrishnan, N. (1991), 'Lion on the prowl' in *Far Eastern Economic Review*, Vol. 151, No. 21, 23 May.

Balasubramaniam, Arun (1987), *The Brantas Project: An Integrated Approach to Water Resources Development in Indonesia*, Institute of Southeast Asian Studies, Singapore.

Beijing Review, Government of China, Beijing.

Bell, Coral (1991), *Agenda for the Nineties*, Longman Cheshire, Melbourne.

Brown, Lester R. (1991), 'The New World Order' in Brown, Lester R., *et al.* (eds), *State of the World*, Norton and Co., New York.

Burgess, P.F. (1989), 'Asia' in Duncan Poore (ed.), *No Timber Without Trees*, Earthscan, London.

Cheung, Tai Ming (1991a), 'Gun barrel politics', in *Far Eastern Economic Review*, Vol. 151, No. 3, 17 January.

Cheung, Tai Ming (1991b), 'Flood dividend', in *Far Eastern Economic Review*, Vol. 151, No. 31, 1 August.

Cheung, Tai Ming, Elizabeth Cheng and Sandy Hendry (1991) 'China 1991' in *Far Eastern Economic Review*, Vol. 153, No. 32, 8 August.

249

China News Analysis, Hong Kong.

Choi, Ki-Sang (1990), 'Status of Energy and Mineral Resources in Korea', Paper given at 12th Joint Conference of Korea/Australia Business Council, Seoul.

Clark, William C. (1989), 'Managing Planet Earth' in *Scientific American*, Vol. 261, No. 3, September.

Clifford, Mark (1991), 'Bright lights, dim cities' in *Far Eastern Economic Review*, Vol. 153, No. 31, 1 August.

Commission for the Future (1990), 'A Sustainable Future for Australia', in WCED, *Our Common Future*, Oxford, Melbourne.

Concepcion, Mercedes B. (1984), 'Population Development in Asian Countries, Causes and Effects' in Hermann Schubnell (ed.), *Population Policies in Asian Countries*, Drager Foundation and Centre of Asian Studies, University of Hong Kong, Hong Kong.

Crouch, Harold (1985), *The Continuing Crisis in the Philippines*, Institute of Strategic and International Studies, Malaysia.

Cuc, Le Trong (1990), 'The Environment in Vietnam', Paper given to Environment Link 1989, Australia.

Daly, G.L. (1989), *The Greenhouse Trap*, Bantam Books, Sydney.

Daly, Herman E. (1977), *Steady State Economics*, Freeman, San Francisco.

Daly, Herman E. and John B. Cobb (1989), *For the Common Good*, Beacon Press, Boston.

Delfs, Robert (1991), 'Saints and sinners' in *Far Eastern Economic Review*, Vol. 153, No. 31, 1 August.

Delfs, Robert (1990), 'China's rivers' in *Far Eastern Economic Review*, Vol. 147, No. 11, March.

Delfs, Robert and Tai Ming Cheung (1991), 'Power to the provinces' in *Far Eastern Economic Review*, Vol. 151, No. 14, April.

Demeney, Paul (1984), 'Population Growth in East and Southeast Asia: a long-term prospect' in Hermann Schubnell (ed.), *Population Policies in Asian Countries*, Drager Foundation and Centre of Asian Studies, University of Hong Kong, Hong Kong.

Economist, London.

Elegant, Robert (1990), *Pacific Destiny*, Crown Publishers, New York.

Emmot, Bill (1989), *The Sun Also Sets*, Simon and Schuster, London.

Environment Agency, Government of Japan (1990), *Quality of the Environment in Japan 1990*, Tokyo.

ESCAP (United Nations Economic and Social Commission for Asia and the Pacific) (1985) and (1990), *State of the Environment in Asia and the Pacific*, United Nations, Bangkok.

ESCAP Secretariat (1989), Paper E.660, Bangkok.

Fesharaki, Fereiden (1989), 'Energy Outlook in the Asia-Pacific Region: Declining Oil Availability and its Impact on Gas Requirements' in *ASEAN Economic Bulletin*, Vol. 6, No. 2, November.

Fewsmith, Joseph, (1988), 'Agricultural Crisis in China' in *Problems of Communism*, Vol. 37, No. 6, November–December.

Fincher, John (1991), 'Rural Bias and Renaissance of Coastal China' in G.J.R. Linge and D.K. Forbes (eds), *China's Spatial Economy*, Oxford, Hong Kong.

Foley, G. with Charlotte Nassim (1981), *The Energy Question*, Second Edition, Penguin Books, Harmondsworth.

Forestier, Katherine (1989), 'The Degreening of China' in *New Scientist*, No.1671, July.

Fujime, Kazua (1990), 'How to Deal with New Subjects of Energy Situations' in *Energy in Japan*, Special Edition, Institute of Energy Economics, Tokyo.

Garnaut, Ross (1989), *Australia and the Northeast Asia Ascendancy*, Canberra, Australian Government Publishing Service.

Gittings, John (1990), *China Changes Face*, Oxford, New York.

Goldstein, Carl (1991), 'Tarnished image' in *Far Eastern Economic Review*, Vol. 153, No. 27, 4 July.

Gourlay, Alan (1988), *Poisoners of the Seas*, Zed Books, London.

Graedel, Thomas E. and Paul J. Crutzen (1989), 'The Changing Atmosphere', *Scientific American*, Vol. 261, No. 3, September.

Grainger, Alan (1990), *The Threatening Desert*, Earthscan Books, London.

Han, Guojian (1990), 'Green the Land', *Beijing Review*, 25 June-1 July.

Handley, Paul (1991), 'Victims of success' in *Far Eastern Economic Review*, Vol. 153, No. 38, 19 September.

Heibert, Murray (1991), 'The Mekong' in *Far Eastern Economic Review*, Vol. 151, No. 8, 21 February.

Hendry, Sandy (1991), 'The heavies' turn again' in *Far Eastern Economic Review*, Vol. 153, No. 32, 8 August.

Hill, H. and J. Mackie (eds) (1989), *Indonesia Assessment 1988*, Australian National University, Canberra.

Holstein, William J. (1990), *The Japanese Power Game*, Charles Scribner and Sons, New York.

Hull, Terence H. (1990), 'Government Involvement in Planning Asian Families: the cases of Viet Nam and the Philippines', Conference Paper, Asian Studies Association of Australia.

Hull, Terence H. (1989), 'Indonesian Population Policy: Fertility Decline in the New Order Period', Conference Paper, Australian National University.

Hull Terence H. and Anne Larson (1987), 'Dynamic Disequilibrium: Demographic Trends and Policies in Asia' in *Asian-Pacific Economic Literature*, Vol. 1, No. 1, National Centre for Development Studies, Australian National University, Canberra.

Inside China Mainland (1991), Taiwan.

Institute of Energy Economics (Japan) (1990a), *Energy in Japan*, Special Edition, Tokyo, Japan.

Institute of Energy Economics (Japan) (1990b), *Energy Demand Forecast for the Pacific Basin in 2000, 2030*, Tokyo.

Johnstone, Bob (1991), 'False economies' in *Far Eastern Economic Review*, Vol. 153, No. 38, 19 September.

Jones, Gavin (1991), 'Population, Resources and the Environment' in Wang Jiye and Terence Hull (eds), *Population and Development Planning in China*, Allen and Unwin, Sydney.

Kato, Saburo (1991) 'Regrouping for Earth' in *Look Japan*, Vol. 36, No. 418, January.

Keesings Record of World Events, Longman, Harlow (UK).

Klintworth, G. (1989), *China's Modernisation*, Australian Government Publishing Service, Canberra.

Liu Guoguang (ed.) (1987), *China's Economy in 2000*, New World Press, Beijing.

Liu Zheng (1984), 'China' in Hermann Schubnell (ed.), *Population Policies in Asian Countries*, Drager Foundation and Centre of Asian Studies, University of Hong Kong, Hong Kong.

Magrath, William and John Doolette (1990), 'Strategic Issues in Watershed Development' in *ASEAN Economic Bulletin*, Vol. 7, No. 2, Institute of Southeast Asian Studies, Singapore.

McBeth, John (1991a), 'Position vacant' in *Far Eastern Economic Review*, Vol. 151, No. 24, 13 June.

McBeth, John (1991b), 'Power to the patron' in *Far Eastern Economic Review*, Vol. 151, No. 3, 17 January.

McBeth, John (1991c), 'Roads to the rebels', in *Far Eastern Economic Review*, Vol. 151, No. 15, 11 April.

McBeth, John (1991d) 'The forces be with you', in *Far Eastern Economic Review*, Vol. 151, No. 24, 13 June.

McBeth, John (1989) 'The boss system' in *Far Eastern Economic Review*, Vol. 145, No. 37, 14 September.

McCormick, John (1989), *Acid Rain*, Earthscan, London.

McDowell, Mark A. (1990), 'The Development of the Environment in ASEAN' in *Pacific Affairs*, Vol. 62, No. 3.

McNamara, Robert (1984), 'Time Bomb or Myth: The Population Problem', *Foreign Affairs*, Vol. 62, No. 5, Summer.

Mindich, Jeffrey H. (1991), 'Intractable River Pollution' in *Free China Review*, Vol. 41, No. 10, October.

MITI (Ministry of International Trade and Industry, Japan) (1990a), 'The New Earth 21' in *News from MITI*, NR-382(90-11), June.

MITI (1990b), *The Global Environmental Challenge: Japanese Initiative* in *Technological Breakthrough*, July.

MITI (1990c), *The Research Institute of Innovative Technology for the Earth*, August.

Murata, Tokujii (1989), 'Poisoning the Environment through Waste Management' in *Japan Echo*, Vol. 16, No. 4, Winter.

Nakatika, Toru (1991), 'The Takeoff of the East Asian Economic Sphere' in *Japan Review of International Affairs*, Vol. 5, No. 1, Spring–Summer.

Nakano, Takamasa (1986), 'Environmental Policies in Japan' in Chris Park (ed.), *Environmental Policies: An International Review*, Croom Helm, London.

Nester, W.R. (1990), *Japan's Growing Power Over East Asia and the World Economy*, St Martin's Press, New York.

New Zealand Official 1988–89 Yearbook, Department of Statistics, Wellington.

Ogawa, Yoshiki (1990), 'Energy Consumption and Global Warming' in *Energy in Japan*, Special Edition, The Institute of Energy Economics, Tokyo.

Pan, Lynn (1990), *Sons of the Yellow Emperor*, Secker and Warburg, London.

Pardoko, Henry (1984), 'Indonesia', in Herman Schubnell (ed.), *Population Problems in Asian Countries*, Drager Foundation and Centre of Asian Studies, University of Hong Kong, Hong Kong.

Pearce, David, Anil Markandya and Edward B. Barbier (1989), *Blueprint for a Green Economy*, Earthscan, London.

Pearman, G.I. (ed.) (1988), *Greenhouse: Planning for Climate Change*, Commonwealth Scientific and Industrial Research Organisation, Australia.

Poore, Duncan (ed.) (1989), *No Timber Without Trees*, London: Earthscan.

Reksohadiprodjo, Sukanto (1987), *Asean Cooperation in Coal*, Institute of Southeast Asian Studies, Singapore.

Rivkin, Jeremy (1989), *Entropy: Into the Greenhouse World*, Revised Edition, New York: Bantam Books.

Sagawa, Naoto (1990), 'Energy Conservation: Its Roles and Future Potentials' in *Energy in Japan*, Special Edition, Institute of Energy Economics, Tokyo.

Sakiyama, Teruji (1979), 'Policies in Pollution, Aquaculture and Coastal Management in Japan', *Marine Policy*, Vol. 3, No. 1.

Sandhu, K.S. (1992), in Desmond Ball and David Horner (eds), *Strategic Studies in a Changing World: Global, Regional and Australian Perspectives*, Canberra Papers on Strategy and Defence No.89, Strategic and Defence Studies Centre, Australian National University, Canberra.

Sasaki, Yoshiyuki (1991), 'The Tragedy Persists' in *Pacific Friend*, Vol. 18, No. 10, February.

Savadove, Bill (1991), 'Something for the children', in *Far Eastern Economic Review*, Vol. 153, No. 38, 19 September.

Schlossstein, Steven (1991), *Asia's New Little Dragons*, Contemporary Books, Chicago.

Schubnell, Herman (1984), 'Population development in industrialized and non-industrialized countries and its effects on population growth', in Herman Schubnell (ed.), *Population problems in Asian Countries*, Drager Foundation and University of Hong Kong, Hong Kong.

Schwarz, Adam (1991a), 'Growth strains superstructure' in *Far Eastern Economic Review*, Vol. 151, No. 16, 18 April.

Schwarz, Adam (1991b), 'Empire of the son' in *Far Eastern Economic Review*, Vol. 151, No. 11, 14 March.

Seager, Joni (ed.) (1990), *The State of the Earth*, Unwin Hyman, London.

Segal, Gerald (1990), *Rethinking the Pacific*, Clarendon Press, Oxford.

Smil, Vaclav (1988), *Energy in China's Modernization*, Sharp, New York.

Smil, Vaclav (1984), *The Bad Earth*, Sharp, New York.

Smil, Vaclav (1976), *China's Energy*, Praeger, New York.

Song, J. and J.Y. Yu (1984), 'The Stability of Population and Population Control Policies' in Hermann Schubnell (ed.), *Population Policies in Asian Countries*, Drager Foundation and Centre of Asian Studies, University of Hong Kong, Hong Kong.

Tan, Boon Ann (1984), 'Malaysia' in Herman Schubnell (ed.), *Population Policies in Asian Countries*, Drager Foundation and Centre of Asian Studies, University of Hong Kong, Hong Kong.

Tanaka, Masuru (1990), 'Taking Out the Trash' in *Look Japan*, Vol. 34, No. 417, December.

Tasker, Rodney (1991), 'Class 5 digs in' in *Far Eastern Economic Review*, Vol. 153, No. 31, 1 August.

Tiglao, Rigoberto (1990), 'Power to the plutocrats' in *Far Eastern Economic Review*, Vol. 149, No. 28, 12 July.

Tirasawat, Penporn (1984), 'Thailand' in Herman Schubnell (ed.), *Population Policies in Asian Countries*, Drager Foundation and Centre of Asian Studies, University of Hong Kong, Hong Kong.

Toichi, Tsutomu (1989), 'Development of the Natural Gas Market in the Asia-Pacific Region' in *ASEAN Economic Bulletin*, Vol. 6, No. 2, Institute of Southeast Asian Studies, Singapore.

United Nations, Division of International Economic and Social Affairs, *Population Growth and Policies in Mega-Cities* (1986) Metro-Manila, 5 (1987) Bangkok, 10 (1989) Jakarta, 18, United Nations, New York.

Van Wolferen, K. (1990), *The Engima of the Japanese Superstate*, Papermac, London.

Vermeer, Eduard (1990), 'Management of Environmental Pollution in China', *China Information*, Vol. 5, No. 1, Summer.

Wang, Hong (1991), 'Population Planning in China' in Wang Jiye and Terence H. Hull (eds), *Population and Development Planning in China*, Allen and Unwin, Sydney.

Whiting, Allen (1989), *China Eyes Japan,* University of California Press, Berkeley.

World Bank (1989), *Philippines Environment and Natural Resource Management Study*, World Bank, Washington DC.

World Commission on Environment and Development (1990), *Our Common Future*, Oxford University Press, Melbourne.

World Commission on Environment and Development (WCED) (1987), *Our Common Future*, Oxford University Press, New York.

Wu, Chung-tong and Xu Xueqiang (1991), 'Economic Reform and Rural to Urban Migration' in G.J.R. Linge and D.K. Forbes (eds), *China's Spatial Economy*, Oxford, Hong Kong.

Xin, Dingguo (1988), 'The Present and Long-Term Energy Strategy of China' in J.P. Dorian and D.G. Fridley (eds), *China's Energy and Mineral Industries—Current Perspectives*, Westview, Boulder and London.

Yan, Hao (1991), 'Population and Development Planning in China' in Wang Jiye and Terence H. Hull (eds), *Population and Development Planning in China*, Allen and Unwin, Sydney.

Yang, Xiaobing (1989), 'Countering the Surge in Population' in *Beijing Review*, Vol. 32, No. 11, 13–19 March.

Yih, Hong-Ting (1990), 'Taiwan's Energy Strategy and Projects in the 1990s', Paper given to Fourth Mineral and Energy Forum, Pacific Economic Cooperation Conference, Dallas, Texas, Chinese Taipei Economic Cooperation Committee, Taipei.

Yuasa, Toshiaki (1990), 'Japan's Energy Demand Scenarios and Environmental (CO_2) Problems' in *Energy in Japan*, Special Edition, Institute of Energy Economics, Tokyo.

Zablan, Zelda C. (1984), 'Philippines' in Herman Schubnell (ed.), *Population Policies in Asian Countries*, Drager Foundation and Centre of Asian Studies, University of Hong Kong, Hong Kong.

Index